Britain's Island Fortresses

Britain's Island Fortresses

Defence of the Empire 1756–1956

Bill Clements

Pen & Sword
MILITARY
AN IMPRINT OF PEN & SWORD BOOKS LTD
YORKSHIRE - PHILADELPHIA

First published in Great Britain in 2019 by
Pen & Sword Military
an imprint of
Pen & Sword Books Ltd
47 Church Street
Barnsley
South Yorkshire
S70 2AS

ISBN 978 1 52674 030 4

A CIP catalogue record for this book is available from the British
Library

Typeset in Ehrhardt by
Mac Style Ltd, Bridlington, East Yorkshire
Printed and bound in the UK by TJ International Ltd,
Padstow, Cornwall

Pen & Sword Books Ltd incorporates the imprints of Pen & Sword
Archaeology, Atlas, Aviation, Battleground, Discovery, Family
History, History, Maritime, Military, Naval, Politics, Railways,
Select, Transport, True Crime, and Fiction, Frontline Books, Leo
Cooper, Praetorian Press, Seaforth Publishing and Wharncliffe.

For a complete list of Pen & Sword titles please contact
PEN & SWORD BOOKS LIMITED
47 Church Street, Barnsley, South Yorkshire, S70 2AS, England
E-mail: enquiries@pen-and-sword.co.uk
Website: www.pen-and-sword.co.uk

Contents

Preface   vi
Introduction   viii

Chapter 1   Bermuda   1

Chapter 2   Jamaica   32

Chapter 3   St Helena   56

Chapter 4   Antigua and St Lucia   80

Chapter 5   Ceylon   101

Chapter 6   Mauritius   133

Chapter 7   Ascension Island   159

Chapter 8   Singapore   180

Chapter 9   Hong Kong   214

Appendix: Artillery Guns and Mortars   250
Notes   254
Glossary   260
Bibliography   263
Index   266

Preface

The development of the British Empire over one hundred and twenty years between 1793 and 1913 brought with it a requirement to provide bases for the Royal Navy which, during those years, was the primary defensive arm of Britain and the Empire. These bases enabled the Empire to expand and, while Gibraltar and Malta are well documented, little appears to have been written about a number of important islands which provided support for the Royal Navy in terms of dockyard and victualing facilities.

This book cannot, through limitations of space, cover each of the island fortresses in great detail. Rather the aim is to bring to the reader's attention this somewhat neglected area of historical research. Some of the islands described are very small, others very large, but in every case each provided important, even vital, support in maintaining what came to be referred to as the *Pax Britannica*.

Readers may wonder at the omission of Malta from the island fortresses here described. My reason for this is that much has already been written about this historic and gallant island, and to do justice to it would have required a book in itself.

As always when writing a book, I have been assisted by a number of people. My thanks go to Dr Edward Harris who so kindly gave me accommodation and a magnificent conducted tour of the Bermuda forts. Thanks go also to HE Mr James Dauris and his staff in the British High Commission in Colombo for facilitating my access to Fort Ostenburg in Trincomalee, and to Captain (ASW) N.A. Usayasiri of the Sri Lankan Navy who arranged my tour of the fort and the harbour. Mrs Alice Bagshaw on St Lucia kindly gave me access to the La Toc Battery which she has worked so hard to restore.

I must also thank a number of persons and institutions that have made available photographs which provide illustrations for this book. They include Derek Bird, John Cartwright of the Fortress Study Group, Philippe La Hausse de Louvrière, Brigadier (Retd) Desmond Longfield and the Sentosa Leisure Group.

Finally, I must acknowledge and thank Charles Blackwood for drawing all the maps, without which this book would be very much the poorer, and the Fortress Study Group Committee for a financial grant towards the reproduction fees that have had to be paid for the use of a number of illustrations.

Although I have visited all the locations covered in this book most of my research has been carried out at the National Archives, the National Army Museum and the British Library in London. As always, the staff of these three great institutions have been unfailingly helpful.

I must also thank my editor Irene Moore for the tactful way in which she ensured that numerous failings in grammar and spelling in my manuscript, not to mention an occasional error of fact, did not go unnoticed and slip into the published work.

I have made every effort to find the copyright holder of each of the pictures and plans used to illustrate this book, and to obtain permission to publish. A number are from newspapers and books that are long out of copyright. If, however, I have unwittingly infringed an owner's copyright I can only apologise and say that I have tried to find the owner but failed.

The aim of this book has been to record the history and importance of a large number of British colonial fortifications. I hope this record will be of interest not just to those readers with a specialized interest in fortification, but also to those interested in the history of the British Empire.

Bill Clements
Stamford 2019

Introduction

It is, perhaps, something of a truism to say that the British Empire was acquired through trade rather than conquest. Certainly, battles were fought and territory gained, but in most cases this was the result of necessity and not deliberate policy. At the beginning of the eighteenth century Britain's empire lay almost entirely in the west, in America and Canada, and a number of islands in the West Indies. These West Indian islands included Jamaica and Barbados, together with the Bermudas and St Helena in the North and South Atlantic.

It was the Seven Years War that saw the acquisition of French territory in Canada and the capture of Gibraltar and Menorca from Spain, together with the eclipse of French influence in India. While Gibraltar and Menorca provided the increasingly powerful Royal Navy with strategic bases in the Mediterranean, the British were also obtaining influence and territory in India through the actions of the Honourable East India Company (HEIC). The HEIC had established trading posts and forts at Calcutta (Kolkata), Bombay (Mumbai) and Madras (Chennai) and as a result was now firmly established as a major power in India.

Throughout the eighteenth century no deliberate attempt was made to obtain bases for the Royal Navy which, in this age of sail when the range of ships was dictated more by the need for fresh water than for any other commodity, ships could be careened on beaches to be repaired by the ship's carpenter and his mates. However, at the end of that century with the loss of the American colonies after the American War of Independence and the war with France, Spain and the Dutch Republic, the bulk of the British Empire now comprised Canada, India and some West Indian islands.

However, the increasing importance and expanding role of British overseas trade required protection and the British Government now appreciated that overseas bases were needed, albeit mainly to re-provision Royal Navy ships. In the North Atlantic the Bermudas provided a strategic base for any operations against a hostile United States, while in the South Atlantic St Helena was the only stopping place for vessels on voyages between Britain and India. In the West Indies Jamaica remained the main base for the Royal Navy's West India

Squadron, but with the loss of Menorca, ceded to Spain under the Treaty of Paris in 1783, Gibraltar remained the only British base in the Mediterranean.

In 1793 Britain declared war on Revolutionary France and the blockade of French ports and the security of British trade became the main priorities of the British Admiralty. War with Revolutionary France became war against Napoleon Bonaparte and gradually more territory and bases were acquired including Malta, the Cape of Good Hope, Mauritius and Ceylon. When the war ended the route to India was, effectively, secure.

Subsequently further territories and bases became part of the Empire when Ascension Island in the South Atlantic was occupied in 1816 to prevent any attempt to rescue Napoleon from St Helena; Singapore was acquired by Stamford Raffles for the HEIC in 1819 and Hong Kong became British as a result of the Convention of Chuenpi in 1841 which was subsequently ratified by the Treaty of Nanking the following year at the end of the First Opium War between Britain and China. The Royal Navy had now secured bases in every ocean except the Pacific and these bases secured British supremacy at sea enabling the Royal Navy to gradually assume the role of the 'World's Policeman'.

The naval bases spread along the route to India were vulnerable to capture by an enemy force and so, in the last decade of the nineteenth century, there developed a competition for resources between the Royal Navy and the Army. Supporters of the navy argued on the principle that a strong navy would maintain the security of the home islands and the empire overseas. Those supporting the army argued in opposition that Britain was vulnerable to invasion from the Continent without prior warning, and that the fleet could not guarantee to prevent an enemy force landing. Nor, it was argued, could the Admiralty guarantee the invulnerability of British possessions overseas and, therefore, those ports and harbours must be provided with strong fixed defences.

This debate came to be known as 'The Blue Water School' versus the 'Bolt from the Blue School' and between 1890 and 1900 this was hotly debated. Finally, the matter was settled in 1896 when the Colonial Defence Committee stated that *'The maintenance of sea superiority has been assumed as the basis of the system of Imperial defence against attack from over the sea'*.[1]

The committee then went on to differentiate between the defences required for the four overseas military ports, or Imperial Fortresses as they were termed: Gibraltar, Malta, Halifax and Bermuda, and the coaling stations. Military ports were to be defended for the protection of the dockyards and to afford secure bases of operation for the fleets. The coaling stations were to be defended in order to furnish secure coaling depots for the mercantile marine and to form secondary bases for naval action in the surrounding waters, giving the Royal Navy facilities for coaling and in some cases refitting.[2] It was then agreed by the government that the strength of the Royal Navy should be maintained at what was termed the 'Two Nation Standard', that is that the strength of the Royal Navy should always be not less than the strength of the next two largest navies combined.

Defence of the overseas bases was a particularly delicate subject at this time as so many were armed with obsolete guns and poorly garrisoned. In the days of a navy comprising ships equipped only with sail, the fixed defences provided for the ports and harbours were masonry forts and batteries armed with smooth-bore, muzzle-loading (SB) guns. The responsibility for the provision of these defences was shared between the War Office, which provided the garrison, the Board of Ordnance (until 1855), which was responsible for the fortifications and providing the guns, and the Colonial Office which, usually reluctantly, shared in the overall financial costs of the works.

Indeed, the problem of the financing of the fortifications in colonial territories was to be hotly disputed between the home authorities and the colonial governments throughout the time they were in use, the dispute hinging upon whether these fortifications were for Imperial defence, or for the defence of the colony. Certainly, the matter of expense was to be an ever-increasing problem. Technological advances in guns and warships quickly made both the old masonry fortifications and the guns that armed them obsolete, requiring them to be rebuilt and rearmed frequently at ever-increasing expense.

The Warships

The design of warships did not change materially between the middle of the seventeenth century and the accession to the throne of Queen Victoria in 1837. For two hundred years the line-of-battle ship, with sails as its motor power and armed with broadside batteries of smooth-bore guns, was the supreme arbiter of naval power. It was the invention of the marine steam engine that revolutionized warship design.

Steam power was first used in commercial shipping, initially to power tugs to move the larger sailing ships in commercial harbours. The Royal Navy was suspicious of this new form of propulsion since the new engines were inefficient, consuming large quantities of coal, while the large paddle wheels made the ships vulnerable to the fire of enemy guns. The Royal Navy restricted the new form of propulsion to smaller warships classed as 'steam corvettes' and by 1860 some of these steam warships had seen action in Burma and China.

However, it was the invention of the screw propeller in 1837, together with an improvement in the efficiency of marine steam engines, that ensured the adoption of steam power by the Royal Navy for major warships. Initially, steam was used as an auxiliary form of propulsion in older sailing line-of-battle ships, which were re-fitted, and then in new screw battleships, though still with sail as their primary form of propulsion.

Prior to 1858 all the battleships in the Royal Navy were wooden-hulled, but during the Crimean War the French made use of a number of armoured floating batteries against Russian coastal defences at Kinburn. These batteries proved to be very successful since they were almost invulnerable to the fire of the Russian shore batteries and forts armed with smooth-bore guns. This invulnerability was not lost on the French navy, and in 1859 the French launched the first ocean-going ironclad warship, *La Gloire*, which was followed by three more ships of the same class. In the words of a French naval officer at the time: '[France] *has command of the Channel at the present moment.*'

The Royal Navy wasted no time whatever in designing and building their answer to *La Gloire* and her sister-ships. In May 1859 the keel was laid of HMS *Warrior*, the first ocean-going warship in the world to be built entirely of iron, with additional armour of iron backed with teak. The vessel was completed in October 1861 and her sister-ship, HMS *Black Prince*, a year later. The two ships had an armoured belt 4½ inches (11mm) thick, backed by a further 18 inches (457mm) of teak. The teak provided additional protection from iron splinters resulting from an enemy shot or shell striking the iron armour. When completed the two ships were the largest and most powerful in any navy at that time. Both were steam-propelled and had a top speed of 14 knots.

HMS *Warrior* and HMS *Black Prince* revolutionized naval tactics as they were fast, no longer reliant upon the wind, and were heavily armoured and armed with Armstrong breech-loading rifled (RBL) guns and 68-pdr SB guns. However, there was still the drawback that these ships lacked endurance when using steam power alone, so the importance of British colonial possessions as coaling stations quickly became apparent.

The American Civil War (1861–65) saw the further development of ironclad warships. The United States used the term 'monitors', and these provided practical evidence of the effectiveness of naval armour against solid shot fired by smooth-bore guns. Suddenly ships had become invulnerable

HMS *Warrior*, the world's first armoured iron-hulled warship. The restored warship is preserved as a museum ship at the National Museum of the Royal Navy in Portsmouth. (*Author*)

to the fire of coastal artillery, and the introduction of armoured turrets on these ships enabled the largest calibre guns to be mounted and fired almost independently of the direction of the ship.

Monitors were essentially coast defence ships; steam powered and with a low freeboard, they had poor sea-going qualities. Nevertheless, a number of these vessels were built for the Royal Navy and colonial navies. The monitor HMVS *Cerberus* was built for the navy of the colony of Victoria for the defence of Melbourne, while two others, HMS *Abyssinia* and HMS *Magdala* were ordered by the India Office for the defence of Bombay.

Because the range of steam-powered warships was limited by the amount of coal that could be carried in their bunkers, sail remained as an auxiliary form of propulsion for the next ten years. This was a time of experimentation in the design of warships for the Royal Navy, but in 1869 the keel of a revolutionary new warship HMS *Devastation* was laid down. Completed in 1873, HMS *Devastation*, dispensed with masts for sails and had an increased freeboard when compared with monitors, which gave the ship improved sea-going qualities. The ship carried 1,800 tons of coal, enough for a cruising radius of 9,200 miles (14,720 kms) at 5 knots, or 2,700 miles (4,320 kms) at a full speed of 12½ knots. On trials the ship, armed with four 12-inch RML guns in two armoured turrets, proved to be a steady gun platform and a good steamer. HMS *Devastation* thus proved to be the prototype of a new class of warship.

In this period of experimentation in ship design the Royal Navy struggled to combine effectively steam propulsion, weight of armour and fuel capacity, losing both HMS *Vanguard* and HMS *Captain* to inherent design faults in the process. The efficacy of marine steam engines improved rapidly both in reliability and power with the invention of reciprocating and double and triple expansion engines. With increased power for less fuel the range of operation of warships with the new engines increased dramatically.

Development of armour plate and guns also proceeded apace. In 1862 the armour on HMS *Warrior* consisted of iron plates 4½ inches (114mm) thick backed by 18 inches (457mm) of teak. By 1873 the armour plates on HMS *Devastation* were 12 inches (304mm) thick backed by 18 inches (457mm) of teak. By 1888 the new battleship HMS *Trafalgar* had a belt amidships 20 inches (508mm) thick. This produced a difference of 3,500 tons displacement between the old HMS *Warrior* and the later HMS *Trafalgar*.

The armament of the British ships also changed enormously in the period between 1860 and 1890. As the thickness of armour on foreign warships

HMS *Devastation* was the first ocean-going battleship not to be equipped with sails. It was a mastless turret ship and the forerunner of the capital ships of the twentieth century. (*Author's collection*)

increased, it became clear to the Royal Navy that rifled muzzle-loading guns were no longer suited to naval use, because in order to penetrate enemy armour the gun had to be made ever larger. However, any attempt to increase the barrel length in order to increase the muzzle velocity was restricted by the problem of loading the gun. In the larger British battleships this was partially overcome by lowering the barrel muzzle to deck level and loading the gun hydraulically through an aperture in a fixed armoured *glacis* on the deck in front of the turret. This, of course, meant that loading the gun became slower and was also potentially dangerous because there was always the possibility of loading a second charge and shell on top of a misfire. This happened aboard HMS *Thunderer* in 1879, causing an explosion that killed eleven men. All this led, finally, to the conversion of Their Lords of the Admiralty to the policy of mounting breech-loading guns in Royal Navy ships.

The new armament included the very largest 12-inch (304mm) and 13.5-inch (342mm) BL guns and even an enormous, but ultimately unsuccessful, 16.25-inch (412mm) BL gun, as well as smaller quick-firing guns. The latter used fixed case ammunition, where the charge and warhead were in a brass shell case, developed to counter the new and fast torpedo boats and torpedo boat destroyers then coming into service with all navies.

By the end of the nineteenth century there had been startling advances in the construction of warships and their armament. These advances meant that all existing coastal defence forts and batteries were now obsolete, so new guns and new methods of construction became necessary to provide adequate protection against the threat of large high-explosive shells fired with improved accuracy from greater distances offshore.

The Guns

As with warships, between the age of Queen Elizabeth I and the mid-years of Queen Victoria's reign little changed in the design of artillery other than an improvement in metallurgy. In the Georgian period the standard naval and coastal defence guns were smooth-bore 24-pdr 50cwt and the 32-pdr 63cwt guns. It was in 1821, however, that the first major change in the design of guns occurred when a French officer, Colonel Henri-Joseph Paixhans, demonstrated a method of firing explosive shells from artillery guns as opposed to high-angle howitzers and mortars.

Although it was some fifteen years before the French finally adopted the Paixhans' system for general use, it was not long after that the British developed and introduced into service the 8-inch (203mm) and 10-inch (254mm) SB shell guns, primarily for sea service. The 8-inch shell gun was preferred by both the Royal Navy and the Army since it was lighter and could be mounted on a standard pattern carriage and traversing platform.

The French interest in rifled ordnance was matched in England by the work of a number of inventors including William Armstrong, Joseph Whitworth, and Alexander Blakely. Guns had traditionally been manufactured of cast iron but this material had serious limitations, being deficient in tensile strength, thus restricting the size of the gunpowder charge. Steel was not dependable at this date, so the gun makers turned to using wrought iron. As we have seen Armstrong developed a rifled breech-loading (RBL) gun as early as 1854 and this gun was notable for the fact that instead of being cast in one piece, as were the smooth-bore guns, it was built-up by means of shrinking a number of wrought iron tubes, one upon another, to provide the necessary strength. After four years of trials an ordnance committee recommended the adoption of this gun, and in 1859 Armstrong was appointed Superintendent of Rifled Ordnance at the Royal Gun Factory at Woolwich.

There is some doubt as to whether this method was Armstrong's own idea or whether he pirated the design from Alexander Blakely. Certainly, Blakely patented a method of constructing gun barrels in layers only to have his design ridiculed by the Board of Ordnance. Armstrong, however, presented

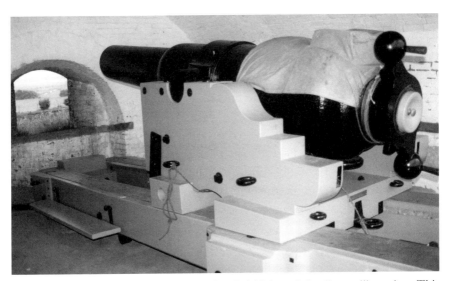

The Armstrong 7-inch RBL gun was the first British breech-loading artillery piece. This example is mounted in a Haxo casemate at Fort Nelson, the Royal Armouries Museum of Artillery in Portsmouth. (*Author*)

his patents *gratis* to the Crown on completion of successful trials of his gun and was immediately granted a knighthood.

Rifled guns were also developed by Joseph Whitworth who produced breech-loading guns with hexagonal rifling of his own unique design. These guns were produced between 1854 and 1867 and their construction differed from that of Armstrong's guns in that they were made of wrought iron cylindrical tubes forced over each other by hydraulic pressure rather than by heating and shrinking. The performance of these guns was impressive and in every way comparable with Armstrong's guns, but despite this the War Office took the decision to adopt the latter, probably influenced by the fact that the Crown already held the patents.

Armstrong's breech-loading system was not a success and there were a number of accidents because of a weakness in sealing the breech. Added to this was the fact that in trials the Armstrong 7-inch (177mm) RBL gun, designed for use both by the Royal Navy and in coastal fortresses, proved to be less effective against armour than the 68-pdr SB gun. It was for this reason that in 1864 a committee was set up to compare the performance of the Armstrong and Whitworth guns. A trial was ordered by the War Office to compare the performance of each manufacturer's breech-loading and muzzle-loading guns. Both Armstrong and Whitworth had taken the precaution of developing a muzzle-loading rifled gun and in the trial all the guns, including an Armstrong RBL gun with a modified breech action, performed satisfactorily. However, the committee reported in 1865 that the muzzle-loaders were superior to the breech-loaders in all respects including ease of working the guns and cost of manufacture.

A series of trials over a period of some ten years confirmed the superiority of rifled ordnance, but both the Royal Navy and the Army held vast numbers of cast iron smooth-bore guns, including over 10,000 32-pdrs of various weights and 8-inch shell guns. Various attempts had been made to rifle smooth-bore guns without success, but in 1862 a cavalry officer, Major Palliser of the 18th Hussars, solved the problem of the re-use of these guns by inventing a method by which a wrought iron rifled liner could be inserted into the barrel and expanded into place by firing a proof charge. Trials showed that the liner so strengthened the converted guns that they were now more powerful than the original smooth-bores. Two thousand of these 'rifled converted' guns were made by converting some of the 32-pdr 58cwt and 56cwt guns, together with a number of 8-inch shell guns and 68-pdr 95cwt guns, into 64-pdr RML guns of 71 and 58cwt respectively and the 80-pdr 5-ton RML gun.

It soon became clear, however, particularly to the Royal Navy, that the Palliser converted guns were insufficiently powerful to deal with the ever-increasing thickness of armour of the new foreign ironclad warships currently under construction, many in British shipyards. New, larger and heavier muzzle-loading guns were needed to defeat this threat.

The first of the new guns to be manufactured in any number were the 64-pdr Mk III gun and the 7-inch 7-ton RML. These were followed by the 8-inch 9-ton gun of which only a few were produced. As the thickness and strength of armour plate increased a new gun was required by both the Royal Navy and the Army, and the result of this requirement was the 9-inch (228mm) gun weighing 12 tons. This gun was first produced in 1866 and a shell fired from it could penetrate 9 inches of iron plate at 1,000 yards (923m). This weapon was subsequently followed by the 10-inch (254mm) 18-ton RML, the armour-penetrating capability of which was now almost 12 inches (304mm), the 11-inch (279mm) and 12-inch (305mm) RML guns each of 25 tons and the 12.5-inch (317mm) which weighed 38 tons.

Later and larger guns were even heavier culminating in the giant Armstrong 17.72-inch (450mm) 100-ton RML gun, two of which were sent to Malta and two to Gibraltar, while eight were exported to Italy to arm the battleships *Duilo* and *Dandalo*. However, none of the large RML guns were sighted to fire beyond 6,000 yards (5,530m).

At this time experiments were being carried out in the use of slow-burning gunpowder as the propellant for guns. When compared with the standard

An 11-inch 25-ton rifled muzzle-loading gun, one of the larger RML guns. This gun is mounted on its original iron carriage and traversing slide at Fort George, Bermuda. (*Author*)

powder used in charges at that time, the new slow-burning powder expended much less energy in the initial explosion so accelerating the projectile for a much longer time. However, to obtain the full effect of this slower combustion a gun with a much longer bore was required. Since the muzzle-loading guns mounted in both casemates and turrets tended to have a limitation on the overall length of the gun, it was almost impossible to take full advantage of this new development.

This problem could be overcome by mounting the muzzle-loading guns in an open gun pit firing *en barbette*. This was cheaper to construct than an armoured casemate and the gun could be traversed over a greater arc than a gun in a casemate. To the British authorities it seemed that the gunners manning a gun in an open pit would be more vulnerable to enemy fire, particularly when loading the gun. This problem had been addressed by Captain Alexander Moncrieff of the Edinburgh Militia Artillery who designed a counter-weight mounting which enabled 64-pdr and 7-inch RML guns to be loaded by the gun crew within the gun pit. The gun was then raised to fire by releasing the counterweight and then, when fired, the recoil forced the weight upwards again and the barrel sank down into the gun pit for re-loading. However, this form of mounting was not suitable for the heavier guns and the slow rate of fire of muzzle-loading guns meant that large numbers of guns were needed to cope with the increased speed of warships, particularly the new torpedo boats and torpedo boat destroyers, currently coming into service.

By the mid-1880s Armstrong had successfully overcome the problem with his breech-locking mechanism inherent in his earlier designs and, with the advent of reliable breech-loading guns, it became necessary to ensure maximum use was made of this improved rate of fire. In 1887 the Inspector General of Fortifications, Lieutenant General Sir Lothian Nicholson, submitted a strongly worded report to the committee 'To consider Plans for the Fortification and Armament of our Military and Mercantile Ports',[3] chaired by the Secretary of State for War, the Rt Hon Edward Stanhope. The Inspector General stated his opinion that:

'Up to about 1876 the 80-ton or 100-ton RML guns were the most powerful in service…but the production of slow-burning powder, giving a vastly increased charge in a long gun, with a greatly reduced strain upon the material of the gun, has caused a complete revolution in artillery, enabling the range and penetrative power of the new type of guns to be largely increased…making it possible for ships armed with these guns to bombard our coast defences without coming within range of the short RML guns with which the works are armed.

The introduction of new type BL guns of long range and high penetrative power into the armament of our coast defences is, therefore, obviously of the highest importance and most pressing necessity'.

By the 1880s Friedrich Krupp in Germany had produced effective steel breech-loading guns which forced the Royal Navy and the British Army to change from muzzle-loading guns to breech-loaders. For coast defence the Army adopted the 6-inch BL guns Marks IV and VI and the heavier counter-bombardment 9.2-inch BL guns Mark I and IV. These guns were mounted on a new 'disappearing' mounting, the hydro-pneumatic mounting developed by the Elswick Ordnance Company which replaced the old Moncrieff counterweight mounting and permitted a heavier weight of gun to be mounted. The gun on the new mounting, like the Moncrieff mounting, was loaded below the parapet of the gun pit, then being raised to fire, but, unlike the Moncrieff mounting, the hydro-pneumatic mounting could take guns up to 23 tons. An armoured shield with an aperture for the gun barrel covered the top of the gun pit through which the gun was raised to its firing position and this provided additional protection for the gun crew.

The hydro-pneumatic mounting was adopted by the War Office and used in a number of locations, particularly overseas for use with both the 6-inch close defence and the 8-inch and 9.2-inch BL counter-bombardment guns. Although the rate of fire of these new guns on hydro-pneumatic mountings

This photograph of a 9.2-inch HP gun shows it in the raised position and firing. (*Author's Collection*)

was still relatively slow and the maximum range constrained because no carriage could be developed to elevate the gun beyond an angle of twenty degrees, it was, nevertheless, faster than the fire of the RML guns, and offered increased range and accuracy.

As a result of trials, it became clear that it was actually unnecessary to load the new breech-loading guns under cover in a gun pit. A warship was, essentially, an unstable gun platform and the trials proved that the gun crews were no more vulnerable to the fire of a warship in an open gun pit firing *en barbette* than in a hydro-pneumatic gun position and the rate of fire was greatly increased as was the range. So, from the early 1900s, the open gun pit became the standard emplacement for British coast defence guns.

Although the 6-inch and 9.2-inch BL guns were considered to be effective against light and heavy cruisers, the rate of fire was still too slow to adequately counter an attack by the new torpedo boats and torpedo boat destroyers, many of which by the 1890s had a speed of over 20 knots. For the anti-torpedo-boat role a quick-firing gun of sufficiently large calibre to enable it to fire a heavy shell was required. Neither the 6-pdr QF gun nor the larger 12-pdr QF fired a shell heavy enough to damage seriously these fast and agile ships. So the preferred weapon for the role was now the 4.7-inch (120mm) QF gun which fired a shell weighing 45lbs (20kgs). Although termed a quick-firer, the 4.7-inch gun fired separate-loading ammunition with the charge contained in a brass cartridge case, but the rate of fire was still considerably faster than the 'breech-loaders' using bagged charges.

A larger quick-firing gun, the 6-inch QF, was also developed at this time. Controversy had arisen as to what was the best system of breech-closure, the cased charge and quick-firing gun or the bag charge and the breech-loading gun. In order to obtain the benefits from the speed of loading the quick-firing gun the Royal Navy equipped a number of ships with this type of gun and a number were adopted for use in coast defence, particularly where there was a need to defend the port from 'tip and run' attacks from heavier warships. The defences of a number of colonial ports, including Singapore, were equipped with these guns, until the advent of the 6-inch BL Mk VII gun.

By 1898 it was clear that the latest marks of breech-loading guns were far superior to the largest calibre muzzle-loading guns used for coast defence. At a conference held on 8 December 1898 to recommend breech-loading guns to replace muzzle-loaders, the Director of Artillery stated that the 9.2-inch Mk IX or X BL gun had, when the barrel was a quarter worn, a penetrative effect nearly 50 per cent greater than a new 12.5-inch RML gun. It could be fired three times faster and the cost of the projectile was less than half that of the 12.5-inch RML gun. Equally, the 6-inch Mk VII BL gun, also when a quarter worn, had a penetrative effect 20 per cent greater than a 10-inch RML gun. It could be fired six times faster than the RML and the projectile cost about a quarter of the price of a 10-inch shell.[4]

In 1905 the Admiralty and the War Office set up a joint committee which was directed *'to report what additions or alterations, if any, are necessary to the existing fixed defences of all defended ports at home to suit modern conditions'.* The president of the committee was General J.F. Owen with four other members, two from the Royal Navy and two from the Army. This committee was to have great influence on future policy concerning Fixed Defences in the United Kingdom and overseas.

The Owen Committee, as it became known, took as the basis for its considerations the fact that the ports of the United Kingdom (and by inference colonial ports as well) might be subjected to three classes of naval attack. These were: Class A – Attack by Battleships; Class B – Attack by Armoured Cruisers; and Class C – Attack by Unarmoured Cruisers, Torpedo Boats and Block Ships.

After much consideration the committee settled on four types of gun with which to arm the fixed defences. For defence against Class A and Class B attack the 9.2-inch BL Mk X gun was selected in preference to the 12-inch BL gun on the grounds that the angles of elevation and the descent of shells did not differ sufficiently to affect the long-range shooting, but in barrel life and rapidity of fire the 9.2-inch gun was greatly superior.[5] For defence against Class C attack the requirement was for rapidity of fire combined with as great a weight of shell as could be provided. The committee, therefore, recommended the 6-inch BL Mk VII gun and the 4.7inch QF Mk V gun as being the most appropriate for this role. However, the 12pdr 12cwt QF gun which was already installed in port defences as an anti-torpedo boat gun, was retained in service.

After the First World War efforts were made to improve the maximum ranges of both the 6-inch Mk VII gun and the 9.2-inch Mk X gun. Thought was given to developing a 55° mounting for the 9.2-inch gun, and a 70° mounting for the 6-inch gun, enabling the latter to act in both a coast defence and an anti-aircraft role. Financial constraints and technical problems resulted in both these developments being dropped. However, a new 6-inch BL gun, the Mark XXIV on a 45° mounting, was introduced immediately prior to the outbreak of the Second World War with an increased maximum range of 24,500 yards (22,600m).

Although the idea of a 55° mounting for the 9.2-inch gun had been abandoned, a modification of the existing Mark V 15° mounting was produced which increased the elevation to 35°. This Mark VII mounting increased the maximum range to 36,700 yards (33,670m) and was provided with power traverse and elevation and a power-driven rammer. The simple shield of the Mark V mounting was replaced by a large, rectangular, splinter-proof gun house.

The 9.2-inch Mk X and the 6-inch Mk VII BL guns, with the 4.7-inch Mk V and 12-pdr QF guns remained the mainstay of British coast defence until the disbandment of coast artillery in 1956.

The Forts and Batteries

The introduction of armoured steamships and rifled guns by the French alarmed the British public and, as a result of newspaper pressure, the British Government set up a Royal Commission in 1859 to consider the defence of the naval ports. The commission's report in 1860 brought about a major programme of defence works to improve the defences of Portsmouth, Plymouth, Chatham and Milford Haven, the Royal Navy's principal bases in England and Wales.

It was the experiences of the American Civil War that showed that the days of high-walled masonry forts were now over. The effect of the fire of the new rifled guns demonstrated that brickwork and masonry fortifications, no matter how thick, could quickly be demolished. In Britain tests carried out against Martello towers on the English south coast in Sussex had clearly proved the superiority of rifled guns over smooth-bore guns, and similar trials were conducted by the Prussian Army against the small fortress of Juliers with similar results. In Sussex the tests were carried out using two smooth-bored guns, a 32-pdr and a 68-pdr, against Tower No 49, while against Tower No 71, on the beach at Eastbourne, three new rifled guns, an Armstrong 7-inch RBL gun firing a shell weighing 100lbs (45kgs), a 40-pdr RML gun and an 80-pdr RML gun were used. The tests were conclusive: Tower No 71 was quickly demolished, but Tower No 49 was damaged but still serviceable.

In response to this advance in artillery technology the military engineers developed new forts that were polygonal in plan, a design that superseded the old bastion fortification and provided a greater range of horizontal fire for the guns. Instead of standing proud, these forts were now sunk into the landscape, with earthwork ramparts 50 feet (15m) thick and scarped with brick or stone. The fort was surrounded by a deep ditch and *glacis*, with *caponiers* for the

An aerial photograph of Crownhill Fort, Plymouth. This was one of the new style forts built as a result of the Royal Commission on the Defence of the Naval Ports in 1860, to withstand the fire of rifled artillery. (*Courtesy of the Landmark Trust*)

defence of the ditch. These forts were extensive in size, enabling a large number of guns to be mounted on the ramparts and in casemates, and with a brick or masonry keep securing the gorge and including accommodation for the garrison. On the Continent a system of detached forts affording mutual support was developed which became known as the 'Prussian System'.

The slow rate of fire of the large rifled muzzle-loading guns meant that it was necessary to mount a large number of these guns in the forts on two levels, with the guns at the lower level mounted in casemates, frequently protected by iron shields. Additional protection for some of the guns on the ramparts was provided by mounting them in Haxo casemates which were brick or concrete structures that covered the gun. However, as in all cases where guns were emplaced in casemates, the arc of fire was considerably restricted when compared to those mounted on the ramparts or in gun pits firing *en barbette*. The War Office believed such positions could be vulnerable to enemy shellfire, particularly when loading a muzzle-loading gun and as a result the 'Disappearing' mounting was developed.

In the 1860s and 1870s the most influential British military engineer involved in the design of fortifications was Major William Jervois, the Assistant Inspector General of Fortifications, later Deputy Director of Fortifications and adviser on fortifications to numerous colonial governments. Jervois was also instrumental in designing a large number of major forts throughout the British Empire, many of which were notable for the use of armour to protect the guns, and for the elaborate, almost medieval, design of the gates and domestic buildings.

Although the Royal Commission on the Defence of the Naval Ports, which sat in 1859–60, had resulted in the construction of large forts to defend Portsmouth, Plymouth, Chatham and Milford Haven from land attack, these were quickly made obsolescent by the introduction of the new breech-loading rifled guns.

It now became clear to military engineers that for defence against attack from the sea, large forts, even those sunk into the ground and protected by a large *glacis*, were no longer the best form of defence. Now a number of batteries each consisting of two or three breech-loading guns mounted *en barbette* in gun pits could provide an adequate, and much cheaper, form of defence. This had been demonstrated by the successful Turkish defence of Plevna against the Russians in 1877, where the defenders used earthwork fortifications, and at the bombardment of Alexandria in 1882 by the British Mediterranean fleet. At Alexandria it was found that guns emplaced behind earthworks proved relatively immune to the British shells.

As a result, a standard design for sea batteries began to appear comprising gun pits for two 6-inch or 9.2-inch BL guns with underground magazines and crew accommodation built between or adjacent to the guns, and a battery command post to the rear or, occasionally, between the gun pits. In some batteries the gorge was closed by an earth bank, but more often it was closed with just an 'unclimbable' iron fence and barbed wire. Close defence was provided by machine guns on the parapets or field carriages. This reflected the view then current that once an enemy force had landed it was unlikely that a battery could be successfully defended no matter how strongly protected.

In order to engage enemy ships by night, in particular the modern fast torpedo boats, gun batteries were now supported by powerful searchlights, known to the military as Defence Electric Lights (DELs). Brought into service after extensive trials in the 1880s, the DELs were of two types: the moving light which had the role of acquiring a target and then following it so enabling the guns to engage, and the fixed light which illuminated a specific area of water. The DELs were controlled from an Electric Light Control Station, usually co-located or adjacent to the Battery Command Post, and manned by men of the Royal Engineers Fortress companies until 1940 when the Royal Artillery took over the role.

With the advent of the First World War many batteries had dispensed with the earth bank and were constructed quite simply as pits, each with a concrete apron in front acting as a small *glacis*. The Battery Command Posts were now more sophisticated, frequently including a telephone exchange as well as the DEL director's position. Local defence was now provided by a number of pillboxes as well as barbed wire.

On the outbreak of the Second World War most coast defence batteries and forts remained much as they had been in the previous war twenty-one years before. However, defence against air attack was now vitally important and steps were taken to protect the guns by providing all-over splinter-proof shields, and frequently providing many of them with concrete overhead cover. While once again, as in the case of the old masonry casemates, this cover limited the traverse of the guns but, weighed against the danger of air attack, this was considered to be an acceptable limitation. Only in Singapore, where the guns were sited primarily to counter attack from the sea, did this limitation prove to be a major problem when endeavouring to counter a land attack.

Today many of the massive polygonal masonry forts still stand testament to the design and workmanship of their designers and builders. However, the later sea coast batteries, particularly the emergency batteries built in the Second World War, have proved to be more transitory, often demolished because the commercial value of the sites in the eyes of developers and councils outweighed their historic value.

Submarine Mining

A new form of defence for harbours, submarine mining, was developed in the latter half of the nineteenth century. Submarine mining, that is the laying of electro-contact and observation mines, which were known as 'torpedoes' prior to 1870, was introduced into the British Army in 1871. It was an additional form of defence for ports and harbours, with the role becoming the responsibility of the Royal Engineers. The mines used were the electro-contact type containing 100lbs of guncotton, moored on the surface and activated by being struck by a ship, and the observation mines of either 250 or 500lbs of guncotton laid on the sea bed and fired electrically from an observation post ashore.

In 1873 the first submarine mining company, 4 Company RE, was formed and a section was sent to set up submarine mining establishments at Bermuda and Halifax. Subsequently the company also sent detachments to Ceylon and Jamaica in 1878. In the same year detachments from 33 Company RE were sent to Hong Kong, Mauritius and Singapore, and in 1886 these three detachments, together with the Ceylon detachment, became companies in the newly-formed Eastern Battalion RE. However, the Eastern Battalion was short-lived and the four companies, together with the company at Jamaica, became independent local companies manned by locally-enlisted personnel with a cadre of regular Royal Engineers officers, NCOs and specialists.

The submarine mining branch of the Royal Engineers had a short history, being in existence for only thirty-five years, and in 1905 the role was transferred to the Royal Navy which, shortly afterwards, closed it down. In 1905 ten of the submarine mining companies were converted into Fortress Companies and continued to have responsibility for manning the searchlights and other electrical installations, including the electrical generators, in the forts and batteries manned by the Royal Garrison Artillery.

The Board of Ordnance and the Defence Committees

The command and control, management and supply of an army in peace and war is a complex business. Prior to 1855 the responsibility for commanding and supplying the British Army had been split between the Commander-in-Chief, with his headquarters at the Horse Guards, and the Board of Ordnance. The Board of Ordnance, under the Master General of the Ordnance, was responsible for the supply of arms and ammunition, the construction of fortifications and barracks and command of the three technical corps, the Royal Artillery, the Royal Engineers and the Royal Sappers and Miners, the latter having been formed in 1812. It should be noted that in 1805 the Royal Engineers was a very small corps totalling 121 officers assisted by thirty-seven surveyors and draftsmen of the Corps of Royal Military Artificers, though by 1815 this number had doubled.

The Board of Ordnance traced its origins to the Royal Arsenal at the Tower of London. Queen Elizabeth I appointed the Earl of Exeter as Master General of the Ordnance so emphasizing the importance of the development, production and supply of artillery and other weapons to the nation. Over the centuries the Board of Ordnance grew in importance, its responsibilities extending beyond the supply of weapons and ammunition to the armed forces of the Crown, and growing to include the supply of all kinds of stores and the design and construction of fortifications and other military buildings.

The Board of Ordnance, like the Board of Admiralty, comprised both civilian and military members. The senior member of the Board was the Master General of the Ordnance who was also a member of the Privy Council and, as such, was the government's principal military adviser with a seat in the Cabinet. Subordinate to the Master General were the Lieutenant

General and the Surveyor General, the former being responsible for the armaments and fortifications and for the technical corps of which the Master General was commander-in-chief, while the latter was responsible for the manufacture and supply and custody of munitions. Other officers of the Board were the Clerk of the Ordnance, the Clerk of the Deliveries, and the Principal Storekeeper. Only the Master General and the Lieutenant General were soldiers, the other four being civilians. The Board was assisted by two civil servants, the Secretary to the Ordnance and the Chief Clerk to the Clerk of the Deliveries.

In practice command of the Royal Engineers, together with the responsibility for the design and construction of fortifications devolved upon a third soldier, the Inspector General of Fortifications (IGF), who answered directly to the Master General and was always an officer of the Royal Engineers. The Inspector General of Fortifications, assisted by the two civil servants, formed a small executive committee responsible for the day-to-day decisions on fortifications and buildings made in the name of the Board of Ordnance. When the Board and the Inspector General required advice on the planning and construction of fortifications it would be advised by a body known as a Committee of Engineers, comprising two or more senior officers of the Royal Engineers. In each military district and overseas colony there was a Commanding Royal Engineer with a number of Royal Engineers officers subordinate to him.

In each district the Commanding Royal Engineer, together with the senior Royal Artillery officer, was a member of a body known as the Respective Officers. This body was a miniature reflection of the Board of Ordnance itself and included the local Surveyor and the Storekeeper. These officers supervised expenditure in the military district.

The Royal Engineers officers in the district were responsible for preparing a detailed financial estimate for any building or fortification to be constructed, and this estimate was submitted to the Board of Ordnance in London through the local Commanding Royal Engineer. Work could not start until the authority to do so was received from the Board and this, in practice, could be a long time, since the Board was notorious for the length of time it could take before authorizing work to start. Once work started the local Respective Officers strictly monitored the letting of contracts and supervised the expenditure to the last farthing. The only way this delay could be short-circuited was if the local commander-in-chief was prepared to authorize the works as 'Field Works', in which case they were financed from the Commander-in-Chief's budget.

The supervision of expenditure was clearly necessary in view of the large sums of money involved in building and maintaining fortifications at home and throughout the Empire. In view of the British Government's almost permanent state of financial stringency, the Board of Ordnance was always subject to the jealous eyes of both the Cabinet and the Treasury. The Cabinet decided the level of Army expenditure while the Treasury supervised the Commissariat, and both suspected the Board of Ordnance of waste and being a drain on the public purse. Although subject to much criticism, the Board had a champion in the Duke of Wellington, both as Master General and Prime Minister, and as long as he lived no changes in the organization of the Board were possible.

Wellington's death in 1852 coincided with a campaign against large military expenditure, particularly overseas. The responsibilities of the Board of Ordnance in the colonies ceased shortly after the duke's death, and the Board, under further attack by Lord Grey and other reformers, particularly after its failure to provide the necessary support for the Army in the Crimean War, was abolished in 1855.

Commissions and Committees

The demise of the Board of Ordnance brought the responsibility for the construction and arming of fortifications directly under the Master General of the Ordnance and the Inspector General of Fortifications. In 1859 the Inspector General became directly responsible to the Secretary of State for War for the execution of all engineer works and in 1862 his title was changed to Inspector General of Engineers and Director of Works; but in the role of Inspector General of Engineers he was responsible to the Commander-in-Chief.

In 1870 the reforming zeal of the Secretary of State for War, Edward Cardwell, resulted in the reorganisation of the Commander-in-Chief's staff and the archaic situation where the Commander-in-Chief was answerable only to the Sovereign was finally ended. In that year he was made subordinate to the government by Royal Order. As an indication of his changed position the Commander-in-Chief's headquarters was moved from the Horse Guards to the War Office in Pall Mall and a number of new committees were set up. One of these was the new and powerful Naval and Military Defence Committee. This committee took over the strategic decision-making role on all aspects of fortification at home and overseas. It had a number of technical sub-committees to advise it. These included the Heavy Gun Committee which advised on the provision of heavy guns and the armament of forts and batteries. In 1884 the newly established Royal Artillery and Royal Engineers Works Committee took over the role of the Heavy Gun Committee. This latter committee sat until 1895 when it was abolished and its role taken on by the War Office Works Department.

The Naval and Military Defence Committee was in existence until 1888 when a Royal Commission with the Marquis of Huntingdon as president was set up '*To inquire into the civil and professional administration of the Naval and Military Departments, and the relation of those Departments to each other and the Treasury.*' The commission recommended the '*formation of a naval and military council*', and a Joint Naval and Military Committee was established which met from 1891. The Permanent Under-Secretary for War was the president and the naval members included the First Sea Lord, the Admiral Superintendent of Naval Reserves, the Director of Naval Ordnance and the Director of Naval Intelligence. The War Office was represented by the Adjutant General, the Inspector General of Fortifications and Works, the Director of Artillery and the Director of Military Intelligence. The committee was formed for the consideration of questions of coast defence in which the Admiralty and the War Office were jointly interested.

At the same time the defence of the colonies and British overseas coaling stations was not neglected. In 1877 a committee on the Defence of Commercial Harbours and Coaling Stations was set up, to be quickly followed the next year by the establishment of the first Colonial Defence Committee to advise on the defence of the colonies. The Secretary of State for the Colonies directed that a local defence committee should be set up in each colony. The first Colonial Defence Committee was to be short-lived and was disestablished in 1879. However, in the same year, following the Russian War scare of the previous year, a further Royal Commission with Lord Carnarvon as president was set up with terms of reference that required it '*To Enquire into the Defence of British Possessions and Commerce Abroad*'. The commission, known informally as the Carnarvon Commission, sat for two years from 1879 to 1881.[6]

The commission heard evidence from colonial governors, senior military officers and other interested parties and produced three reports. It transpired that the newly elected Liberal government of William Ewart Gladstone was actually hostile to the aims of the commission, and the reports were not made public until 1887. However, the reports did result in the establishment of the second Colonial Defence Committee in 1885 and colonial governors were directed to set up local defence committees to submit plans for the defence of each colony to the Colonial Defence Committee. These local committees were to comprise the senior military and government officers in the colony, resembling the Respective Officers of the old Board of Ordnance.

The Colonial Defence Committee was in existence until 1904 when, as a result of the Esher Committee's recommendations for the re-constitution of the War Office, made after the debacle of the Second Boer War, it was subsumed into the new Committee of Imperial Defence as the Colonial Defence sub-committee, and subsequently as the Oversea Defence Committee, in which guise it lasted until 1939. Prior to 1914 there were three other permanent sub-committees which were the Home Ports Defence sub-committee, the Co-ordination of Departmental Action sub-committee and the Air sub-committee.

In 1923, in order to co-ordinate joint service planning, the Chiefs of Staff Committee was established where the three heads of the services, Army, Royal Navy and Royal Air Force met to discuss and agree defence matters. In 1928 a Joint Planning sub-committee was set up to carry out detailed planning for the Chiefs of Staff.

The Committee of Imperial Defence, an *ad hoc* committee with the role of advising the Cabinet on defence matters, existed from 1904 until the start of the Second World War in 1939. The Committee was chaired by the Prime Minister, with members comprising cabinet ministers, the heads of the armed services and key civil servants, depending upon the matter under review. After the First World War the permanent sub-committees included the Chiefs of Staff Committee, the Defence Committee, which became the Joint Oversea and Home Defence Committee, and a number of sub-committees set up to consider specific subjects. Examples of the latter were the Singapore sub-committee which considered the siting and arming of the Singapore naval base and the Coast Defences sub-committee that advised on the arming of the coast defences at home and abroad.

With the outbreak of the Second World War the Committee of Imperial Defence was replaced by the War Cabinet set up by the Prime Minister, Winston Churchill. The Chiefs of Staff Committee continued reporting directly to the War Cabinet, together with a number of other committees that included the Port Defence Committee and the Defence of Bases Committee, both responsible for allocating weapons and their priorities.

As we will see the Board of Ordnance and the various committees and commissions will appear frequently in the subsequent chapters of this book.

'are entirely worn out (the Drummer excepted) the others are like all draughts
[sic] *the worst men, for there are none of them but have some defects, as*
ulcered legs, the remains of Venereal Taints, and from their great propensity
to drinking rum renders a cure impossible. The whole including the Officers
are thirty in number, and there are not three sober men amongst them, or men
on whom any reliance could be placed.'[4]

Captain Thomas Cunningham made a thorough inspection of the island's
batteries recommending that a number should be abandoned and others
replaced by towers. Most of the large forts and batteries he found to be still
in need of repair with many guns and carriages unserviceable. He therefore
made a number of recommendations which included the rebuilding of Upper
Fort Paget, and so removing the necessity of maintaining Smith's Fort, Town
Cut Battery and Fort Popple, together with plans for a new work in place of
the old Fort St Catherine. These included a new lower battery to command
the eastern channel into Murray's Anchorage. He also reviewed the defences
of the Ferry and recommended that only one Martello tower rather than the
two recommended by Debutts should be built there.

Cunningham's recommendations for the defence of the naval establishment
on Ireland Island were for a tower on the north-western point of the island
and a second tower on a hill 750 yards (692m) from the first, in conjunction
with a ditch across the island aligned with the second tower. The tower on
the point was to be a large three-gun tower similar to those being built on
the English east coast, admitting that *'These towers I know only by description,*
having never seen a plan.'[5]

Major Cunningham, as he had now become, left Bermuda in 1816 without
seeing his recommendations implemented. However, work was subsequently
started on the new fort on Paget's Island, to be named Fort Cunningham
on the orders of the governor; on the new Fort St Catherine and on the Martello
tower planned for Ferry Point.

It was only with the arrival of Major Thomas Blanshard in 1822 that work
on the defences of the Royal Navy dockyard commenced. He was to stay in
Bermuda for some eight years, but his initial task was to prepare a report on
the state of the existing fortifications and to recommend new works for the
defence of the island.

By 1823 Hamilton was the principal trading port on the island, and Murray's
Anchorage and the Great Sound were the principal anchorages, with the only
entrance through The Narrows. The critical areas of the island to be defended

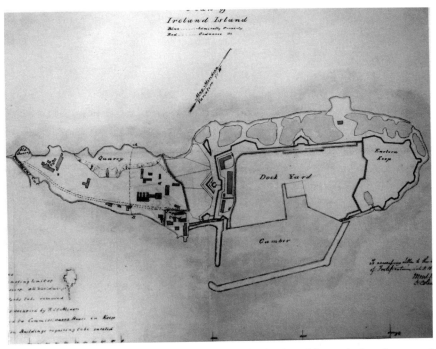

Plan of Ireland Island in 1855. The plan shows the bastioned keep, dockyard area and fortified land front. (*TNA MPHH 1/683*)

were the entrance to The Narrows, Hamilton itself and Ireland Island, with the strategic importance of St George's now much reduced.

Blanshard reported that Fort Cunningham, the pentagonal redoubt on Paget Island mounting ten 24-pdr SB guns on traversing platforms, was now completed, but Fort St Catherine which, in his words '*has been constructed on a more expensive scale than was at first intended*', was still in the course of construction, as was the Martello tower at Ferry Point. At the dockyard the ditch for the Entrenched Line across the island was under construction.[6]

Captain Blanshard's report was completed in 1823 and, apart from the defences of the dockyard, his main recommendations for new works were:

a. Completion of Fort St Catherine for seven 24-pdr SB guns in two batteries.
b. Completion of the Martello tower at Ferry Point.
c. Construction of a permanent work for five guns on traversing platforms on Retreat Hill, a hill 160 feet (50m) high in the rear of Fort St Catherine.
d. Construction of a redoubt on a lower hill to the south of Retreat Hill to protect that hill, and to mount three heavy guns on traversing carriages.
e. Construction of a small work at Spanish Point opposite Ireland Island to keep an enemy at greater distance from the Royal Navy dockyard.

f. Construction of a small work on Matilda Hill, 1,100 yards (1,015m) from the dockyard.

g. Construction of a small work on Signal Hill on St George's Island which would add to the security of St George's.

The 'small work' to the south of Retreat Hill was to become the Western Redoubt, later to be known as Fort William. This was to be a square masonry bomb-proof tower of three storeys surrounded by a deep ditch and mounting four heavy guns on the roof. An *epaulement* was a bank raised to protect a fortification and the Western Redoubt *epaulement*, the only such construction in Bermuda, was designed to mount four guns to command the town and harbour of St George's and the approaches to the latter from both the east and west.

Much of Major Blanshard's attention was, however, to be directed towards the fortification of the dockyard itself and the Entrenched Line in particular. In his report he stated: '*Since Major Cunningham wrote his report it has been determined to form a more extensive Naval Establishment and also that a Breakwater of larger dimensions should be constructed.*'[7] As a result Blanshard recommended enclosing the rear of the Entrenched Line and recommended a *caponier* that would also act as a barrack in place of the proposed Martello

Ferry Point Martello Tower. Completed in 1823, this tower, similar in design to the English South Coast towers, was one of the last Martello towers to be built. (*Author*)

tower. In Blanshard's design the Martello tower was replaced by a detached *caponier* in the centre of the ditch, entered by means of a tunnel to a bridge across the ditch, and mounting four carronades providing flanking fire along the ditch. An additional form of defence was provided by a *ravelin* covering the *caponier*.

Blanshard also had the practical idea of using the stone from the areas of cliff to be scarped in the construction of the breakwater and also proposed that two batteries should be constructed at the point of Ireland Island in place of the Martello tower proposed by Cunningham.

Two years after receiving Major Blanshard's report the Duke of Wellington, then Master General of the Ordnance, instructed Lieutenant Colonel Edward Fanshawe RE to proceed to Bermuda in order to examine the current state of the defence works, particularly as regards the security of the dockyard and the approaches to Murray's Anchorage. Fanshawe was to report on:

a. The efficiency of the works and their present state.
b. The probable period of completion.
c. Whether, when completed, they will effectively ensure the security of the dockyard and anchorage, or what further measures should be adopted to preserve to Great Britain this important station.[8]

Fanshawe's first recommendation was to reject the proposal that the beaches and landing places should be defended with batteries or towers and, instead, suggested that the island should be defended by a mobile force comprising a corps of infantry supported by a brigade of field artillery. He then approved Fort Cunningham, as it had been completed, and also Fort St Catherine which was still unfinished, though in the case of the latter fort he recommended that the upper walls of the D-shaped tower should be thickened in order to support an arch to the roof on which two heavy guns could be mounted.

Where the dockyard was concerned Colonel Fanshawe approved Blanshard's plan to scarp the cliff on the northern side and building revetments where necessary, together with bastions. The sea front was to be protected by a curtain wall and bastions, and it would seem that the Royal Navy dockyard in Bermuda was one of the last positions in the Empire to be defended by a bastion trace.

The Land Front formed a defensive masonry line across Ireland Island with a ditch in front of it and the main entrance to the dockyard was defended by the *couvre porte* and the South Orillion, the latter also acting as a defence for the short arm of the breakwater. Because of the rising ground on which it was built, the eastern *demi-bastion* of the Land Front rose above the South Orillion and, as a result, the five 24-pdr SB guns positions on the demi-bastion were, rather unusually, terraced one above the other.

The final fortification of the sea side of the Land Front was not completed until 1842 when the Right Advance was built to enfilade the western shore of Ireland Island. The Right Advance stood alone, separated from the Land Front by the main ditch, and the work itself was divided into two parts, separated by a subsidiary ditch, with a single 32-pdr SB gun mounted on the section nearest to the Land Front, and two similar guns mounted on the section closest to the sea. Access to the Right Advance was through a cave and tunnel system from the yard of the Casemate Barracks.

The Admiralty proposed that the main dockyard area should be separated from the adjacent Ordnance area by a wall which Major Blanshard proposed should be built in such a manner that guns mounted on it would, together with the guns of a large casemated barracks which it was proposed to build to accommodate Royal Marine personnel, bring fire to bear on the interior of the dockyard should an enemy force a landing through the basin. Blanshard's plan for a wall across the dockyard was approved by Colonel Fanshawe and this resulted in the Ordnance area becoming a fortified keep or position of last defence.

The design for the redoubt on Retreat Hill was also approved, but Fanshawe recommended two further redoubts on St George's Island. One was to be sited on St George's Hill, about 1,100 yards (1,015m) from Retreat Hill in a position to command the approaches to Murray's Anchorage from the west, and a second, smaller, redoubt on a small hill about 300 yards (276m) to the east of the summit of Retreat Hill. This second redoubt would command the southern approach to Fort St Catherine and its guns would also be able to bear on the ship channel. The redoubt on St George's Hill, named Fort George, was to be almost identical with Fort William, though without the *epaulement*, while the Eastern Redoubt, later named Fort Albert, was to be a pentagonal masonry redoubt with a ditch and *glacis*, mounting seven 32-pdr SB guns.

In order to carry out the work on the fortifications a company of the Royal Sappers and Miners had been posted to Bermuda in 1819 but, even with slaves allocated to the work, work on the fortifications proceeded slowly as a general workforce was lacking in the small population. In 1824 some 300 convicts were dispatched from Britain to supplement the labour force. Further drafts of convicts were sent over the next two decades to be accommodated on prison hulks at the dockyard, or in barracks on Boaz and Watford Islands.

Fort George. This aerial photograph shows the two 11-inch 25-ton RML guns which armed the fort, still in position today. (*Dr Edward Harris*)

The Duke of Wellington received Colonel Fanshawe's report and approved its recommendations in a Minute dated 27 November 1826.[9] The Minute is interesting as it lays out in detail the construction responsibilities of the Admiralty and the Board of Ordnance for the construction of the dockyard. The enclosure of the dockyard was to be the responsibility of the Admiralty, together with the eastern line, the northern boundary and the western extremity of the wharf on which the left flank of the Entrenched Line was to be constructed. The Ordnance was to be responsible for the fortifications and also the necessary powder magazines, cooperage, shifting house and ordnance store for the Navy.

In the Duke's Minute there is the first reference to the construction of a '*Casemated Building on two stories* [sic] *in Rear of the Entrenched Lines.....the Summit of this Building is to form a cavalier four feet* [1.2m] *above the Parapet of the Works and it is to be separated from the Terreplein of the Rampart by a Ditch area 12 feet* [3.7m] *wide....This Building will afford accommodation for 400 Men with Officers besides Stores.*'[10]

In 1842 a dispute occurred between the Governor, Colonel Reid RE, and the Board of Ordnance over the use of Royal Engineers personnel to deepen the entrance to St George's Harbour and to make alterations to a naval building at the request of the Admiral. Reid also criticized aspects of the defences still under construction. Governor Reid made his views known regarding potential flaws in the design of a number of the works then under

The Casemates barracks in the dockyard. Built to accommodate 400 men, it also acted as a *cavalier*. (*Author*)

construction in a letter to Lord Stanley, the Secretary of State for War and the Colonies, dated 1 May 1842. It would appear that Governor Reid's views, despite his previous distinguished service in the Royal Engineers (he had been at the siege of Badajoz in 1812), were not taken seriously by the Board of Ordnance in London. A clerk has annotated his letter to Lord Stanley with the following comment:

> '*I assume that this* [letter] *must be sent to the Ordnance, and I think it not amiss to observe that Colonel Reid who is a man of remarkable talents and actions, having written very copiously during the last three years on the Naval and Military defences of Bermuda has, as I cannot doubt, from what I have seen and heard, acquired at the Ordnance the reputation of being needlessly importunate and busy. Whether this be so or not I do not pretend to judge; but I know that when once a man has earned that reputation he may convey the most important suggestions to little purpose; and as far as, in utter ignorance of his science, I can presume to judge it seems to me that many of the suggestions made in his Despatch, and the Enclosure to it, merit very serious regard.*'[11]

Governor Reid's criticisms may have been well founded for an American agent, Albert Fitz, in a secret dispatch to the United States Department of State describing the naval and military strength of the British West India

Islands dated 21 July 1842 reported that in Bermuda the walls of the dockyard embraced a space of thirty acres (12 hectares) and that *'upwards of 100 guns are already on the walls, and the works are not yet complete'*.[12]

Of the other works of defence that Albert Fitz managed to inspect, Fort Cunningham was described as *'the oldest and feeblest permanent work upon these islands'*, while Fort Victoria on Retreat Hill was described as *'a complete bomb-proof work, of the first class, and great strength; mounting eighteen 32-pdrs, and two 32-pdr carronades'*.[13] Fort St Catherine he considered to be *'a strong work'* that mounted sixteen 32-pdr and 64-pdr guns, but Fort Albert, the Western Redoubt, was, apparently, *'not quite finished, but already mounts seven 32-pdrs, is bomb-proof, and has a ditch'*.[14] Finally, Fitz describes the work on George's Hill being under construction and designed to mount four 64-pdr guns.

Interestingly, in view of what the future would hold for Bermuda, Fitz noted that at the dockyard two steam vessels were constantly kept in commission, for the purpose of towing vessels, and cruising among the islands.

A Time of Change

The years between Major Blanshard's departure in 1830 and the outbreak of the Crimean War in 1853 were peaceful and a time in which Britain was the world super-power, with the Royal Navy unrivalled in its strength and professionalism. As a result, however, the British Government took the opportunity, as it always has done in time of peace, to reduce the expenditure on defence to an absolute minimum. Construction work on expensive fortifications was cut back, so work on the defences of Bermuda proceeded slowly.

In 1857 a committee under the chairmanship of Colonel A.J. Hemphill, the officer commanding the troops on Bermuda, assisted by the senior Royal Artillery and Royal Engineer officers on the island and a Royal Navy officer, was assembled on the instructions of the Secretary of State for War to report on the defence of the island. While noting that the principal defence of Bermuda against attack by major warships lay in the northern belt of reefs enclosing Murray's Anchorage and the dockyard, the committee made the point that there was one deep channel off the eastern side of the island that was navigable for such ships and which it was essential to secure. Therefore, the eastern fortifications were the key to the defence of the island.

The committee recommended the rearming of all the major forts, Forts Cunningham, Victoria, Albert, George, St Catherine and the Western

Redoubt with heavier guns. Indeed, the committee noted that the Western Redoubt, only recently completed, was not yet armed.

One immediate effect of the committee's report would appear to have been the dispatch of HMS *Terror*, an iron-hulled floating battery, to Bermuda. Mounting sixteen 68-pdr SB guns, HMS *Terror* had been designed for use against the Russian Black Sea batteries in the Crimean War but had only been completed after the end of that war. Instead, it was sent to Bermuda, subsequently becoming the Royal Navy receiving and base ship until decommissioned in 1902.

However, the outbreak of the American Civil War in 1861 re-emphasised the strategic importance of Bermuda, particularly in relation to a potentially hostile United States. Although no attempt was made by the United States to threaten the island during the war, steps were taken to reinforce the armament of the forts. The majority of the guns were still the older 32-pdr and 24-pdr SB guns, but a number of more powerful guns had been sent to the island. In 1863 Bermuda's armament included twenty-three Armstrong 110-pdr 82 cwt RBL guns, forty-nine 8-inch SB shell guns and twenty-eight 68-pdr 95 cwt SB guns.

Colonel William Drummond Jervois RE, Deputy Director of Fortifications at the War Office, was dispatched to Bermuda to inspect the existing works and make recommendations regarding improvements required as the result of the recent introduction of rifled ordnance, as well as the use of iron plate in the construction of fortifications. Colonel (later Lieutenant General Jervois) was, with General Sir Charles Pasley RE, one of the two greatest experts on fortification the British Army was to produce. During his career he was to travel throughout the British Empire advising on and designing works of fortification in almost every dominion and colony. Indeed, it has been said of him, rather unkindly, that he was '*bound and determined to erect on any barren rock or parcel of land on which the Union Flag has been raised a lasting memento to his gifted skills wherein expense seemed a secondary consideration*'.[15] Despite that, Jervois was a professional military engineer to his fingertips, aware of all the latest developments in fortification and ordnance.

On his arrival in Bermuda in 1865 Jervois found that some effort had been made to provide the forts with heavier guns. Fort Cunningham had been rearmed with four of the new Armstrong 110-pdr RBL guns and nine 68-pdr 95 cwt SB guns. A new battery had also been built at Buildings Bay on the eastern shore of St George's Island, probably as a result of the Hemphill Report.

Jervois saw the main priorities for defence as being the Main Channel (The Narrows) and St George's Island, with the defence of Castle Harbour and the dockyard as secondary priorities. He realized that the new rifled guns were much more powerful than the old smooth-bore weapons and, on inspecting the existing fortifications, he quickly realized that neither their construction nor their armament could resist the latest iron-clad warships mounting rifled ordnance.

Jervois considered that Fort St Catherine was particularly vulnerable to the fire of enemy warships attempting to enter the Main Channel and recommended that it be replaced by a 'powerful work'. He had in mind a battery mounting thirty guns in two tiers, but he realized that building such a large battery would take two or three years once its construction had been approved by the War Office. Jervois was no doubt well aware that obtaining War Office approval could be a long-drawn-out business.

As a temporary expedient Jervois proposed that the parapets of the existing fort should be rebuilt incorporating 'Gibraltar' shields to protect the embrasures. A 'Gibraltar' shield was a laminated iron shield constructed of three plates of wrought iron held together by bolts with nuts at the rear that covered each embrasure leaving an aperture in the centre for the muzzle of the gun. Two H-beams reinforced the shield, one at the top and one at the bottom, and triangular supports of riveted iron plates provided support at

A Gibraltar shield, one fitted to an embrasure in Fort Cunningham. (*Author*)

barbette on the north-west face of the fort to fire over the approach to the dockyard. For land defence there were four 64-pdr (Palliser Conversion) RML guns mounted two on the south face and two on the east face of the fort, but no guns were mounted in the flanking galleries. The fort was completed in 1881 but only had a short service life being abandoned in 1901.

All three forts were substantial works, not unlike those built in the same period to defend Portsmouth. It rather seems that once again the Royal Engineers designers had exercised their talents, probably influenced by Colonel Jervois, for constructing elaborate and expensive works. In 1889 Major General W.H. Goodenough RA inspected the works and defensive positions on Bermuda, and made the following interesting comment in his report to the War Office on the forts of the Prospect Hill Position:

'*There is a line of forts, Langton, Prospect, and Hamilton, the intervals of which are to be filled by field defences in wartime for the defence of Hamilton and to deny Spanish Point to the enemy. The forts are protected by such enormously deep and wide ditches that they are practically invulnerable. Siege operations, involving considerable time and work, would be required to reduce them. One must not grumble too much at having an article too good for the purpose for which it is required, but I must say that the expense of construction of these works, from their enormous and costly ditches down to the speaking tubes with their china mouthpieces, was lavish in the extreme, and far beyond what was necessary.*'[18]

To which an anonymous hand has annotated the words 'Hear Hear' in the margin!

In his report of 1869 Colonel Jervois had recommended the construction of a line for the defence of the dockyard between Ely's Harbour and the Great Sound on Somerset Island where the island narrows to a neck of land 500 yards (461m) wide, to be known as the Somerset Position. Jervois recommended that the position be defended by a ditch and parapet across the full width of the neck, with a small keep in the centre. In 1886, however, although the position appears to have been completed, it was not armed at that date.

In the early 1870s the majority of the guns on the walls of the dockyard keep were old smooth-bore muzzle-loaders. Jervois had recommended the addition of heavier rifled muzzle-loading guns and by 1886 these had been installed. One 10-inch 18-ton RML gun had been mounted on each of B, C, D, F, G, and H Bastions, and a single 64-pdr (Palliser Conversion) RML gun on the curtain wall between C and D Bastions and between D and E Bastions. Three

7-inch RBL guns were also mounted, one on E Bastion, one on G Bastion and one in the Flagstaff Battery. In addition, some twenty–eight assorted smooth-bore guns and carronades were still mounted on the walls of the dockyard keep and the Land Front.

Jervois also recommended the construction of a battery for three 9-inch 12-ton RML guns on the shore of Whale Bay to defend the entrance through the reef known as Hog Fish Cut. This battery was duly constructed and was operational by the end of the 1870s providing covering fire for the line of 'torpedoes', or submarine mines, laid as an additional form of defence.

Personnel of the Royal Engineers Submarine Mining branch had been dispatched to Bermuda in 1873 and six minefields had been laid. Two minefields were laid to defend the Narrows Channel, with a further two to defend the entrance to St George's Harbour and Castle Harbour Passage, one off Paget's Island and one off St David's Head. All four minefields were covered by the fire of the guns of St George's Island. The remaining two minefields were on the other side of the island, one to defend Hog Fish Cut which was covered by the fire of Whale Bay Battery; and one at Daniel's Head further north which was undefended.

The Royal Navy Dockyard

By 1869 the Royal Navy dockyard was fully established with barracks for the Royal Marines and seamen manning the gunboats, storehouses, magazines, boiler and engineering shops and smithy, thus enabling the base to maintain all types of vessels allotted to the Royal Navy's North America and West Indies Station. However, the base lacked a dry dock for the refitting of ships and the construction of a dry dock on Ireland Island had, on investigation, proved to be impracticable due to the porous and fissured nature of the Bermuda limestone. The Admiralty solved this problem in 1866 by ordering the largest floating dry dock to have been constructed up to that date. The dry dock was completed in 1869 and was towed to Bermuda by the ironclads HMS *Agincourt* and HMS *Northumberland* as far as Madeira with the paddle sloop HMS *Terrible* linked to the stern of the dock to assist in manoeuvring. At Madeira the towing ships were changed and HMS *Warrior* and HMS *Black Prince* took over for the final stage to Bermuda. The dock then remained in use at Bermuda until 1906 when it was replaced by Admiralty Floating Dock No 1.

The Bermuda floating dock with a *Pelorus* light cruiser undergoing a refit c.1897. (*Author's Collection*)

In 1857 the floating battery HMS *Terror* had been sent to Bermuda to act as the receiving and base ship, but with the arrival of the floating dock the Admiralty decided to take a hand in the defence of the island. HMS *Terror* was joined in 1868 by two experimental gunboats, HMS *Viper* and HMS *Vixen* each armed with two 7-inch RML guns and in Bermuda they acted as floating batteries in defence of the dockyard. Both vessels were towed to Bermuda as they were considered unfit for seagoing service but on arrival at Bermuda they were used more as steam tugs rather than as part of the defences. HMS *Vixen* was subsequently sunk in Hog Fish Cut in 1896 to block the channel.

It would seem that the Admiralty regarded Bermuda as a dumping ground for unseaworthy experimental ships as in 1869 HMS *Scorpion*, an armoured turret ship mounting four 9-inch RML guns in two turrets, joined the two gunboats to act as guardship and for coast and harbour defence. The ship was laid down in 1862 at Laird's shipyard at Birkenhead ostensibly as the Egyptian *El Tousson* but actually she was being built secretly for the government of the Confederate States of America. The British Government seized the ship in 1863 and it was completed and commissioned into the Royal Navy as HMS *Scorpion*, remaining in Bermuda until sunk as a target in 1901. In 1898 the ironclad ram HMS *Hotspur* was sent to Bermuda to replace *Scorpion* followed, in 1904, by a second ironclad ram HMS *Rupert*, continuing the tradition of sending old outdated ships with poor seagoing qualities.

In January 1889 the recently established Royal Artillery and Royal Engineers Works Committee (RA & RE Works Committee) reviewed the defences of Bermuda. The armament of the forts and batteries at that date was:

Fort Cunningham	2 × 12.5-inch 38-ton RML guns
	5 × 10-inch 18-ton RML guns
	2 × 9-inch 12-ton RML guns
Fort Albert	4 × 10-inch 18-ton RML guns
Fort Victoria	3 × 11-inch 25-ton RML guns
	8 × 64-pdr RML guns
Fort George	2 × 11-inch 25-ton RML guns
	2 × 64-pdr RML guns
Fort St Catherine	5 × 10-inch 18-ton RML guns
	3 × 64-pdr RML guns
Alexandra Battery	5 × 9-inch 12-ton RML guns
Fort Langton	3 × 10-inch 18-ton RML guns
	4 × 64-pdr RML guns
Fort Prospect	6 × 64-pdr RML guns
Fort Hamilton	7 × 64-pdr RML guns
Ireland Island	6 × 10-inch 18-ton RML guns
	15 × 64-pdr RML guns
Whale Bay Battery	3 × 9-inch 12-ton RML guns
Scaur Hill	2 × 64-pdr RML guns

The main recommendation of the committee involved the installation of 10-inch and 11-inch High Angle Fire RML guns in Forts Albert, George and Victoria. The committee recognized the fact that although the guns of St George's Island could effectively prevent an enemy from entering the Narrows Channel, there were no guns capable of holding an enemy at such a distance that it would be impossible to bombard each fort successively.

Additionally, the committee recommended the removal of the two 9-inch RML guns from the north-west face of Fort Cunningham and the mounting of two of the new 4.7-inch QF guns in this position, also the removal of one of the 10-inch RML guns from the casemate battery of Fort St Catherine. The committee further proposed that Alexandra Battery should be re-constructed to mount two 10-inch RML guns and two 4.7-inch QF guns. For the defence of Ireland Island and the dockyard the committee proposed that four 10-inch High Angle Fire guns should be mounted together with three of the new 9.2-inch BL guns on hydro-pneumatic mountings.

Three months later, as we have seen, Major General Goodenough, the Inspector of Artillery, visited Bermuda and reviewed the recommendations of the RA & RE Works Committee. In view of the possible delay in the production of the 10-inch and 11-inch High Angle Fire guns he proposed their replacement by 9-inch High Angle Fire RML guns, though in the case of Fort Victoria he believed that the ravelin on which it was planned to mount a High Angle Fire gun was too small for such a weapon.

Reviewing the defences of the dockyard, Goodenough believed that there was insufficient space to mount the 9.2-inch guns and he recommended that the armament should be changed to three 6-inch BL guns 'of the latest type'.[19] He also proposed that the number of 64-pdr RML guns in the forts should be reduced, and at Fort St Catherine, rather than removing the 10-inch RML gun from the casemate battery, one of the guns from the south-east face should be removed instead. He also recommended the dismantling of Whale Bay Battery.

This was the situation in Bermuda as the British Army turned finally from a reliance on muzzle-loading guns and adopted breech-loaders.

The Breech-Loading Era

The Naval and Military Defence Committee now proposed that all the RML guns on the island should be removed, with the exception of the two 12.5-inch guns mounted in Fort Cunningham, and for the defence of the Narrows channel a new battery should be constructed on St David's Island to be armed with two 9.2-inch BL guns and two 6-inch BL guns. Alexandra Battery, together with Forts Cunningham and Albert, were each to be armed with two 6-inch BL guns and Fort Victoria with three 9.2-inch BL guns. All these weapons were to be 'of the latest type'.[20]

Despite the Defence Committee's authorization breech-loading guns were slow to arrive in Bermuda. In 1896 two 6-inch BL Mk VII had been mounted in Alexandra Battery in place of the five 9-inch RML guns, and three 4.7-inch QF guns were mounted on the Keep of the dockyard and three more in Whale Bay Battery in place of the three 9-inch RMLs. All the other heavy RML guns remained in position, but all the 64-pdr RML guns had been removed from the establishment with the exception of four mounted at Fort Langton.

On 20 January 1899 a conference was held at the War Office *'to consider and report on the tables showing BL and QF guns recommended to be supplied in place of RML guns'*. The conference reviewed the Naval and Military Defence Committee's proposals for Bermuda and considered the defence approved

Aerial view of Fort Cunningham with positions for two 6-inch Mk VII BL guns clearly visible with the armoured face immediately below. (*Dr Edward Harris*)

for the Narrows to be unnecessarily strong and recommended the reduction of one of the three 9.2-inch BL guns proposed for Fort Victoria and the two 6-inch BL guns proposed for Fort Cunningham.

At Fort Langton the proposal was to mount two 6-inch BL guns in lieu of the three RML guns mounted there, but the conference believed these weapons were not required, while on Ireland Island four 6-inch BL guns were to be substituted for the three 10-inch RML guns and four 12-pdr QF guns for the three 4.7-inch QF guns.[21] The recommendation of the substitution of the 12-pdrs for the 4.7-inch guns seems strange since at this time the opposite was occurring in the United Kingdom and elsewhere in the Empire. The recommendation does not appear to have been implemented as the three 4.7-inch QF guns remained in place, one each on Bastions A, B and G. However, two 12-pdr QF guns were subsequently mounted as the only armament on the Land Front.

The Defence Committee also proposed to make permanent the line of field defences to defend Hamilton and Spanish Point, currently only to be constructed in time of war. However, the Defence Committee believed such a line would be vulnerable to enfilade fire from enemy ships lying off the southern end of the line, and so recommended that a new battery be constructed at the southern end of the line, near Hungry Bay, for three 9.2-inch BL and two 6-inch BL guns. The conference, however, preferred an armament of two 9.2-inch and four 6-inch BL guns.

Despite the Defence Committee's proposals, the armament situation on the island remained as it was in 1896 until 1904 when the Defence Plan showed both Fort Cunningham and Fort St Catherine as being without guns, though Fort Cunningham was being remodelled to mount two 6-inch BL Mk VII guns on the roof of the fort. Fort Victoria was now armed with two 9.2-inch BL Mk X guns and the armament of the Keep at the dockyard was now four 6-inch BL Mk VII guns and three 4.7-inch QF guns. The only RML guns remaining mounted were the four 10-inch guns mounted on Fort Albert and the two 11-inch guns at Fort George. For defence of the South Shore the Defence Plan recommended the construction of new batteries at Cataract Hill and Turtle Hill, but no action was taken on this proposal.

In 1905 the submarine mining branch of the Royal Engineers was abolished; minefields were no longer part of the defences of Bermuda and 27 Submarine Mining Company RE became 27 Fortress Company RE. Consequently, the number of DELs was reduced to three concentrated moving lights, one at St David's Battery and two at Fort Cunningham, of which one was mounted in reserve.

By 1906 Fort Cunningham had been rearmed with the two 6-inch BL Mk VII guns while Fort Albert and Fort George had been disarmed so that the island's armament now consisted of:

Fort Victoria	2 × 9.2-inch BL Mk X (15°) guns
Fort Cunningham	2 × 6-inch BL MK VII (15°) guns
Alexandra Battery	2 × 6-inch BL Mk VII (15°) guns
Ireland Island (The Keep)	4 × 6-inch BL Mk VII (15°) guns
	3 × 4.7-inch QF guns
Whale Bay Battery	3 × 4.7-inch QF guns

The guns of the dockyard consisted of a 6-inch Mk VII gun on C, D, E, and F Bastions and 4.7-inch QF guns on A, B, and G Bastions, with two 12-pdr QF guns on the Land Front. Alexandra Battery had been one of the first batteries on the island to receive breech-loading guns, having been converted for the new guns in 1898 but was now to be retained as a practice battery, while the three 4.7-inch QF guns of Whale Bay Battery were to be retained but not manned.[22]

Further changes in the armament occurred two years later in 1908, though these were changes in location rather than number. It was proposed that one of the 9.2-inch BL guns mounted at Fort Victoria should be moved to the new St David's Battery, where a 9.2-in BL gun was mounted in reserve – that

6-inch Mk VII BL gun on Bastion C of the Dockyard Keep. (*Author*)

is without personnel to man the gun – and it was also proposed that the two 6-inch BL guns at Fort Cunningham be moved to St David's Battery to act as the Examination Battery for the island. At the Keep on Ireland Island the number of 6-inch guns was reduced to three, with the fourth gun remaining mounted in reserve, and the 4.7-inch QF guns had been removed.

It was at this time that Germany came to be considered the major threat to Great Britain's security bringing about a major shift in Admiralty policy. Admiral 'Jacky' Fisher, the First Sea Lord, took the decision to concentrate the major ships of the fleet in Home waters and the Mediterranean and scrap dozens of outdated and unseaworthy vessels. A result of this policy was the down-grading in importance of a number of naval bases including Bermuda and Halifax. In 1904 the Owen Committee had defined the defences of the major ports and harbours at home and abroad based on three forms of attack. Bermuda had been classified as possibly subject to Class B attack, attack by armoured cruisers, but in 1910 it was decided that, under the conditions then existing, the defences of the island did not need to be maintained on a scale greater than that required to resist a raiding attack by unarmoured cruisers.[23]

Therefore, the defences of the island were further reduced and immediately prior to the outbreak of the First World War the guns manned by 3 Garrison Company RGA and the Bermuda Militia Artillery, the latter founded in 1895, were:

St David's Battery	2 × 9.2-inch BL Mk X guns on Mk V mountings (one mounted in reserve) 2 × 6-inch BL Mk VII guns on Mk II CP mountings (Examination Battery)
Fort Victoria	1 × 9.2-inch BL Mk X gun on Mk V mounting
Ireland Island	3 × 6-inch BL Mk VII guns on Mk II CP mountings (The Keep)

The World Wars 1914–1945

The First World War impinged little on Bermuda, though the regular troops of the British garrison were soon withdrawn for service in Europe. The RGA company was replaced by men of the Bermuda Militia Artillery who manned the guns of the coast defences until the end of the war. A regular company of the RGA returned to Bermuda in 1919 but it was withdrawn, together with the Fortress Company RE, in 1928. The only gun battery on the island to be maintained and operational was the 6-inch gun battery at St David's which acted as the island's examination battery in wartime.

With the approach of war in 1938 the War Office took the decision to improve the defences of Bermuda by constructing a new 6-inch BL battery to defend the south shore of the island and deter a raider from bombarding the dockyard from that side of the island. The site chosen for the new battery was high ground in the rear of Warwick Camp, an old British Army training camp

St David's 6-inch gun battery manned by personnel of the Bermuda Militia Artillery c.1935. (*Dr Edward Harris*)

Warwick Camp 6-inch gun battery c.1970. (*Dr Edward Harris*)

and rifle range. The battery was completed and operational in 1940. The guns were manned by men of the Bermuda Militia Artillery and the searchlights by the Bermuda Volunteer Engineers, a unit formed in 1931.

In 1941, following the Destroyers for Bases agreement signed with the United States in 1940, the Americans took over the defence of the island from the British and initially established four new batteries. Two of these batteries were armed with First World War vintage 8-inch BL railway guns, two guns on Scaur Hill and two between Fort Victoria and Fort Albert. While the other two batteries, each of two 155mm GPF guns on field carriages, were established, one two-gun battery at Turtle Hill on the south shore and a second on the eastern end of Cooper's Island, overlooking the entrance to St George's Harbour. The 155mm guns were mounted on concrete 'Panama' mounts, circular concrete platforms on which the guns could rotate a full 360°. In 1943 new battery positions each for two 6-inch BL guns were constructed on Tudor Hill on the south shore and between Fort Victoria and Fort Albert. When these batteries were operational the 8-inch railway guns were withdrawn. At the end of the war in 1945 all the American coast defence guns were removed.

In 1941 the approved armament for Bermuda included four 9.2-inch Mk X guns on 35° mountings, though no priority had been allocated for their manufacture.[24] As late as 1946 the Defence of Bases Committee were reviewing the armament of Bermuda with plans to install four 9.2-inch BL Mk X guns on 35° mountings, two on Scaur Hill, with another on Ireland Island and one at St George's, though the actual location of this last gun was not made clear. In addition, a battery of three of the latest 5.25-inch dual-purpose anti-aircraft/coast defence guns was planned for St David's Island.

Perhaps, not surprisingly, the plan for the new British gun batteries was never implemented and in 1953, when the Coast Artillery branch of the Royal Artillery was disbanded in the British Army, the guns of St David's Battery were removed. However, the guns of Warwick Camp Battery remained in place, unmaintained, until removed in 2015 to be used as display pieces at the refurbished Alexandra Battery.

Chapter Two

Jamaica

The Early Years

Jamaica, originally claimed for Spain by Christopher Colombus in 1509, remained under Spanish rule until 1655 when it was taken by an English force sent out by Oliver Cromwell with the objective of capturing Santa Domingo (Haiti). The English ships were under the command of Sir William Penn and the troops were commanded by General Robert Venables. Having failed to capture Santa Domingo the English force invaded Jamaica and established the main English settlement at the end of a narrow strip of land at the entrance to the harbour of present-day Kingston. Originally called Cagway, the name of the settlement was soon changed to Port Royal.

Kingston Harbour is one of the finest natural harbours in the world and, as such, became an important base, firstly for privateers and Letters of Marque operating against Spanish shipping in the wars of the late seventeenth and eighteenth centuries, and also as a base for ships of the Royal Navy. As Jamaica increased in importance as a sugar-producing island so the need to defend it against Spain and France also increased.

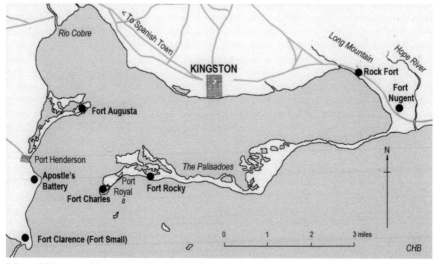

Map of Kingston Harbour. (*Charles Blackwood*)

'With respect to the general state of the Fortifications on the Coast, they are truly in a dreadful condition. The fact is, my Lord, they have been the repeated Jobs of ignorant avaricious men, who had assumed the name of Engineer.'[2]

With money now available he set about completing the defences originally planned by his predecessor. He strengthened the parapet of Fort Augusta, increasing it to a thickness of 18 feet (5.5m), and constructed a musketry wall in advance of the landward side of the fort to protect the Royal Navy powder magazine which lay outside the walls of the fort.

Work was also carried out on the old Fort Castillo to construct a circular battery for seven 32-pdr SB guns. Fort Castillo was an estate house built originally by Sir James Castillo in 1693 at the head of Kingston Harbour. Sir James, of Spanish origin, was a naturalized British citizen who was the Factor of the Spanish Asiento of Port Royal, and, in the same year, was given permission *'to enclose his dwelling with imbattled* [sic] *walls'.*[3] General Campbell also ordered the construction of a number of redoubts to defend the Hope River valley, an earthwork line at the rear of Rock Fort called Cleland's Line and a redoubt above Fort Castillo.

General Dalling, General Campbell's predecessor, had planned further defences to protect Port Royal. Through lack of funds the plan had lain in abeyance until the requisite funding was produced in 1781. At General Campbell's direction work commenced on the excavation of a dry ditch round the south and west fronts of Port Royal itself, and a hornwork for twenty guns with a dry ditch, a Place of Arms, a covered way and a *glacis* in front. This work was designed by two Royal Engineers officers, Colonels Mercer and Mackerras, and comprised two *demi-bastions* flanking a front and, on completion in 1783, was known as the Polygon Battery. Subsequently the fortification was named Prince William Henry's Polygon in honour of the third son of King George III who visited Jamaica while serving as a midshipman. Four years later Prince William Henry's Polygon was badly damaged in a hurricane and remained unrepaired for the next twenty years.

Since there was a fear that an enemy force could avoid the harbour and land south of Salt Pond Hill and march on Spanish Town or Kingston from the west, two private citizens took it upon themselves to build batteries to defend the Salt Pond area. In his Memoir of Jamaica in 1782 Major General Campbell describes the two batteries as Fort Johnston and Fort Small. Fort Johnston, built by a David Johnston who owned the land on which it was built south-west of Salt Pond Bay, consisted of a guardhouse, a semi-circular

Remains of Fort Small, Kingston. (*https://fsgfort.com/fortfinder*)

platform and a magazine. The role of the battery was to engage an enemy landing force and the armament appears to have been four 12-pdr and five 6-pdr SB guns.

Fort Small was of a similar design, but its role was to engage enemy ships supporting a landing force, and for that reason it was more heavily armed than Fort Johnston mounting eight 24-pdr SB guns and one 10-inch mortar. The *Jamaica Almanac* of 1784 notes that the captain of Small's Battery was David Small, but, strangely, there is no reference to Fort Johnston, which throws the date of its completion into some doubt.

War with Revolutionary France and Napoleon 1793–1815

Jamaica was little affected by war with Revolutionary France as little attention was paid to colonial territories by the warring powers. As a result, little attention was paid to the island's forts and batteries which were the responsibility of the colonial authorities rather than the Board of Ordnance. However, it would seem that Fort Small was repaired in the early 1790s and, mounting five 24-pdr SB guns, was renamed Fort Clarence in 1799 in honour of Prince William, Duke of Clarence, the future King William IV.

The situation, however, changed dramatically in 1803 with the recommencement of the war with France after the collapse of the Peace of Amiens. As part of a plan to lure Nelson away from the blockade of French ports and to enable the French fleet to support the invasion of Britain, Napoleon concocted a scheme by which three fleets should be sent across the Atlantic to the West Indies under the command of three noted French admirals, Villeneuve, Ganteaume and Missiessy. In 1805 only Villeneuve and Missiessy reached their destinations, and only the latter had some success briefly occupying Dominica and reinforcing the French garrison on Santa Domingo (Haiti), while Villeneuve quickly returned to France with Nelson in hot pursuit.

The rumours of an imminent French invasion and the arrival of Admiral Missiessy with five ships-of-the-line and four frigates concentrated the minds of the members of the Jamaica House of Assembly wonderfully. Throughout the history of the colony there had always been a reluctance to vote money to build and maintain the island's defences. However, the rapidly approaching threat of a French invasion caused the governor, Lieutenant General George Nugent, to attempt to make some impression on the outstanding repairs required for the forts.

General Nugent proposed repairs to Fort Castille and the construction of a new circular gun platform for six 24-pdr SB guns and a tower mounting one 12-pdr SB gun on a traversing carriage on the hill above the fort. This would enable the fort to effectively defend the approaches to Rock Fort and the ground between it and the Hope River. In honour of the governor the name of the fort was changed to Fort Nugent.

View of Kingston Harbour from Apostles Battery c.1800. (*Author's Collection*)

The general also authorized the raising of a European Garrison company with a strength in 1805 of one captain, two subalterns, and seventy-nine Other Ranks. The company was to be stationed at Apostles Battery and Fort Clarence to reinforce the Royal Artillery garrison and the Dutch Emigrant Artillery, a unit which was subsumed into the Royal Foreign Artillery in the same year.

General Nugent's successor as governor in mid-1805 was Lieutenant General Sir Eyre Coote who, on his arrival and in view of what was then considered to be an imminent threat of French invasion (though, unknown to the British on Jamaica Admirals Villeneuve and Missiessy had returned to France in July of that year) set out on an inspection of the island's defences. He presented the results of his inspection in a letter to Lord Castlereagh, the Secretary of State for War and the Colonies, dated 23 March 1806 saying:

'Immediately on my becoming invested with the chief command, I lost no time in making a most minute inspection and accurate survey of the Forts, Stores, and Depots of all kinds in the vicinity of Kingston, the result of which has been to convince me that nothing can be worse than the state of Fortifications intended for the defence of the Island, and above all the important works of Port Royal.'[4]

In a further letter two months later he continued his criticism of the fortifications stating:

'The coast fortification of this colony consists of Forts and Batteries, numerously distributed along the Coast, at an enormous expense, and with the most glaring want of judgment – In fact, they are for the greater part totally useless, possessing of Fortifications nothing but the name, as in the construction of them jobbing, and individual advantage, have been the principal, if not only consideration.'[5]

The Shipley Report

General Sir Eyre Coote was so disturbed at the state of the island's defences that he requested the Board of Ordnance to send a senior Royal Engineers officer to inspect and report on the existing defences. The Board selected Brigadier General Charles Shipley RE, an officer with vast experience of the Caribbean having been the Commanding Royal Engineer of the Windward and Leeward Islands from 1796 to 1805, and who had recently been appointed brigadier general to the forces in the West Indies.

Brigadier General Shipley carried out a complete inspection of the forts and batteries on the island and in his report strongly castigated their condition. He made no attempt to mince his words, stating in a letter to General Morse, the Inspector General of Fortifications in London:

'I have no hesitation in saying that the Existing Defences are totally inadequate to the security of the island which is by far the most valuable and important of any British Possession in the West Indies'.

He went on to say:

'Works badly contrived, and worse Executed – Unserviceable Guns – Decayed Gun Carriages – Corroded Shot – Great deficiency of the necessary Stores and Ammunition – and damp Powder Magazines – Such is the by no means exaggerated description of most of the Forts and Batteries.'[6]

Referring to the problem that the construction and repair of fortifications was a matter for the colonial authorities he continued:

'But it demands imperiously that no more money should be wasted on irrational Plans, Conceived in Error, Acted upon without Energy, but persisted in with the Confidence and Obstinacy of Ignorance. And above all it is requisite the Legislature of the Colony should go hand in hand with the British government by a liberal and extended understanding upon the Subject.'.[7]

Believing that a permanent and effective plan of defence for the island was practicable with suitable co-operation between the colonial and British military authorities – though he suspected that such co-operation might be difficult to achieve – Brigadier General Shipley made numerous recommendations for improvements to the defences. Both Prince William Henry's Polygon and Fort Augusta had been damaged, the former by a hurricane and the latter by an earthquake and subsidence which had resulted in the right *demi-bastion* and nearly a quarter of the curtain of the land front being sunk on its foundations and completely split in places. Shipley proposed the repair of the existing fortifications and new works at Rock Fort, Prince William Henry's Polygon and two marine batteries to be built on shoals in Old Harbour, a bay to the south of Kingston where the French had landed in 1694.

Curtain wall and bastion of Fort Augusta showing the hurricane and earthquake damage still visible today. (*Author*)

To further strengthen Rock Fort, Shirley proposed repairing an old masonry redoubt on the hill above the fort known as Spanish Fort and linking it to Rock Fort by means of a loopholed wall to act as a covered way. At Prince William Henry's Polygon, he was of the opinion that there was little point in repairing the defences, but instead proposed the construction of a circular Martello tower, 30 feet (9.2m) in diameter in the centre of the Polygon. However, this tower and the two marine batteries in Old Harbour were never built.

With the defeat of the combined French and Spanish fleet at Trafalgar the threat to Jamaica of invasion was sharply diminished and, as a result, little was done to improve the defences other than the strengthening of Rock Fort

Fort Nugent Martello tower. The tower still retains the concrete battery command post for the 9.2-inch BL gun built in the Second World War. (*Author*)

and the construction of the Martello tower mounting a single 12-pdr SB gun overlooking Fort Nugent. Brigadier General Shipley had recommended that the 24-pdr guns at Fort Nugent should be replaced by lighter 12-pdr SB guns, as a faster rate of fire could be achieved with these guns making them more effective against an infantry attack but once again no action was taken by the colonial authorities.

Indeed, in a report on the state of the forts and batteries in Kingston Harbour in 1812 it was clear that the colonial government had done little to maintain them or provide the appropriate stores and ammunition. In 1812 the armament of the forts and batteries comprised the following:

Fort Charles	King's Line	10 × 26-pdr SB guns (Foreign)
	Queen's Line	8 × 24-pdr SB guns
	Prince Frederick's Line	nil
	Hanover Line	30 × 24-pdr SB guns
		2 × 18-pdr SB guns
	Prince of Wales's Line	16 × 32-pdr SB guns
		1 × 26-pdr SB gun (Foreign)
	Redan Battery	8 × 26-pdr SB guns (Foreign)
Prince William Henry's	Left Flank	4 × 24-pdr SB guns
Polygon		2 × 2 × 8-inch SB Howitzers
Fort Clarence		5 × 24-pdr SB guns
Fort Clarence Blockhouse		8 × 4-pdr SB guns
Apostles Battery		9 × 42-pdr SB guns
		3 × 32-pdr SB guns
Fort Augusta		48 × 24-pdr SB guns
Rock Fort		13 × 24-pdr SB guns
		2 × 4-pdr SB guns (Foreign)
Fort Nugent		6 × 24-pdr SB guns
Fort Nugent Upper Battery		nil
Fort Nugent Martello Tower		1 × 12-pdr SB gun (Foreign)[8]

The majority of the armament consisted of iron guns mounted on iron or wooden garrison carriages and many of these carriages were unserviceable when the report was written. The foreign guns found in some of the West Indies forts at this time were captured French bronze guns.

Eight years after the 1812 report Captain George Barney RE was directed to report on the island's defences and he found them still to be in a dire condition. He noted that the whole of the defences, magazines, barracks, and stores (with the exception of the new barracks at Up Park Camp and the Arsenal at Kingston) were the property of the colony and in a further statement he made it clear that the colonial authorities were continuing to

Rock Fort. The photograph shows the rear of the casemates and the ramp to the *terreplein*. (*Author*)

show a marked reluctance to spend money on defence works, particularly in a time of relative peace. Captain Barney concluded that the defences so long neglected and allowed to go to ruin would cost at least £100,000 to repair.[9]

Captain Barney inspected all the forts and batteries of Kingston Harbour and found that most of the guns and carriages were in a poor state. At Rock Fort he found shrubbery growing out of the masonry, no tampions for the guns and these had not been scaled or painted, indeed one of the guns had fallen through its wooden carriage from decay. At Fort Augusta no repairs had been carried out to the land front *demi-bastion* and the curtain wall, while Fort Clarence and the Apostles Battery, though still armed, appeared to Captain Barney to have been abandoned.

In 1829 it would seem that while some repairs had been made to the defences these clearly did not include Fort Augusta which, in 1824 had been declared a health hazard because of its proximity to the swamp. In the same year the Board of Ordnance ordered a supply of guns and carriages for Jamaica including three 18-pdr SB guns for Fort Nugent. The provision of these guns appears to have been in answer to Brigadier General Shipley's recommendation some twenty-three years earlier that 12-pdr guns should replace the heavier 24-pdr guns. Interestingly the Board of Ordnance, never noted for the speed of its deliberations, substituted a reduced number of 18-pdr SB guns in place of the previously recommended 12-pdrs, giving as its reason that '*no iron traversing platforms had ever been constructed for so small a calibre of gun*'.[10]

Five years after this, in May 1834 both Fort Augusta and Apostles Battery were placed in a state of care and maintenance and transferred to the Barracks Department.

Naval Base and Coaling Station

By the middle of the nineteenth century, thanks to the superiority of the Royal Navy, there was no major threat to the British possessions in the West Indies. The only two countries that were considered to pose some slight threat were France and the United States. In the 1850s Britain and France were allies engaged in the Crimean War with Russia and, although the Russian Far East Fleet posed a potential threat to Britain's colonies in the Far East, Russia's Baltic and Black Sea Fleets were blockaded by the Royal Navy and had no access to the Atlantic. The United States, though geographically closer to the Caribbean, was not considered any threat despite occasional diplomatic contretemps, as the United States Navy was only a fraction of the size of the Royal Navy.

The fact that there was no immediate threat meant that the Jamaican House of Assembly continued to be reluctant to provide funds for the maintenance of the defences. However, the decline of the sugar industry as a result of the British Government's Sugar Duties Act in 1846, which removed Jamaica's favoured status as Britain's primary supplier of sugar, together with ensuing racial and religious tension, resulted in a period of civil unrest culminating in the Morant Bay Rebellion in 1865. This rebellion so alarmed the colonial authorities that they formally requested Britain to impose direct rule and in 1866 Jamaica became a Crown Colony.

The resultant change in government meant that responsibility for the defence works now rested with the British War Office under the Secretary of State for War and the Commander-in-Chief of the Army, but still little attempt was made to improve the island's fortifications. The garrison comprised one British infantry battalion and three battalions of the West India Regiment under the command of a major general. By 1875 the garrison, now commanded by a colonel, had been reduced to one British infantry battalion and one battalion of the West India Regiment, though there had been some up-grading of the armament of the forts which at that date comprised eighteen 8-inch SB guns and twenty-six 32-pdr SB guns.

The importance of Port Royal as a naval base remained despite its lack of a graving dock for the new iron-hulled steamships. Although Bermuda was the main Royal Navy dockyard for the North America and West Indies Station,

Port Royal was designated as a first-class coaling station and continued as the main base for Royal Navy ships in the western Caribbean.

In 1872 the governor of Jamaica wrote to the Colonial Office to complain that Port Royal in its current state was absolutely indefensible and *'in the absence of British ships-of-war would be at the mercy of a gunboat'*.[11] In January 1875 the Admiralty drew the attention of the Secretary of State for War to the state of the island's defences and the Inspector General of Fortifications, Lieutenant General Lintorn Simmons, concurred with the governor's view, commenting that nothing had been done to improve the defences since the governor's letter.

In 1878 the Defence Committee in reviewing the temporary defences of the coaling stations approved the allocation of ten 7-inch 6½-ton RML guns for the defence of Kingston, five of these guns to be mounted at Fort Charles, three at Fort Rocky and two at Apostles Battery. In addition, provision was made for six light guns, 64-pdr RML guns, to be installed whenever they could be spared together with submarine mines to block all the channels leading into the harbour with the exception of the eastern channel. The total cost was estimated at £26,600.

Four years later, in 1882, the Inspector General of Fortifications issued a Memorandum on the Defences of Jamaica. The Memorandum showed that the emplacements for the RML guns had been completed for a new battery at Port Royal Point, also for the guns to be mounted in the Hanover and Prince of Wales's Line at Fort Charles and at Rocky Point. At Apostles Battery the emplacements were only partially completed.

The approved armament for Jamaica was:

Port Royal Point Battery	3 × 7-inch 6½-ton RML guns *en barbette*
	2 × 64-pdr RML guns Moncrieff mountings
Prince of Wales's Line, Port Royal	1 × 7-inch 6½-ton RML gun *en barbette*
Hanover Line, Port Royal	1 × 7-inch 6½-ton RML *en barbette*
Rocky Point Battery	3 × 7-inch 6½-ton RML guns *en barbette*
	2 × 64-pdr RML guns Moncrieff mountings
Apostles Battery	2 × 7-inch 6½-ton RML guns *en barbette*

As yet, however, none of the approved guns had been mounted. In 1884 Prince William Henry's Polygon was transferred to the Admiralty as building development in front of it removed its effectiveness as a defence work.

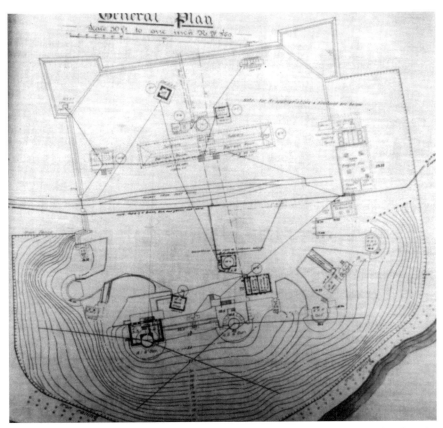

Plan of Rocky Point Battery c. 1920. The plan shows the two bastions defending the rear of the battery, possibly the last bastion defences to be built by the British Army. (*TNA WO 78/4905*)

Front reached crisis level. To maintain sufficient troops to man the harbour defences forty men from the 1st Battalion, The West India Regiment, the current infantry garrison, were attached to 66 Company RGA.[18]

With the end of the war in November 1918 there was no longer any requirement to maintain the Kingston defences in a state of alert. In December the outlying forts, Rocky Point Battery and Fort Clarence were demobilized, as was the Jamaica Militia Artillery, though still retained as a part-time volunteer unit.

Throughout the inter-war period a company of gunners was retained in Kingston with 66 Company RGA being relieved by 10 Heavy Battery RA in 1925 after the amalgamation of the Royal Garrison Artillery and the Royal Field Artillery. However, in 1929 and until the outbreak of the Second World War the Royal Artillery garrison in Kingston was reduced to 2 Heavy Battery

Rocky Point Battery. The photograph shows the two 6-inch Mk VII gun positions, one on each side of the central block. (*Author*)

RA in cadre strength. The only change to the defences was the substitution of two 6-inch Mk VII BL guns for the old 6-inch QF guns at Fort Clarence in 1937, with the fort becoming the examination battery for Kingston. One of these guns was subsequently transferred to Rocky Point Battery, probably to replace an unserviceable gun in the battery, and at some date in the 1930s the approved armament of Rocky Point Battery was reduced to a single 6-inch MK VII BL gun.

The Second World War

The outbreak of war on 3 September 1939 saw the mobilization of the Jamaica Militia Artillery and the manning of Kingston harbour defences. These were:

Fort Nugent	1 × 9.2-inch Mk X BL gun
Fort Clarence (Examination Battery)	2 × 6-inch Mk VII BL guns
Rocky Point Battery	1 × 6-inch Mk VII BL gun

However, as in the First World War Jamaica was little troubled by events in Europe. Initially, the threat was deemed to be from German surface raiders. but the sinking of the German pocket battleship *Graf Spee* and a number of merchant ships armed for raiding reduced this threat almost completely. A threat from U-boats to ships in the harbour remained, but this did not prevent the withdrawal of the British garrison to be replaced by a new formation, the North Caribbean Force. This force and its counterpart, the South Caribbean Force, was established to incorporate the mobilized elements of the defence forces of the various Caribbean islands together with those of British Honduras and British Guiana.

The Jamaica Militia Artillery was subsumed into the North Caribbean Force as 1, 2, 3, and 4 Coast Batteries, with 1 Coast Battery manning the gun at Fort Nugent, 2 Coast Battery the gun at Rocky Point Battery and 3 Coast Battery the guns of Fort Clarence. Two 75mm QF guns were dispatched to Turks Island, a dependency of Jamaica, and these were manned by the men of 4 Coast Battery.

Under the terms of the Destroyers for Bases Agreement between the United States and the United Kingdom signed in September 1940, the United States established two bases in Jamaica, an Army Air Force airfield, Vernam Army Airfield near Clarendon, and a United States Navy seaplane base on Goat Island, both west of Kingston. For the defence of Goat Island, the United States Army provided four 155mm mobile guns on Panama mountings manned by personnel of 327 Coast Artillery Battalion, with two coast artillery searchlights. Four 37mm anti-aircraft guns manned by men of Battery A of 425 Coast Artillery Battalion were provided for the defence of Vernam Field, though that does raise the question as to where the air threat to the airfield would come from.

In October 1944 1 and 3 Coast Batteries NCF at Fort Nugent and Fort Clarence ceased to be operational and the guns were placed in care and maintenance. One of the 6-inch guns from Fort Clarence was moved to Rocky Point Battery which continued in an operational role until July 1946 when the Jamaica Militia Artillery element of the North Caribbean Force was disbanded.[19] This finally brought to an end the coast defences of Jamaica.

Chapter Three

St Helena

The First Fortifications

Situated in the middle of the South Atlantic is the small volcanic island of St Helena. With a total area of 47 square miles it lies 1,200 miles (1,920 kms) from the continent of Africa and 1,500 miles (2,400 kms) north-west of Cape Town. The island is mountainous and almost completely surrounded by precipitous cliffs with only a few practical landing places. Behind the sheer and barren cliffs, the island, although mountainous, is green and fertile. The highest point is Diana's Peak, some 2,600 feet (800m) high. It was this abundance of vegetation, a plentiful supply of fresh water and a single, comparatively safe, anchorage that attracted the island to passing

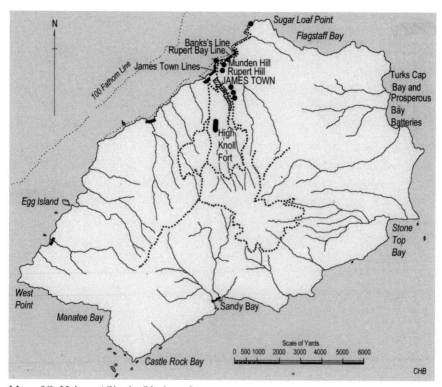

Map of St Helena. (*Charles Blackwood*)

ships. The island was discovered in 1503 by the Portuguese navigator Joao da Nova who arrived there on the birthday of Saint Helena, mother of the Roman Emperor Constantine.

Although St Helena had been known to the Portuguese since its discovery in 1503, they had never formally claimed sovereignty of the island and the first English interest came in 1588 when an English sea captain, Thomas Cavendish, landed on the island. Between 1588 and 1657 English, Portuguese, Spanish, and Dutch ships all visited the island without making any attempt to claim it. However, the Anglo-Dutch wars of the mid-seventeenth century forced the English Honourable East India Company to claim the island in 1657, two years after the capture of Jamaica, in order to provide the Company's ships with a re-supply base, since the Dutch occupation of the Cape of Good Hope prevented English ships obtaining supplies there.

The Dutch briefly occupied St Helena in 1672–73 but were ejected by an English force under the command of Sir Richard Munden. It was after this brief Dutch occupation that the Court of Directors of the HEIC decided that the island must be fortified if it was to be retained by the Company and so, in 1673, the HEIC developed the island into a major fortress.

The first fortification to be built was the castle at the small settlement of James Town which overlooked the only sheltered anchorage. James Town was situated in a sheltered valley, one of a number that run down to the sea in the north-west corner of the island. The other valleys are Rupert's Valley and Bank's Valley, to the north of James Town and Breakneck Valley, Friar's Valley, and Lemon Valley to the south of the settlement. The castle was essentially a triangular fort with three bastions, two facing the sea and the third, on the landward side, at the apex of the triangle formed by the walls. The castle mounted eighteen guns that are described in the St Helena Records as being *'one demi-cannon, five whole culverins, five demi-culverins and six sakers'*.

The flanks of the castle were each secured by a battery for two guns and by a wall extending to the vertical cliffs on each side of the valley. These defences were strengthened by the construction of a battery on Munden's Point, the northern arm of the James Town bay. In addition, two guns were mounted in a battery known as Banks' Platform, also known as King William's Fort, on Sugar Loaf Point. Inland a two-gun battery was placed on the ridge overlooking James Town, and at Prosperous Bay on the north-east of the island a guardroom was built to be used as a lookout post. In 1678 the HEIC Records also showed that there was a battery of five guns sited just a short distance from the small landing place at Lemon Valley. This battery was first known as Sprague's Platform, but the name was then changed to Berkley's (or Bearkley's) Platform.

The Eighteenth Century Fortifications

James Town Lines

In 1708 Governor Roberts had the castle that exists today built in the rear of the old James Fort, together with a massive curtain wall that acted as a retaining wall for the castle and a second line of defence behind the original wall. This was completed in 1714 and by 1734 the defences of James Town were reported to comprise two substantial curtain walls and two *demi-bastions*, the latter probably being on the sites of the original flank batteries. James Valley was now defended by a fully fortified 'Line' with access provided at the eastern end across a drawbridge. In 1727 it was stated that there were seventy-nine guns of assorted calibres mounted in the James Town lines with a further fourteen mounted in Munden's Battery, placed 80 feet (24m) above the sea. In 1767 a Captain Mitchel pointed out the severe disadvantage of having a perpendicular rock face at the rear of the guns and proposed moving the battery to the top of the hill. The siting of a battery on the top of Munden's Hill did not occur, however, until later in the century.

By the end of the eighteenth century a dry ditch had been dug on the seaward side of the line running the complete length of the line. The ditch was completed in 1787 and by that date a total of thirty-two modern guns were mounted on it.

James Town Lines c.1860, showing the centre bastion and ditch. (*Royal Geographical Society*)

Banks' Lines

Between James Town and Sugar Loaf Point, about 3 miles (5km) to the north, there were two more narrow valleys where the HEIC felt an enemy could land. Closest to Sugar Loaf Point was Banks' Valley Bay, and it was decided to fortify the entrance to the valley on the seaward side by building a line of fortifications to support the old two-gun battery on Banks' Platform, known originally as King William's Fort. The importance of Sugar Loaf Point lay in the fact that any ship approaching James Town was forced by the south-east trade winds to keep close inshore as they passed Banks' Bay.

As early as 1678 there were a number of guns defending Banks' Bay, some reports give the number as three, others as five, and by 1727 the number of guns had been increased to seven and a defensive wall across the mouth of the valley was in the course of construction. These guns were very necessary as they acted as an examination battery enforcing the governor's orders that all ships approaching James Town must identify themselves on reaching Banks' Bay.

Banks' Lines comprised a curtain wall 8 feet (2.4m) thick closing off the seaward end of the valley. Built of rubble stone, it had stone platforms and embrasures for the seven guns. Because a small stream ran down the valley a tunnel was built in the wall to allow the water through and this was defended by a portcullis. Behind the gun platform there was a single-storey barrack building providing accommodation for the garrison and behind the barrack there was a small cookhouse. The rear of the battery was enclosed with a wall and a track, described on a nineteenth century plan of the lines as a 'Military Road', led up the valley to James Town.

On the right flank of Banks' Line and overlooking the line there was another battery position known as the 'William and Mary Battery', probably the old King William Fort, and subsequently renamed Half Moon Battery or Upper Lines. This battery mounted eleven guns firing *en barbette* and mounted on stone platforms.

The importance of Banks' Point and Sugar Loaf Point was further emphasized by the construction of additional batteries in the 1770s along the line of the cliff face from Half Moon Battery north to Crown Point. A road was built into the cliff face connecting Middle Point, Crown Point and Buttermilk Point. These were small gun positions, each mounting one or two guns and they were sited so that there was a continuous line of guns stretching from Crown Point to Banks' Valley Bay. The Buttermilk Point battery was frequently referred to as the Lower Crown Point Battery and immediately below this battery there was a position for a single gun approached by a

Banks' Lines as it is today. Although partly ruined, the main gun platform and the outlet for floodwater still stand. (*Author*)

staircase built within the rock face. This position was sometimes referred to as Pirie's battery.

Most of the guns were 18-pdr SB guns and the magazines to store the powder and shot were excavated in the cliff face behind Half Moon Battery and between Middle Point Battery and Repulse Point Battery. The siting of the magazines within the cliff face is a feature of the St Helena fortifications, and the thick rock provided excellent protection from enemy gunfire. Each magazine comprised a short entrance passage with two rooms opening from it, each about 6 feet (1.8m) by 8 feet (2.4m) in size. Other examples of rock magazines are to be found at Sandy Bay on the east coast and on the path leading to another Half Moon battery at Lemon Valley Bay.

Rupert's Bay

Between James Bay and Banks' Bay lies the larger Rupert's Bay, named after Prince Rupert, brother of King Charles I, who is alleged to have anchored there once on his return from a voyage to India. Strategically not as important as Banks' Valley Bay, it did, however, provide a tactical landing place and any enemy invasion force, after landing, could move up the valley and then approach James Town from the rear. Rupert's Bay had, therefore, to be defended and so a fortified line was built to close off the entrance to the valley from the sea. As early as 1678 eight guns had been placed at Rupert's Bay, but work on the line was not completed until 1707. In 1727 a report noted that *'Rupert's was defended by nine guns some of which were small 4-pdrs.'*[1]

Work on the Rupert's Valley line was contemporaneous with the construction of Banks' line but, because of the size of the mouth of the valley, the line was considerably longer, nearly 550 yards (500m) in overall length. There were eventually stone platforms for fourteen guns and living quarters for soldiers in barrack accommodation a little way up the valley. The wall of the line was 5 feet (1.5m) thick, and, in places, 20 feet (6.1m) high. As with the line across Banks' Valley there was a tunnel through the wall to enable the water flowing down the valley to escape to the sea. In fact, the tunnel proved to be inadequate for its role, for in 1787 Rupert's line was reported as being wrecked by a flood and the line was described as being in such a state that repair would be equal to building a new fortification![2]

Chubb's Rock Batteries

Three single-gun batteries were established on Chubb's Rock, a rocky headland between Munden's Point and Rupert's Bay. These batteries were known as Upper Chubb's Rock, Middle Chubb's Rock, and Lower Chubb's Rock. Originally the batteries were armed with old guns and they were vulnerable to damage by the sea. On 12 November 1737 the seas were so high that a gun was washed off Lower Chubb's Rock. The gun was described as a demi-culverin of 43cwt. This was a gun with a calibre of 4½ inches (114mm) which fired a round shot weighing nine pounds.[3]

Although the *Records* are not clear on the armament of the Chubb's Rock batteries it would seem that three 9-pdr SB guns were mounted there until the later years of the eighteenth century when they were probably replaced by three 12-pdr SB guns.

Sandy Bay Lines

On the southern side of the island there was one possible landing place for an enemy force and this was the small cove known as Sandy Bay from the fact that the valley opened out onto a wide gravel beach. Although partially protected by a spit of land known as Horse's Head, and by a hill called Crown Point opposite it, Sandy Bay was a dangerous place to approach as it was exposed to the prevailing south-easterly wind.

A small temporary battery for two guns had been authorized for the defence of the bay in 1695, but the main line of fortification was not built until the middle of the eighteenth century.[4] Because Sandy Bay was as far from James Town as it was possible to be on the island and because there was a track leading directly up to Diana's Peak, the highest point, the HEIC directed that the bay should be strongly fortified. Once again the decision was taken to wall off the beach, but at Sandy Bay this involved the construction of two separate walls because two valleys, Sandy Bay and Broad Gut, debouch onto the same beach separated by a promontory known as Beach Hill.

The walls at Sandy Bay were second only to the Rupert's Bay lines in length being over 400 yards (365m) long. The main section of the wall on the western side was a properly constructed fortification with a ditch and *glacis*. There was a small bastion for guns firing through embrasures and on the right of the bastion there was the usual tunnel to permit floodwater through to the sea. The two sections of the wall were linked by connecting steps around Beach Hill which were protected by a wall on each side.

Since Sandy Bay was such a distance from James Town the troops manning the line were required to live at Sandy Bay. This garrison was accommodated in two single-storey buildings built along the inner side of the western curtain wall and in additional buildings to the rear of the line. A cookhouse building was also provided, also built against the inner side of the western wall, and a magazine was cut into the western side of Beach Hill. There was also a substantial parade ground behind the wall. These buildings and the wall were much damaged by a flood in 1781 but were subsequently repaired.

The eastern wall across Broad Gut was not protected by a ditch and *glacis*, but again there was a tunnel, protected by a portcullis, to allow stream water through to the sea. There was no bastion but simply a small gun platform for two guns, firing through embrasures, in the centre of the wall. In the eighteenth century these were long guns, probably 6-pdr SB or 9-pdr SB guns but subsequently, probably early in the nineteenth century, two 24-pdr carronades were mounted on the platform. The substitution of carronades for the earlier long guns may have resulted from the fact that carronades were better suited to this particular position. This was because the angle of the eastern curtain wall prevented these two guns from firing at approaching ships and only permitted enfilade fire along the main beach. In 1863 a photograph by John Lilley showed that the lines and buildings were well maintained, but six years later, in 1869, a second photograph taken by a Colonel Swinton showed the lines abandoned and the buildings derelict.

Behind the walls defending the beach two further gun positions were constructed with a platform for a single gun on Beach Hill, the promontory in the middle of the beach, and a second position, also for a single gun, on the heights of Crown Point on the eastern side of the bay. In addition, a three gun battery was built on Horse's Head, the western headland of the bay that provided shelter for a landing place on the rocks between the headland and the beach. Using the rocky outcrops of the headland as natural protection,

Sandy Bay Lines showing the main gun platform, floodwater outlet, and the flanking wall with two gun embrasures at the other end of the beach. c.1860. (*Royal Geographical Society*)

three stone gun platforms were built together with a small stone magazine and a guardhouse. The battery was armed with four guns, three 24-pdr carronades and one 18-pdr carronade. These guns were obviously selected because of the confined nature of the site, and because of the short range over which ships entering the bay would be engaged by the guns of the battery.

Depth was provided to the defence of the beach by another battery approximately 2,500 yards (2,290m) inland covering the track leading from the beach. This battery, at a spot called Lemon Grove, was for four guns on stone platforms, and was also provided with a small stone magazine.

Lemon Valley Lines
To the west of James Town the steep cliffs would seem to preclude any attempt at landing from the sea, but there were a number of narrow valleys – Breakneck Valley, Young's Valley, Friar's Valley and Lemon Valley – which provided possible, though difficult, approaches. Two of these valleys, Young's and Friar's Valleys, were so narrow that it was decided that gun platforms on either side of Goat Pound Ridge, the spur between the two valleys, would be sufficient to prevent an enemy using these approaches. Breakneck Valley was the closest to James Town and any ships approaching would be observed and fired on from guns at James Town or on Ladder Hill, so it was considered sufficient simply to provide a wall at the beach end of the valley.

However, Lemon Valley was a different matter as it was a spectacularly deep valley, broader than the others and, although it was a steep climb to the high ground, it was a possible landing place and invasion approach that had to be defended; it was where the Dutch landed in 1672. Initially the valley was defended by siting five guns to cover the bay together with a magazine and a guardhouse. These defences were originally known as 'Sprague's Platform', but on a map of 1764 it appears that the name had changed to 'Berkley's Platform' by which time the number of guns had been reduced to four, two on each side of the valley. Subsequently, the position was renamed Lemon Valley Fort.

The early defences of Lemon Valley were subject to damage from flooding and by 1717, in a letter to the directors of the HEIC, they were described as *'now decayed and ruinated* [sic] *the Platform broke down these six years'.*[5] Despite this it was not until the middle of the eighteenth century that steps were taken to improve the Lemon Valley defences. A fortified line 200 yards (183m) long was then built between the steep cliffs on each side of the valley, completely closing it off. The wall was 20 feet (6.1m) high and 8 feet (2.4m) thick along the indented centre section that formed the *terreplein* of the battery. Here six guns were mounted on stone platforms firing through embrasures. The two flank sections of the line were at an angle to the centre section and were narrower in width, being only 3 feet (0.91m) thick. Again, there was a tunnel through the wall with a portcullis to allow floodwater to exit from the valley behind the wall and, in this case, the tunnel was located under the centre of the gun platform.

A report of 1777 by a Major James Rennell described the wall as being of better construction than any of the others. Behind the gun platform there was a single-storey barrack building and two or three smaller buildings, probably cookhouse and magazine. Major Rennell also recommended additional gun positions to defend the valley and these were subsequently built including another 'Half Moon Battery' sited on the lower part of the cliff on the left flank of the line. A narrow path was hewn out of the cliff to provide access to the new battery and a magazine was built into the cliff face half way along the path. The Lemon Valley Half Moon Battery was armed with four 18-pdr SB guns.

Lemon Valley Bay was also protected by three-gun positions on Goat Pound Ridge, a steep sided ridge to the north of the bay. Three platforms were situated, one on the north side of the ridge, a second on the eastern side, and the third on the western side. These were simple rubble stone platforms built into the steep sides of the ridge with a total of five guns, one 12-pdr

Lemon Valley Lines. (*Author*)

SB and one 6-pdr SB long guns, and three 12-pdr carronades, mounted two on both the north and west platforms and one on the east. There was also a small guardhouse and a magazine on the east side. An interesting aspect of the carriages of the guns in these positions, and others mounted on Ladder Hill and at Powell's Valley, was that their carriages were modified to permit the guns to fire at considerable angles of depression up to 45°. Similar depression carriages were provided for guns mounted high on the Rock of Gibraltar.[6]

Thompson's Valley
The only other valley to be fortified in the eighteenth century was Thompson's Valley in the south-west of the island. Here a long, deep valley led up from a small bay to Thompson's Wood on the central ridgeline, so providing access to the centre of the island. Once again the valley was defended by walling it off at the seaward end, but here an additional form of defence was provided by the construction of a square musketry tower, sometimes referred to as a Martello tower. The tower was built on an outcrop of rock approximately 100 feet (30.4m) above the bay. The base of the tower was 19 feet (5.8m) by 22 feet (6.7m) square and about 25 feet (7.6m) in height. It was entered at first floor level and had a single row of musketry loopholes also at first floor level. Below the tower there was an open gun platform for a single gun.

Thompson's Bay was defended by two further gun positions, East Battery and West Battery, each sited on the flanks of the bay to provide crossfire in conjunction with the gun under the tower. Both were positions for two carronades, one 68-pdr SB and one 18-pdr carronade at East Battery and two 18-pdr carronades at West Battery, and there was a small guardhouse behind the West Battery. The East Battery had positions for two guns mounted on wooden platforms, but the two guns at West Battery were mounted on stone platforms.

Half way up the west side of the valley there was a position for one gun. The position was similar in size to East and West Batteries and was known as Eagle's Eyrie. Access to the battery was difficult and it is likely that it was abandoned by the end of the Napoleonic War. The one gun mounted there was a carronade, either an 18-pdr or a 12-pdr. The choice of this weapon for the battery was probably due to the fact that carronades were much lighter than long guns and easier to move into positions that were difficult of access.

The East Coast Defences

Prosperous Bay and Turk's Cap Bay, both on the north-east side of the island, were also considered vulnerable points where a landing was possible. Indeed, it was at Prosperous Bay that the English landed in 1673 to retake the island from the Dutch after the latter's brief occupation of the island.

Prosperous Bay is a wide bay overlooked by steep cliffs with two possible landing places separated by the height of Horse Point. The northern valley is overlooked by Turk's Cap, and behind it there is a ridge with precipitous sides while to the south the other landing place is backed by the cliffs of Horse Point.

No attempt was made to build walls to secure these valleys, instead a number of batteries and a tower were built with the aim of preventing any enemy landing force making their way inland up either valley. At the northern end of Prosperous Bay two batteries were built on the ridge behind Turk's Cap Bay. Cox's Battery, for two guns, was built on the edge of the cliff overlooking Turk's Cap and was supported by a similar battery, Gregory's Battery, about 650 yards (595m) behind Cox's Battery. Both were simple gun platforms without protection, standing at a height approximately 750 feet (230m) above the bay, and from this position were able to dominate both the northern valley and Turk's Cap Valley on the other side of the ridge.

On the northern side of Turk's Cap Bay there was a further battery built about 1734. The eight guns, probably iron 6-pdr 20cwt SB guns, were mounted behind an earth embankment firing through embrasures rather than just mounted on an open platform. In the rear of the battery there was a magazine and a guardhouse. This battery may well have been built on the site of an older one since it is sometimes known as 'Portuguese Battery' or 'Dutch Battery'. The *St Helena Records* for 24 July 1734 state:

> '*The Battery for eight guns; Guard House and Powder Room are near finished at Turk's Cap Valley. If attacked it must be by boats for being directly to windward no ship durst venture near enough to throw their shot on shore for besides the danger of a lee shore there is a hedge of Rocks about half a mile off hardly fifteen feet (4.8m) under water and the ground all over this Bay is very foul'.*[7]

The battery was, apparently, erected at the charge of the plantation owners but by the beginning of the nineteenth century it appears to have been abandoned.

The southern landing place, where the English had landed in 1673, was defended by three batteries and two towers. At beach level there was a battery for two guns, marked on some maps as Jefferies' Battery. Beside it was a square musketry tower large enough to accommodate twenty or thirty men. About 100 feet (30m) above the beach there was a second, smaller tower with a single row of loopholes, and close to it a gun platform for a single gun, thought to have been a 9-pdr SB gun.

A description of the defences of Prosperous Bay in 1850 was probably an accurate description of the batteries and towers sixty years earlier. The report said:

> '*Prosperous Bay is defended by a stone tower to the south-west loopholed for musketry on the west edge of a rugged watercourse and within effective range. A spur projects into the valley to the north-west of the tower, with a tower and battery on the east end overlooking the sea and 150 feet [48m] above. Its fire sweeps the coast to the north and east and would render the tower untenable if captured. The inland communication with the battery is by a winding track up a steep slope as far as 600 feet [183m] above the sea defended by a gun and guardhouse and very difficult of access'.*[8]

The first of these towers was actually sited on the beach close to the sea and, unlike the tower on the spur, it had loopholes at the top of the tower and on the first floor and was considerably larger than the spur tower.

The gun and guardhouse defending the track formed a small battery known as Holdfast Tom and it stood 600 yards (550m) behind the beach, and 1,056 feet (322m) above it on the north side of the southern, or main, valley. The battery name relates to an incident when the English landed in

Prosperous Bay in 1673 to retake the island from the Dutch. Then a slave named Tom scaled the cliffs above Prosperous Bay with a rope that was then used to assist the English troops to ascend. With its extensive field of fire for its four guns, it dominated any attempt to leave the beach and move up the valley.

The Inland Fortifications

Away from the coast a number of alarm guns were sited on prominent peaks to warn the James Town garrison of any invasion, but none of these were defensive batteries as such. The main inland fortification built at the end of the century was Ladder Hill Fort. Work to build a battery on Ladder Hill appears to have begun in the early 1780s after the carriage road from James Town to the top of the hill had been completed. When a portion of the garrison mutinied in 1783, they tried to occupy Ladder Hill where, as an account of the mutiny relates, there was a post where there were '*field pieces, mortars and various ammunition*'.[9]

In 1797 additional efforts were made to improve the defences of Ladder Hill and Governor Brooke relates that Ladder Hill had been strengthened by a tower mounting two 12-pdr SB guns to aid in covering the rear of Ladder Hill works, and by a battery of two 18-pdr SB guns on a point over the sea.[10] A barrier gate had also been built with works to flank it on the road leading from the town to the hill.[11] In addition to the tower, Governor Brooke proposed

Ladder Hill Fort. The ladder to the top of the hill was built on the foundations of the old Inclined Plane which was used to bring stores to the fort. (*Author*)

that Ladder Hill should be fortified on the landward side by a line capable of sustaining a siege (in case of an enemy carrying any of the sea defences) so as to form an inland post.

It would seem that the tower built by Governor Brooke was the round tower that now forms part of High Knoll Fort and still stands today, albeit considerably modified from its original 1797 design. Built of rubble masonry, it stands 29 feet (8.9m) high, has a diameter of 72 feet (22.1m), and walls 5 feet (1.5m) thick. The tower is similar in many respects to the Simon's Town tower near Cape Town, and this may not be a coincidence as troops of the St Helena Regiment were part of the expedition sent in 1795 to capture the Cape of Good Hope from the Dutch. The tower was armed with two 12-pdr SB guns, possibly carronades, together with a battery of two 12-pdr SB guns at the base of the tower and was designed to defend the approaches to Ladder Hill Fort from the rear. A print depicting the tower and a small guardhouse was published in London in 1821, but there is no guarantee of the accuracy of this depiction.

Governor Brooke also constructed 'an additional tower' sited in the rear of Ladder Hill. This tower was probably Coleman's Tower, a D-shaped musketry tower now almost demolished, that stood on a cliff that forms part of Stone Top Hill at the head of Young's Valley. The tower would have guarded the approach to High Knoll up Breakneck Valley. Little is known about the design or construction of this tower though it may have supported two gun platforms at New Ground Camp. These two gun positions were shown on a map of 1811 but appear to have been abandoned in the early nineteenth century.

The Nineteenth Century Fortifications

The early years of the nineteenth century saw most of the island's fortifications maintained though there was little likelihood of an attack by a French force. The only new batteries to be built were three single-gun batteries on the south coast that protected Powell's Valley and the bay 3,000 yards (2.75kms) west of Sandy Bay. Cock's map of 1804 shows only two batteries but four years later, in 1808, Barnes' map shows a third battery. The armament of the three batteries was one 12-pdr SB gun, one 9-pdr SB gun, and one 12-pdr carronade all mounted on wooden platforms, and each battery had a small guardhouse and a magazine. Two of the batteries were sited on the east side of the valley and at a height of 1,000 feet (305m) and the role of these batteries was to close what Governor Patton described as the back door to the island by ensuring that no advance into the island could be made up Powell's Valley.

The Round Tower, to the rear of Ladder Hill Fort and which still stands, is referred to on Palmer's military map of 1850 as an 'ammunition tower'. This small tower appears to have been built in the first half of the nineteenth century as a magazine. Certainly, the roof platform was never strong enough to mount a gun, there are no musketry loopholes and the wall of the tower is thin.

The arrival of Napoleon in 1815 to start his exile on the island brought about the final flurry of fortification, mounting smooth-bore guns. By now the whole of the island was well fortified with all the potential landing places and valleys leading from them defended by gun batteries. The garrison, which had consisted of a battalion of infantry (the St Helena Regiment) and three companies of the St Helena Artillery, all HEIC troops, was reinforced by the arrival of the 2nd/53rd Regiment and the 2nd/66th Regiment bringing the total of troops on the island to 2,784 officers and men, with 500 guns in the batteries. At sea the Royal Navy assigned three large frigates to patrol the immediate vicinity of the island.

It was Admiral Sir George Cockburn who brought Napoleon to the island and he remained there until the arrival of the new governor Sir Hudson Lowe in April 1816, and it was he who decided to reinforce the defences of Old Woman's Valley by building a battery on Egg Island. This island is a pinnacle of rock 250 feet (76m) high just off the coast opposite the entrance to Old Woman's Valley. Admiral Cockburn considered the existing wall at the mouth of the valley to be insufficiently strong to defend it and he ordered a battery for three guns to be built on Egg Island. The main battery gun position was circular in shape and mounted three 24-pdr SB guns on stone platforms. There was also a 10-inch (254mm) mortar on a wooden platform and a single 24-pdr carronade, the latter mounted for the defence of the landing place. Adjacent to the main gun position there was a building to accommodate the gunners, a powder magazine and a shot furnace.

The years from 1825 to 1860 saw a decline in the strategic importance of St Helena. The death of Napoleon in 1821 saw the withdrawal of British troops leaving only the original garrison of HEIC troops. A further change in the circumstances of the island resulted from the handover of the island by the HEIC to the British Government in April 1834 and its new status as a Crown Colony. The most immediate result of the change was the disbandment of the HEIC units, the St Helena Regiment and the St Helena Artillery. In their place came the 91st Regiment from England and a detachment of Royal Artillery to man the batteries. The resulting dismissal of the officers and men of the HEIC units caused much hardship on the island, but in 1842 a new St

Helena Regiment comprising five companies was formed in England and was sent to the island to become the garrison until its disbandment in 1865.

One other new battery was constructed during this period. This was Patton's Battery situated on the lower part of Ladder Hill overlooking James Town Lines and the bay. The battery was circular in shape with a rubble stone wall 6 feet (1.8m) high surrounding it, and the battery was accessed by means of a path from the road to Ladder Hill. There is something of a mystery as to when exactly this battery was built. Although it was named after Governor Patton, governor of St Helena from 1802 to 1807, the battery is not shown on the 'Return of Ordnance' dated 31 March 1823 and held in the St Helena Archives. There is, however, mention of the battery in 1841 when the battery is shown in a list of works of defence at St Helena that were to be permanently maintained.[12]

On Palmer's military map of the island dated 29 October 1850 Patton's Battery is noted as being one of the nine main defensive locations on the island still armed and manned, and the armament was given as one 18-pdr SB gun, three 24-pdr carronades, and one 18-pdr carronade. It is assumed that the carronades were sited in the battery in order to engage with short-range flanking fire any attempted landing using ship's boats. The battery was abandoned in the 1860s.

By 1850 the batteries that were scheduled to be maintained were reduced to the following:

James Town Lines	24 guns; 1 carronade & 4 mortars
Munden's Battery	13 guns; 3 carronades & 2 mortars
Chubb's Batteries	2 guns; 1 carronade
Banks' Battery	18 guns; 5 carronades
Sandy Bay Lines	5 guns; 8 carronades
Lemon Valley Lines	10 guns
Ladder Hill Fort	16 guns; 8 carronades & 1 mortar
High Knoll Battery	3 guns; 3 carronades
Patton's Battery	1 gun; 5 carronades

However, by 1860 the strategic position of St Helena had deteriorated still further. The advent of steam propulsion for ships and railways resulted in the opening up of a shorter route to the East via the Mediterranean and the short overland route between Alexandria and Port Suez resulting in a major reduction in the number of ships stopping at the island. In 1862 the War Office, always under government pressure to reduce expenditure to a minimum, converted the St Helena Regiment into the 5th Battalion of the West India Regiment and then disbanded it in 1865. The garrison was then reduced to a single infantry company detached from a line battalion stationed at the Cape, an artillery company and a number of Royal Engineers personnel. Similarly, a reduction in the status of the island from a first class coaling station to a second class station led to a consequent reduction in the expenditure on the maintenance of the fortifications which allowed them to fall into a poor state of repair.

There had been some improvement in the armament of the batteries with the delivery of some heavy 68-pdr SB guns to be mounted on Ladder Hill and in the Rupert's Hill (Munden's Hill) battery. However, the advent of the new rifled guns entering service with the Royal Artillery in the 1860s brought about a reassessment of the defences of St Helena and the decision was taken to concentrate the defences around James Town.

The War Office reviewed the island's armament and decided to send out four of the new Armstrong 7-inch Rifled Breech-loading (RBL) guns and three 7-inch Rifled Muzzle-loading (RML) guns. Two of the 7-inch RBLs were to be mounted on Ladder Hill and two were to be mounted in the remodelled Half Moon Battery at Lemon Valley Bay. This battery was considered to be particularly important as its fire would cross with that of the guns of Munden's Point and Ladder Hill. The three 7-inch RML guns were

Munden's Point casemate for three 7-inch RML guns. (*Author's Collection*)

to be mounted in a new casemate protected by iron shutters to be constructed on Munden's Point, with a small position for a Depression Range Finder on the flank of the casemate.

Initial work on the casemate at Munden's Point started as early as 1863 when a government ordinance warned the people of James Town that 'mining by gunpowder' would be necessary on 22 October of that year at Munden's Battery. In 1868 plans were drawn up for an extension of the casemate to mount an additional two guns. It would seem that these guns were to be heavier 9-inch 12-ton RML guns but their mounting was postponed by the Defence Committee in 1872.

Work on the casemate proceeded very slowly and it had still not been completed by 1878. In that year an interesting experiment was carried out in which the Royal Navy gunboat HMS *Boxer* fired a shell from each of its main guns at the old Munden's Battery. The experiment was designed to observe the effect of heavy shells from modern guns, in this case one 7-inch 7-ton RML gun and one 64-pdr RML gun, on fortifications constructed of the local island stone. A black mark was painted on the battery wall and HMS *Boxer* fired two shells at the battery from a range of 400 yards (370m). Both shells struck the centre of the black mark '*but the aged battery seemed not a bit the worse for it*'.[13] The new casemate was then completed for the 7-inch RML guns.

Work on the batteries had been sporadic with J.C. Melliss commenting in his book *Views of St Helena Illustrative of its Scenery and History* published in 1875 that '*the fortifications are in ruins and neglected, and what new batteries have been undertaken remain in an unfinished state, while the modern guns sent out from Britain lie here and there un-mounted and half buried in rock and debris.*'[14]

This was, however, a rather exaggerated view of the situation since at this time (1870-74) a major military complex was under construction on the island. Work had commenced in 1866 on the construction of new accommodation buildings on Ladder Hill and on a high stone wall surrounding them. In 1873 the new barracks on Ladder Hill was completed to provide accommodation for the Royal Artillery and the new barracks incorporated the old Ladder Hill battery. A small shell-filling room with a vaulted stone roof and a separate shell store were built on the parade ground in front of the barrack accommodation verandah. Both of these buildings had floors a few feet below the level of the parade ground. The main gate to the barracks and the fort was close to the top of the Inclined Plane, a ladder and goods trolley-way connecting the barracks with James Town at the base of the hill.

In 1878, as a result of a war scare and clearly before the changes were made to the tower of High Knoll Fort, the Defence Committee reviewed the defences of St Helena in a report entitled '*A Report on the Temporary Defences of St Helena*'. The report showed that the main armament in place at that time comprised the following:

Ladder Hill Fort	3 × 7-inch RBL guns
	2 × 68-pdr SB guns
Munden's Point Battery	3 × 7-inch 7-ton RML guns
Munden's Hill Battery	3 × 68-pdr SB guns
Half Moon Battery, Lemon Valley	2 × 7-inch RBL guns[15]

The three 7-inch RBL guns in Ladder Hill Fort were mounted in the Sea Face Battery, and the two 68-pdr guns were in the Half Moon Battery beside the signal mast. There were also three 13-inch mortars mounted in a line on stone platforms overlooking James Town in what was known as the Town Face Battery, and eleven 18-pdr SB guns formed a saluting battery between the Sea Face Battery and the Half Moon Battery. In addition to these guns and mortars there were a number of other smooth-bore guns and mortars shown as being in place in James Town Lines. The committee also recommended that the two 9-inch 12-ton RML guns originally approved for Munden's Point and then postponed should be installed.

The committee also reported that although the guns in the casemate at Munden's Point were originally to be mounted behind iron shields, these shields had not been fitted. The short-term solution to the lack of shields suggested by the committee was to be the fitting of a double row of rope mantlets.[16] In addition to the 9-inch RML guns the committee recommended that five 64-pdr RML guns should be mounted on Munden's Hill above the casemate.

The date of the reconstruction of High Knoll Battery into High Knoll Fort is something of a mystery. There is no clear paper trail but there is no mention of the fort as such in the 1850 list of batteries to be maintained, nor in the 1878 report on the temporary defences of the island. However, the same report recommended the move of the two 7-inch RBL guns then at Half Moon Battery in Lemon Valley Bay to High Knoll Fort. It would seem likely, therefore, that it was shortly after this that work was carried out to construct the fort in place of the existing tower and battery. A record plan dated 1895 in the National Archives at Kew[17] shows the reconstructed tower with guns and a signal station, together with accommodation and stores, all within a walled

High Knoll Fort. View from the north-west showing the new wall built round the old tower. (*Author*)

enclosure making High Knoll Fort almost certainly the last such structure to be built in the British Empire.

The new fort was 250 yards (229m) long and 66 yards (60m) wide with stores, a cartridge store, and troop accommodation in its casemates at the southern end, There was a single *demi-bastion* to provide flanking fire on the eastern side of the fort and two others with a similar role on the western side. A shallow ditch was excavated out of the rock along the western wall and the entrance to the fort was through a gateway half way along the western wall. The ditch was crossed by means of a rolling bridge that could be withdrawn into the fort. Adjoining the gate there was a small guardroom. The stone curtain wall varied in height between 30 feet (9.1m) at the northern end and southern ends of the fort, to 20 feet (6.1m) on the eastern and western sides.

No action was taken to mount the two 9-inch 12-ton RML guns on Munden's Hill until 1886 when the Defence Committee approved the mounting of the two guns in two separate emplacements with concrete parapets, magazine and protection for the gun crews. The guns were to replace the three 68-pdr SB guns that were still in that battery. At Ladder Hill Fort the two 7-inch RBL guns were to be replaced by two more 9-inch 12-ton RML guns. The first two 9-inch RMLs had been sent to the island in 1885, to be mounted on Munden's Hill. On Ladder Hill the first emplacement was completed in 1887 and the second in 1890.

These guns then became the main armament of the St Helena defences between 1888 and 1902 and frequent practice firings were carried out during this period. In 1898 it was proposed to mount two 6-pdr QF guns in the Munden's casemate in place of the 7-inch RBL guns. These latter guns had become obsolete as they were out-ranged by the heavier guns on Ladder Hill and were unable to maintain the rapid rate of fire required to deal with the latest fast torpedo boats. In 1892 there had been a tentative proposal to mount 4.7-inch QF guns in place of the 7-inch RBLs in the casemate, but on review the smaller 6-pdrs were considered adequate and, of course, were cheaper.

The Twentieth Century Fortifications

As we have seen in the earlier chapters the production in the 1880s of a successful British breech-loading mechanism for heavy guns eventually led to the introduction of these guns into the British Army and the Royal Navy, and, ultimately, to their arrival on St Helena. These new breech-loading guns, together with the smaller quick-firers, were much more effective than the old rifled muzzle-loading guns but they required a new design of battery position. This usually took the form of two concrete gun positions, each for a single gun, and allowing each gun to fire *en barbette* over a low concrete apron. Between the two gun positions there was either a large underground magazine serving both guns or two, smaller, individual magazines each comprising a cartridge store, shell store, shifting lobby, RA store and RA shelter.

In 1902 the Colonial Defence Committee recommended the installation of the latest 6-inch BL Mk VII guns firing a shell weighing 100 pounds to a range of 12,000 yards (10.9km) to replace the 9-inch RML guns at Ladder Hill Fort and Munden's Hill Battery. The 9-inch RML guns were dismounted and the two on top of Munden's Hill were left *in situ* and can still be seen there today.

6-inch Mk VII BL gun at Ladder Hill Battery. The splinter shield was fitted during the Second World War. (*Author*)

The 7-inch RML guns were removed from the casemate and were disposed of by simply tipping them over the cliff onto the rocks below the point where they too can be seen today. The casemate was then adapted to mount two 6-pdr QF guns on elastic frame mountings. This was done by blocking up the centre RML embrasure and constructing concrete platforms in the other two embrasures on which the new guns were mounted. Three storage lockers for ready-to-use ammunition were built into the blocked-up central embrasure. An additional position was built close to the barrack block on Munden's Point, probably as a practice position as it permitted the gun to fire freely seawards.

The mounting of modern guns to defend James Town improved the effectiveness of the defences enormously. However, without searchlights the guns could only be fired by day. Two 90cm Moveable Beam DELs were authorized for Munden's Point and positions for these lights were built on the rocks below Munden's Point battery, one position immediately above the other, accessed by means of steps and steel ladders. The engine house was built into the rock in a sunken emplacement below the level of the old battery *terreplein*.

During the Second Boer War, from 1899 to 1902, Boer prisoners-of-war were held on St Helena and the garrison was increased considerably by the arrival of units required to guard the prisoners, mostly British militia regiments, or elements of them. However, the garrison was reduced when the war ended in 1902 and the prisoners were released.

With the conclusion of the Boer War the strategic importance of St Helena continued to decline and the War Office was anxious to withdraw the garrison which comprised 100 rank and file of the Royal Garrison Artillery and the Royal Engineers. One proposal put forward by the War Office was that the Admiralty should provide a small garrison, but the Admiralty was not prepared to agree to this suggestion. The War Office finally settled on the plan of holding the personnel and equipment necessary to man the 6-inch BL guns at Woolwich, all to be dispatched to the island when required.

In 1906 the War Office removed the remaining garrison and, when the troops left, the guns were stripped but left *in situ*, with the stripped items returned to Woolwich. The garrison took with them the two small 6-pdr QF guns and the two DELs from Munden's Point.

The St Helena defences remained unmanned until 1911 when the Admiralty took over responsibility for the guns. A small maintenance party of Royal Marines comprising one officer (a captain), two sergeants, ten marines and three RN signallers were sent to the island., together with the stripped items for the guns which were made serviceable again. The searchlights at

Munden's Point were re-installed but the 6-pdr QF guns were not returned to the casemate, which was converted into an oil store for the DEL engines. The Royal Marines maintained a garrison on the island throughout the First World War and up to 1938 when the decision was taken to return the four 6-inch guns to Britain.

This decision was, as it turned out, rather premature. Fortunately, the dismounting of the guns was not to happen as there was a delay in sending out the stores necessary to dismantle them, so they were still in position on 3 September 1939 when war was declared with Germany. The War Office immediately dispatched personnel to form the core of the St Helena Coast Battery RA and the St Helena Fortress Company RE, the latter unit being responsible for manning the DELs, with the remaining personnel being recruited from the islanders themselves.

Major R.J. Longfield RA was the first OC Troops St Helena and he arrived in January 1940 having taken almost three months from the date of his posting order to arrive because of the difficulty of transportation to the island. With the evacuation of the British Expeditionary Force from France in June 1940 Britain was in great danger of being invaded by the Germans. Emergency coast batteries were established all along the coasts of Britain and Northern Ireland, and there was an urgent need for heavy guns to arm these new batteries. The War Office considered that two 6-inch BL guns were sufficient to provide the defence of James Town against German surface raiders or U-boats and ordered the return to Britain of the two guns on Munden's Hill.

The Ladder Hill battery now acted as the examination battery for James Town but saw no action during the war. The only act of war to affect St Helena was the sinking of the RFA *Darkdale* by a U-boat when she was anchored off James Town in 1941. No additional gun positions were built on the island, and, understandably in view of its isolated location, it was not considered necessary to provide the guns with concrete overhead cover against air attack. But in 1942 they were provided with the shield extensions that can be seen on the guns today.

In 1939 the two DELs were found to be unserviceable and the 22HP Hornsby Ackroyd diesel engines that powered the lights were unreliable. The OC Troops was ordered by the War Office to rebuild the now renamed Coast Artillery Searchlight (CASL) positions and two CASLs were sent out from Britain, together with three new Lister 22KW engines which were installed in the engine room. The lower of the two original searchlight positions was abandoned and a new position was built close to the entrance to the casemate on the old Munden's Battery *terreplein*. This was a position that had been

St John's	Fort James
	Cripplegate (Goat Hill)
	Entrenchment
English Harbour	Fort Berkeley
Monk's Hill	Codrington Battery
Falmouth	Blake's Island
Parham	Fort Byam
Old Road	Road Fort
Nonsuch Harbour	Fort Harman
Willoughby Bay	Fort William

These were armed with a total of eighty-four smooth-bore guns.[4]

Governor Mathew made it clear in his report that virtually all the forts and batteries built by the colonial government were poorly designed and, at the time of his report, were in poor condition, with rotten gun carriages and many of the guns in an unserviceable condition. One of the forts criticized by Governor Mathew was Fort Berkeley at English Harbour. The original redoubt had been extended by the construction of a wall pierced for guns, but Governor Mathew condemned the *merlons* between the embrasures as being *'far from Cannon-proof'* saying *'Tis pity they Chuse* [sic] *always to do these things (as they give the money) under their own direction, and of men that never saw a Fort, rather than trouble a Governor that has'.*[5]

The Later Fortifications

War with Spain in 1739 and the outbreak of the War of the Austrian Succession in the following year increased the importance of English Harbour as a base for the Royal Navy. In 1728 the Board of Admiralty had purchased land on the eastern side of English Harbour to provide dockyard facilities for Royal Navy ships and some ten years later the dockyard was expanded to include land on the western side on which careening wharves and storehouses were built. To improve the defences of the harbour steps were taken to enlarge Fort Berkeley under the direction of Captain Charles Knowles RN, the senior officer commanding the Leeward Squadron.

It would seem that Captain Knowles was of the same opinion as Governor Mathew regarding the failings in the design of Fort Berkeley and regarded the fort as an inadequate defence of the harbour so he improved it by constructing a second line of guns, beyond the existing line. The colonial authorities would not contribute to the cost of improving the fort therefore Captain

Knowles used the sailors from his ship HMS *Superb* as the labour force. He went ahead relying on the Admiralty to authorize the financial outlay involved retrospectively. However, it is unclear if and when such authority was given since as late as 1751 the matter remained unresolved, though Captain Knowles was admonished by the Board of Admiralty for his unauthorized work, which he estimated cost £300.

Fort Berkeley, English Harbour. (*Author*)

Knowles appears to have been a keen engineer as well as a sailor for it is believed that he provided the designs for the tower and battery built by the Codrington family to defend their estates on the island of Barbuda, some 40 miles north of Antigua. It is probable, also, that he was involved in the design of a battery that took the place of the line of musketry on the headland opposite Fort Berkeley in English Harbour. The musketry line was enlarged into a horseshoe-shaped battery for eleven guns which was known at first as the

Fort James, St John's. The *terreplein* of the fort with original 24-pdr Blomefield pattern smooth-bore guns. (*Author*)

South-East Point Battery, and, subsequently, as Fort Charlotte. In Freeman's Bay, on the eastern side of the harbour and north of Fort Charlotte, another line of guns was built and shown on maps as the Masked Battery. In 1755 this battery mounted twenty guns.

At St John's a new barracks was built on Rat Island and Fort James was extended by the construction of the 'New Fort', an extension of the old fort to the north-west. This extension to the fort had been planned by Governor Mathew a number of years earlier but never completed. The extension included a *demi-bastion* on the eastern side overlooking the sea and a small hornwork at the northern end with a linking curtain wall. A magazine and barracks were built within the 'New Fort' at this time.

The outbreak of the American War of Independence and the subsequent war with France and Spain once again drew the attention of the British authorities to the state of the island's defences. In 1781 the new governor of the Leeward Islands, Major General Sir Thomas Shirley, arrived in Antigua and, having lost the island of Dominica to the French in 1778, he was well aware of the vulnerability of Antigua to French attack. Although in 1779 his predecessor, William Mathew Burt, had improved the defences by building a fort, Fort Barrington, on Goat Hill where previously there had only been an earth gun platform, little else had been done to improve the island's defences.

General Shirley, believing that a French attack on Antigua was imminent, turned his attention firstly to English Harbour considering that it was

Fort Barrington, St John's. A circular battery with a small magazine and accommodation for the garrison. (*Author*)

important to fortify the heights to the east of the harbour since occupation of which by an enemy force would make the harbour untenable.

However, with the end of the war in 1782 there was little incentive for either the Antigua Assembly or the Board of Ordnance in London to expend large sums on such a fortification. In the same year a young Royal Engineers officer, First Lieutenant Charles Shipley, who was to spend a large part of his career in the West Indies, arrived in Antigua. Charles Shipley also recommended the fortification of the eastern heights above English Harbour, but he considered that Fort Berkeley, armed with seventeen guns, and the Masked Battery, armed with nineteen guns, were both effective defences. He noted that there was a battery of five 9-pdr SB guns at Black's Point on the Middle Ground, the date of the construction of which is uncertain.[6]

By May 1785 General Shirley was still waiting for authority to commence fortifying the eastern heights, writing to Lord Sydney, President of the Committee on Trade and the Foreign Plantations, pointing out that in any future war with France Antigua would be an obvious target for a French invasion force. No authority was forthcoming from London and the Antigua Assembly continued to maintain its stance of refusing to grant any money for further fortification.

Work on the heights was eventually commenced and when General Shirley left Antigua in June 1788 work on the fortification that was to be named after him, Shirley Heights, was well in hand. Work now continued apace under the direction of Captain Charles Shipley RE on the fortifications that were eventually to cover most of the high ground overlooking the harbour. These fortifications were divided into three sections, the Blockhouse, the Ridge and Fort Shirley.

By 1790, gun positions had been built at all three of these positions, together with barracks for a British infantry regiment, another for the Royal Artillery garrison, officers' quarters, a hospital and a magazine. By the following year the Blockhouse battery was armed with two 32-pdr SB guns in a position overlooking the sea; Fort Shirley overlooking Freeman's Bay, a position also known as the Lookout, was armed with two 18-pdr and two 12-pdr SB guns, and also acted as a signal station and the Ridge battery was armed with four 9-pdr SB guns. The heights were further strengthened by the construction of an additional battery for five guns on the highest point, Dow's Hill, beside the house of the general officer commanding the garrison.

The harbour defences were also reinforced by the construction of a second battery at the entrance to the harbour, above the existing South-East Point Battery that had been built in 1745. This was another horseshoe-shaped battery built in the position of the lookout and had a small guard house and

View of English Harbour 1807. The picture shows Fort Berkeley on the left and Fort Charlotte in the foreground. Fort George can be seen, faintly, on a hill in the background of the picture. (*Author's Collection*)

a magazine. This new battery was named Fort Charlotte in honour of King George III's consort.

In 1791 plans were made to improve Fort George on Monk's Hill with the construction of what was termed 'The Great Platform', a *cavalier* for eight guns at the eastern end of the fort overlooking the small hornwork. This was all part of a general plan to improve the defences of English Harbour and Falmouth proposed by a Committee of Engineers. This plan included a review of the defence of the Middle Ground, the peninsula lying between English Harbour and Falmouth Harbour.[7]

The committee proposed the construction of a redoubt and two batteries linked by a road. The redoubt was never built, but a battery for three heavy guns, named Fort Cuyler after the commander of the garrison, Brigadier General Cuyler, was built overlooking the entrance to Falmouth Harbour. Two other batteries were built at this time on the Middle Ground: a single-gun battery, Keane's Battery, to defend the entrance to English Harbour and a two-gun battery at Black's Point, below Fort Cuyler. Further east a single-gun battery was sited to defend the entrance to Indian Creek, the inlet immediately to the east of English Harbour.

However, with the war against Napoleon ending in 1815 the dockyard at English Harbour was gradually run down as its importance to the Royal Navy declined. In 1854 the garrison on the island was finally withdrawn and the batteries and forts, lacking maintenance and disused, had become damaged in an earthquake in 1843 and subsequently ruinous.

The advent of steam in the Royal Navy in the mid-nineteenth century meant that English Harbour was retained as a second-class coaling station. The dockyard was retained on a care and maintenance basis until its position and defences were reviewed in a War Office Memorandum on the Defence of Antigua in April 1881.[8] On the basis that English Harbour should be retained as a coaling station then the approved defences should be:

Fort Berkeley	2 × 10-inch 18-ton RML guns
	2 × 64-pdr Mk III RML guns
Fort Charlotte	3 × 10-inch 18-ton RML guns
Black's Hill	3 × 10-inch 18-ton RML guns
	2 × 64-pdr Mk III RML guns
Shirley Heights	7 × 64-pdr Mk III RML guns
Fort Monk (George)	3 × 6-inch BLR or 7-inch 7-ton RML guns
	3 × 64-pdr Mk III RML guns

In addition, provision was to be made for submarine mines to be laid across the entrance to the harbour.

This defence plan was never to be implemented as, at a meeting of the Defence Committee four years earlier in 1877, the Admiralty had expressed a preference for St Lucia as the coaling station in the eastern Caribbean rather than Antigua, and the dockyard was finally closed in 1889.

This was not the end of coast defence in Antigua. During the Second World War American troops and aircraft were stationed on the island under the Destroyers for Bases Agreement signed by Britain and the United States in 1941. A naval air station was established at Crabbs Peninsula, the eastern arm of Parham Harbour, and an army air base on the northern arm. As a result of the mining of Castries harbour on St Lucia in 1942 by the German submarine *U-66*, Allied merchant shipping was diverted from St Lucia to Parham Harbour as a temporary measure until minesweeping measures could be set in train in Castries harbour. As a result of this and earlier submarine attacks on St Lucia a coast defence battery armed with 155mm guns on Panama mounts was sited to cover the entrance to Parham Harbour and defend the two air bases. Similar guns were also mounted at Wetherill's Point, at the northern end of Dickenson's Bay north of St John's.

In July 1943 there was a change of regime in the French Caribbean islands which closed these islands to German submarines, consequently there was a reduction in the importance of Antigua as an anti-submarine base, and the American naval air base on Crabbs Peninsula was placed in care and maintenance later that year. Coolidge Air Base, the army air base was finally closed in 1949.

ST LUCIA

The Capture of St Lucia

St Lucia, a small island in the Windward Islands in the Eastern Caribbean with an area of some 238 square miles (617 sq kms) lies northwest of Barbados and 40 miles (64 kms) south of the French island of Martinique. Discovered in the early years of the sixteenth century, it was settled by the French in 1638. Subsequently also claimed by the British, it was acquired by the French West India Company in 1666 and became a French colony in 1674. Over the next 130 years the island changed hands frequently as Britain and France struggled for possession, each nation coveting the island's valuable sugar production and excellent harbour. For the British, however, there was the additional strategic reason that possession of the island meant that ships of the Royal Navy could monitor the important harbour of Fort de France on Martinique.

Between 1750 and 1800 the island was occupied three times by British forces; first in 1762 during the Seven Years War, until it was returned to

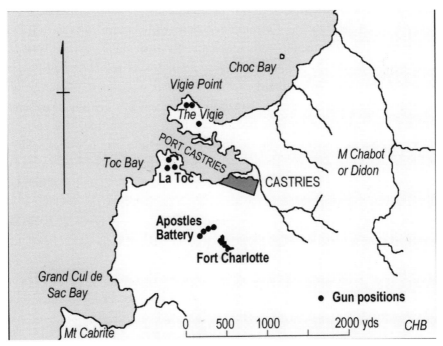

Map of Castries Harbour and defences. (*Charles Blackwood*)

Six-gun Battery, Castries Harbour c.1780. (*Author's Collection*)

France the following year; on the second occasion for five years between 1778 and 1783 during the American War of Independence and, finally, between 1796 and 1802 during the Revolutionary War with France. The island was again returned to France in 1802 under the terms of the Treaty of Amiens, only to be recaptured the following year and finally retained by Britain under the Treaty of Paris signed in 1814.

During the period of their occupation the French fortified the island and established their headquarters initially on the Vigie peninsula. However, in 1765 a large fort was constructed on Morne Fortune, the hill overlooking the town and harbour of Castries, to strengthen the defences. The fort was supported by two redoubts, Prevost and Boucher Redoubts. Additional batteries defended the coast including Ciceron Redoubt overlooking Cul de Sac Bay south of Castries. A half-moon battery for six heavy guns firing through embrasures defended the entrance to Castries Harbour.

In 1778 the British under Admiral Rodney captured St Lucia, established a naval base at Gros-Islet Bay in the north of the island and fortified Pigeon Island, a small, hilly island overlooking Gros-Islet Bay. These fortifications consisted of a battery on the highest point of the south-east corner of the island, somewhat pretentiously known as Fort Rodney, mounting four 24-pdr SB guns on garrison carriages firing *en barbette*. The only other structure in the fort was a small magazine. The approach to the fort was defended by a small musketry redoubt situated in the saddle between the fort and the highest peak on Pigeon Island. A two-gun battery was sited close to the redoubt and a second, larger, two-gun battery was built on the northern side of the island consisting of a masonry platform with the guns firing through embrasures, and with a magazine standing some way behind the platform. These fortifications were built by sailors and marines from Admiral Rodney's fleet, initially from the bomb vessel HMS *Aetna*, and the Muster Book in the National Archives at Kew shows that for a period the island was known as HMS *Pigeon Island*.[9]

Two years after the outbreak of war with Revolutionary France in 1793 Major General Sir Ralph Abercromby was dispatched to the West Indies with a force of 15,000 men with orders to capture the French West Indian possessions. In April 1796 Abercromby landed his troops on St Lucia and besieged the French garrison of 100 French and 2,000 native troops which had retreated within the Morne Fortune fortress. The British force was compelled to advance along a narrow ridge from the west, limited by the steep sides of the ridge and the thick jungle undergrowth. The siege lasted from 26 April to 24 May during which time the French fortress was bombarded by twenty heavy guns and howitzers and fourteen mortars. The final assault was carried out by the 27th (Inniskilling) Regiment of Foot, and the regiment's feat in capturing the fortress was rewarded by General Abercromby who ordered that the regiment's colour should be flown over the fortress for an hour before the Union flag was raised.

The French fort on Morne Fortune was an irregular work about 800 feet (246m) above sea level, overlooking Castries, but set back about 1½ miles (2,363m) from the harbour. The fort was revetted with stone on its north and west sides at an average of 17 feet (5.2m). The west front had a ditch and *glacis*, while the other sides were without ditch or protection.

General Abercromby retained the French fortifications, only constructing three new batteries to defend the western approach to Morne Fortune, the approach that had been used by his force in their assault on the fortress. A battery was established at Abercromby Hill overlooking the approach to the ridge leading to Morne Fortune, and opposite, on Morne Duchazeau, Abercromby placed a gun battery and a mortar battery. These batteries were manned by the Royal Irish Artillery until 1801 when, as a result of the Act of Union, the Royal Irish Artillery was abolished and its personnel incorporated into the Royal Artillery.

Plan of Morne
Fortune, 1823.
(*TNA MPHH
1/198*)

Plan of Morne Fortune, 1823. (*TNA MPHH 1/198*)

Under the terms of the Treaty of Amiens in 1802 St Lucia was returned to France but was only held briefly by the French. With the outbreak of hostilities once again in 1803 Commodore Samuel Hood RN escorted a British force under the command of Lieutenant General Grinfield which retook the island within twenty-four hours. The British retained the island under the terms of the Treaty of Paris in 1814 and it remained a British possession until granted independence in 1979.

Having regained the island in 1803 the British took steps to improve the fortifications. On the western flank of the old Morne Fortune fortress, now renamed Fort Charlotte, a new redoubt, White's Redoubt was built. This was an earthen work, without revetment and situated above the level of the fort as a form of *cavalier*, in order to command the ground below on the east side. Another battery, Shipley's Battery, mounting four guns, adjoined the new redoubt but at a lower level. In 1813 the *redan* at the north-east corner of the fort, which had suffered from subsidence, was remodelled. On the southern side of the fort Boucher Redoubt, an earth work for three guns, defended the approach from Grand Cul de Sac Bay.

Two other earth redoubts built by the French defended the approaches to the fort. One, Prevost Redoubt, defended the approaches from the west, and enfiladed part of the road leading to the fort from Castries, while the second, sited about 200 yards (184m) to the north-west, in the centre of some old French lines, defended the approach on that side.

In addition to the three redoubts on the Morne Fortune incorporated into Fort Charlotte, the British maintained the old French Batteries Seche and Tricolor to defend the approaches to Fort Charlotte from the east, as well as constructing two new batteries, O'Meara's Battery and Morne Freeland battery on the hills immediately overlooking the town of Castries.

Castries and the harbour were defended by the Half-Moon six-gun battery and by further defences on the Vigie and Tapion Rock, at the entrance to the harbour. On the Vigie the original armament was an 18-pdr SB gun at the signal station mounted on the only traversing platform in the island's defences. By 1838 this position had a 24-pdr gun in place of the old 18-pdr and two 13-inch iron mortars. There was another battery for three guns, two 12-pdrs and one 18-pdr French guns, on the northern tip of the Vigie and on the Tapion Rock, the battery consisting of four, one 20-pdr SB gun, one 18-pdr SB gun and two 12-pdr SB guns.

The bays on either side of Castries Harbour were also defended by batteries, Grand Cul de Sac Bay to the south by the old French Fort Ciceron, a small irregular work armed with four guns mounted on garrison carriages behind a masonry parapet. Immediately below Fort Ciceron was a smaller battery for three guns known as Petit Ciceron. Choc Bay was defended by a battery of two 20-pdr SB guns, also on garrison carriages, in a battery constructed of earth and fascines. Like the majority of the guns arming the island's defences these 20-pdr guns were bronze guns of French manufacture and clearly taken into British service when the island was captured.

Pigeon Island, some 9 miles (14.4 kms) north of Castries, was maintained as the main defence of Gros-Islet Bay. In 1805 the armament of Fort Rodney was reduced to three 24-pdr SB guns. On the north of the island the two-gun battery was armed with two 18-pdr SB guns, and in the third battery, Saddle Battery, there was a single 18-pdr gun. Soufriere Bay, south of Castries, was defended by a single battery mounting two guns, one 18-pdr and one 12-pdr SB gun.[10]

In 1805 and again in 1810 the defences of St Lucia were inspected by Colonel Charles Shipley RE, the Commanding Royal Engineer in the West Indies. Shipley found that the batteries and redoubts were generally in a poor state and the guns were either in poor condition or their carriages unserviceable. Since the garrison carriages were made of wood rather than of iron they quickly deteriorated in the wet and humid conditions of the Caribbean.

With the end of the Napoleonic War in 1815 there was no longer any incentive to maintain the St Lucia's defences, particularly as in the days of sail the Royal Navy's Caribbean bases were Port Royal in Jamaica in the west and Antigua in the east, while the main army garrison was on the island of Barbados. A small garrison was retained on the island and work was carried out on the living quarters for the troops both at Fort Charlotte and on Pigeon Island. Indeed, in 1824, authority was given for the rebuilding of the accommodation and hospital on Pigeon Island at an estimated cost of £17,259.17s.4½d.[11]

Coaling Station

In 1872 the Governor of Jamaica drew the attention of the Secretary of State for the Colonies and the Secretary of State for War to the obsolete nature of the defences of the West Indies garrisons. This was followed two years later by the Admiralty drawing the attention of the Defence Committee to the defenceless state of the coaling stations amongst which was included Antigua.[12]

The state of the defences of the coaling stations was formally considered by the Defence Committee at a meeting on 5 June 1877. At this meeting the Admiralty requested that St Lucia should be accepted as a coaling station in lieu of Antigua. The Admiralty considered that the harbour at Castries was larger and deeper than English Harbour on Antigua with a length of 3,000 yards (2,770m), a width of 500 yards (460m) and a depth of nine fathoms (16m) over most of its area. It was also noted that, unlike Antigua, Castries was a major commercial coaling station.

St Lucia had always been seen by the Admiralty as being best suited as a base from which to observe Fort de France, the French naval base on the nearby island of Martinique, but it was also considered to be a suitable temporary base to support a Royal Navy squadron of large armoured vessels in any future conflict with the United States. The harbour could also be easily defended with batteries on the Vigie and La Toc peninsulas. The Defence Committee accepted the Admiralty's request and St Lucia was designated a major naval coaling station.

Between 1878 and 1879 the Colonial Defence Committee produced a report on 'The Temporary Defences of the Coaling Stations'.[13] This report authorized the dispatch of six 7-inch 6½-ton RML guns to St Lucia to be deployed, three on Piton Flore and three on the 'point opposite'.[14] This is clearly a mistake on the part of the committee since the Piton Flore is a mountain in the centre of the island. We must assume that the committee meant the Vigie and La Toc headlands at the entrance to the harbour. A number of 'light guns' were to arm Fort Charlotte and the Redoubt, together with the Choc Bay battery (Fort Ciceron). However, there is no indication that these guns were ever mounted.

As a result of the Admiralty recommending St Lucia as a coaling station, and also the ongoing fear of Russian intentions in Central Asia, in 1881 the War Office issued a Memorandum on the defences of St Lucia. It seems clear from the Memorandum that in 1881 St Lucia was not garrisoned and the existing defences are described as consisting of *'the remains of a few open batteries for the defence of the entrance to the harbour, and of Fort Charlotte, a work strongly situated on the Morne Fortune'*. The latter work was described as being of the nature of a powerful field work containing a barracks, *'not bomb-proof, which in 1856 was capable of accommodating 165 men'.*[15]

As we have seen, the 1880s was a period of considerable technological change in the Royal Artillery. The advent of breech-loading guns meant frequent reviews of the armament of the fixed defences of the ports of the United Kingdom and the Empire. In 1881 the Inspector General of Fortifications and Works, Lieutenant General T.L. Gallwey, issued a War Office Memorandum on the subject which recommended that for defence against naval attack all the guns of the St Lucia fixed defences should be concentrated on the Vigie, and these should be five of the new 10.4-inch BL guns, which were under development at Woolwich, and seven 64-pdr Mk III RML guns. General Gallwey also proposed that there should be a line of defences on the high ground to the rear of Castries to defend the port from a landward attack. He recommended that Fort Charlotte be repaired and a small self-defensible work be constructed on Morne Chabot, and also on Abercromby Hill where a battery had been established when the British captured the island in 1796.

The development of the 10.4-inch BL gun proved more difficult than expected and in 1884 a Report on the Defence of Colonial Possessions Abroad changed the island's recommended armament to three of the new 9.2-inch BL guns on Mk I *barbette* mountings and four 64-pdr Mk II RML guns.[16] However, three years later the guns actually mounted were:

The Vigie	1 × 10-inch 18-ton RML gun
	2 × 64-pdr Mk III RML guns
La Toc	2 × 10-inch 18-ton RML guns
	2 × 64-pdr Mk III RML guns
Morne Fortune	4 × 9-inch 12-ton RML guns
Moveable Armament	4 × 20-pdr RBL guns

Apostles Battery,
Castries with
one of the four
original 9-inch
12-ton RML
guns. (*Author*)

In 1887 it was proposed to change the island's armament yet again, this time to three 6-inch BL Mk IV guns on hydro-pneumatic mountings for Vigie Battery; three 10-inch 18-ton RML guns for La Toc Battery; and four 9-inch 12-ton RML guns on Morne Fortune. By 1899 these guns had been installed, with the 9-inch RML guns in a new battery, Apostles Battery.

However, the Conference on Breech-loading and Quick-firing guns in the same year recommended the removal of the 6-inch BL guns and all the RML guns, considering their rate of fire to be too slow, replacing them with three 9.2-inch BL guns; four more modern 6-inch BL guns; two 12-pdr QF guns and two 6-inch BL howitzers on siege carriages. In 1900 a second battery for two 12-pdr QF guns was approved for St Lucia and the approved armament became:

Vigie	Vigie Battery	1 × 9.2-inch BL gun
		2 × 6-inch BL Mk VII guns
	Meadows Battery	2 × 12-pdr QF guns
La Toc	La Toc Battery	1 × 9.2-inch BL gun
		2 × 6-inch BL Mk VII guns
	Rodney Battery	2 × 12-pdr QF guns
Morne Fortune	Apostles Battery	1 × 9.2-inch BL gun
		2 × 6-inch BL howitzers

La Toc Battery, Castries. The photograph shows one of the 6-inch Mk VII BL gun positions with one of the earlier 10-inch 18-ton RML guns lying on the apron of the gun position. (*Author*)

All the heavy guns were to be on modern *barbette* mountings and the 12-pdr QF guns were to be sited to enable them to fire on the entrance to the harbour with one battery on the Vigie and one on the La Toc peninsula. The 6-inch BL howitzers were to be mounted on siege carriages and were intended to prevent enemy ships lying off in Grand Cul de Sac Bay and bombarding the harbour.

A sophisticated system of fire control was provided for these guns, with four Depression Position Finder cells, one of which included a chart room and telephone room, sited on Telegraph Hill adjacent to Morne Fortune to control the guns of La Toc and Apostles batteries. Four similar cells were sited on the highest point of the Vigie, where the lighthouse stands today, to control the fire of Vigie Battery.

In 1888 there was a single fixed beam DEL placed at the tip of the Point St Victor on the Vigie, and ten years later the number of DELs had been increased to four, with an additional fixed beam light superimposed above the Point St Victor light and two additional search beams, one at Vigie Point and one at Meadows Battery. The engine room and oil store for these lights was sited to the rear of the searchlight on Vigie Point.

At the beginning of the twentieth century the strategic position of St Lucia was to change dramatically. The rise of Germany meant that the British Government now saw that country as the main threat to Britain's world position and, as a result, the major ships of the Royal Navy were concentrated in Home waters. The rapidly increasing strength of the United States Navy also led the new Committee of Imperial Defence to conclude that:

> 'The western coaling stations could not be defended by the garrisons allotted to them against organized expeditionary forces such as might be brought to bear if the British Navy were not able to be employed at full strength in the Western Atlantic…As regards other Powers it is not necessary to contemplate anything more serious than a raid by one or two cruisers.'[17]

While by 'organised expeditionary forces' the committee was clearly referring to the United States, the latter sentence covered the Colonial Defence Committee's view of the danger from Martinique in the very unlikely event of war with France.[18]

The Committee of Imperial Defence requested the Colonial Defence Committee to review the question of the garrison of St Lucia bearing in mind the committee's opinion of the current strategic situation *vis à vis* the island. The garrison at the date of the Colonial Defence Committee's review comprised the headquarters of a British infantry regiment and five companies of the West India Regiment, a total of 1,219 all ranks. At the date of the review the bulk of the St Lucia garrison was stationed on Barbados awaiting the completion of new barrack accommodation on St Lucia.

As a result of the requested review, the Colonial Defence Committee proposed a reduction in the strength of the garrison to four British and two native companies of infantry (650 all ranks), two native infantry companies being considered the equivalent of one British infantry company. The guns were manned by one British garrison artillery company and a newly-formed native artillery company, a total of 321 all ranks. The committee also recommended an increase in the number of native artillerymen and a corresponding reduction in the number of British gunners with a resulting financial saving. The recommended strength of the garrison was to depend on the view of the Admiralty as to whether St Lucia should be retained as a defended naval base considering the changed strategic situation.

Two months after the Colonial Defence Committee report, in December 1904, the Admiralty made it clear that it no longer required St Lucia to be a defended naval base. In the Admiralty's view St Lucia offered no advantage as a base of operations against Germany or Russia, nor did it provide a secure anchorage, despite its defences, against a torpedo boat flotilla stationed at Martinique. In particular, the Admiralty believed that the island would be of no use in a war with the United States although the recent development of the United States into a first-class maritime power made war with that country less likely. The maintenance of a garrison on the island, therefore, would probably, in the end, be equivalent to inviting attack by an overwhelming force. Therefore, St Lucia was now considered to be unsuitable as a base of operations against a maritime power and there did not seem to be sufficient justification for incurring the expense of maintaining a garrison on the island.[19]

The Haldane reforms in the first years of the twentieth century brought about the formation of the British Expeditionary Force of six infantry divisions and a cavalry division and the Territorial Force for Home Defence. This change in organization of the British Army was funded by the disbandment of ten infantry battalions and the withdrawal of a number of overseas garrisons. The St Lucia garrison was withdrawn in 1905 and the batteries were disarmed. Two of the 6-inch Mk VII guns were sent to Jamaica to replace the 6-inch BL HP guns at Rocky Point Battery at Port Royal, and one of the 9.2-inch Mk X guns was sent to arm Fort Nugent at Kingston. This was the situation until the outbreak of the First World War in 1914.

The World Wars 1914–1945

The defence and strength of the garrison of St Lucia had always been premised on a raiding attack by one or two cruisers and a small landing force, but the outbreak of the First World War found the island undefended. Since there was considered to be a possible threat from German raiders, steps were taken to obtain guns from the French authorities on the nearby island of Martinique. The French supplied four 140mm Schneider BL guns which were installed to defend Castries harbour.

With the British Army in 1915 fully engaged on the Western Front and in other campaigns, the problem of manning the guns was solved by requesting the Canadian Government to provide troops to man the island's defences. The Canadian Government agreed to the request and in April 1915 dispatched 6 Company Royal Canadian Garrison Artillery to St Lucia where the company manned the French guns and two 6-inch Mk VII guns removed from Alexandra Battery, the practice battery on Bermuda.[20]

The Canadian detachment comprised personnel of the Royal Canadian Garrison Artillery, the Royal Canadian Engineers and the Royal Canadian Army Medical Corps and numbered 17 officers and 250 Other Ranks. The detachment remained on the island until May 1919 but saw no action.[21]

The island remained disarmed for the next twenty years until the Second World War brought about a rearming of the defences of Castries harbour and the establishment of a USN seaplane base at Gros Islet Bay under the Destroyers for Bases Agreement between Britain and the United States. On 9 March 1942 a German U-boat, *U-161*, approached Castries harbour and fired three torpedoes sinking two merchant ships, the RMS *Lady Nelson* and the SS *Umtata*. The attack on Castries clearly indicated that St Lucia was vulnerable to U-boat attack and should be defended. This was followed by the mining of the entrance to Castries harbour by a German submarine in 1942.

A 4-inch BL Naval gun mounted in one of the old 6-inch gun positions of Vigie Battery. (*Author's Collection*)

The decision was taken to re-establish fixed defences on the island using two guns, a 4-inch BL naval gun and a 12-pdr QF CD/AA gun, manned initially by 4 (British Guiana) Coast Battery, part of the newly-formed South Caribbean Force (SCF), and then by men of 6 (St Lucia) Coast Battery, SCF. The 4-inch gun was mounted on the Vigie using the old gun pit for the No 3 6-inch gun, while the 12-pdr QF gun was mounted in the old gun position at Meadows Battery, also on the Vigie. Additional protection for the harbour was provided by the installation of an anti-torpedo net across the entrance. The two guns were removed in 1946, although part of the mounting for the 12-pdr QF gun may still be seen at Meadows Battery which has been restored by the St Lucia National Trust.

Under the Destroyers for Bases Agreement American bases were also established on St Lucia. Beane Air Force Base was constructed at Vieux Fort in the south of the island and was operational until 1949. A support base was also established at Vieux Fort, but no coast artillery units were provided for defence and the garrison comprised a single infantry company. Beane Air Force Base is now Hewanorra International Airport, the island's main airport.

Chapter Five

Ceylon

Early History

Unlike the majority of island fortresses considered in this book Ceylon, or Sri Lanka to give its modern name, is not a small island but a substantial one with a land area of some 25,000 square miles (64,725 sq kms), or half the size of England, and geographically it hangs like a teardrop off the southern tip of India. Its reason for its inclusion lies in its strategic location on shipping routes to the East in the age of both sail and of steam, and the fact that there were three major harbours defended by fortresses, Colombo, Galle and Trincomalee.

Ceylon has an ancient history dating back more than 125,000 years, but European influence did not arrive on the island until the Portuguese soldier and explorer Lourenço de Almeida discovered the island in 1505. In 1517 the Portuguese took control over most of the coastal area and a number of forts were built in order to maintain this control. The first of these forts was Colombo, built in 1518 and rebuilt in 1554, followed by Matara (1550), Jaffna and Manaar (1560), Galle (1589) and Negombo (1590). In the following century, as a result of intermittent war with the northern kingdom of Jaffna, additional fortresses were constructed at Kalutara (1622), Trincomalee (1623) and Baticaloa (1628), together with a number of smaller forts.

In 1618 the first Dutch traders arrived in search of spices and King Rajasinghe II of Kandy signed a treaty with the Dutch East India Company (VOC) under the terms of which the VOC would remove the Portuguese from the coastal areas that they held. The war between the VOC and the Portuguese was waged between 1638 and 1658 during which time all the principal Portuguese forts fell to the Dutch. Subsequently, the VOC reneged on its treaty with King Rajasinghe II and retained all the coastal area that had been captured from the Portuguese.

The Dutch Fortifications

When the Dutch occupied Colombo they made it their main administrative centre on the island and set about improving the old Portuguese defences.

These new defences stretched for some 2 miles (3.2kms) around the town with four large bastions on the landward side with *counterguards* and *ravelins*, and, on the sea front, there were seven batteries. The sea front was also protected by the natural aspect of the coast which was rocky and with few suitable landing places.

On the landward side additional protection was provided by a ditch and a lake, the latter supplying water to the ditch by means of sluices. The ditch skirted the *glacis* almost to the sea on the south of the fort and was separated from it at these points by a causeway. By cutting through each causeway and opening the sluices, the fort could be completely surrounded by water. There were four gates to the fort, the Water Gate between the harbour and Amsterdam Bastion; the South Gate at Klippenburg Bastion; the Rotterdam Gate between Rotterdam and Hoorn Bastions; and the main East Gate between the Hoorn and Delft Bastions. The harbour to the north of the fort was defended by the Battenburg and Waterpas batteries on the breakwater.

The fort could mount some 300 smooth-bore guns, but it is unlikely that any more than half that number were ever mounted. There were no bomb–

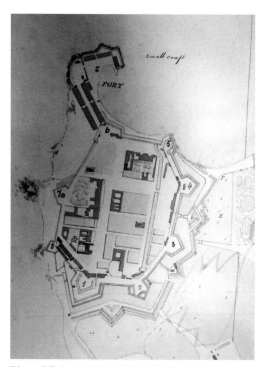

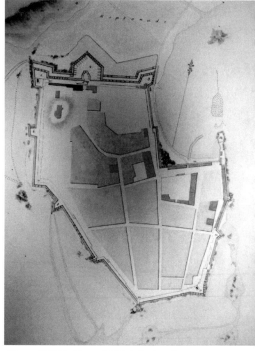

Plan of Colombo Fort, 1827. The bastions are numbered: 1. Middleburg; 2. Rotterdam; 3.Hoorn; 4.Delft; 5.Leyden; 6.Amsterdam; 7.Den Briel; 8. Enkhuizen. (*TNA MPHH 1/10*)

Plan of Galle Fort, 1827. The bastions are: 3.Sun; 4.Moon; 5.Star; 6.Aeolus; 7.Clippenburg; 8.Neptune; 9.Triton; 10.Flagrock; 11.Utrecht; 12. Aurora; 13.Akersloot; 14.Zwart. (*TNA MPHH 1/10*) proof buildings or casemates which made the fort vulnerable in the event of a siege or a naval bombardment.

Galle Fort was only a little smaller than Colombo Fort. Situated on a peninsula and surrounded on three sides by the sea, the main fortifications were on the landward side where the massive Moon Bastion and the Sun and Star bastions effectively closed the gorge of the fort. The other three sides of the fort were defended by a curtain wall more than a mile (1.6kms) long with eleven bastions and demi-bastions. There were four powder magazines within the fort but no casemated barracks or storerooms. The only gate was in the north-facing section of the curtain wall between Sun and Swarts Bastions.

Trincomalee, on the other hand, was not a major centre of population, but it had a deep-water harbour, at that time probably the best between India and China. The Dutch had fortified the harbour by constructing two forts, Fort Frederick and Fort Ostenburg. Fort Frederick stood, and indeed, still stands, on a headland which separates Back Bay and Dutch Bay, facing the open sea and the inner harbour. Fort Ostenburg guarded the entrance to the inner deep-water harbour.

Fort Frederick, like Galle Fort, is situated on a headland with its main defences covering the landward approach at the neck of the peninsula. These defences comprised a wet ditch and a curtain wall flanked by two bastions, Zeeburg and Amsterdam Bastions, and a *ravelin*. On the south-east flank facing Dutch Bay

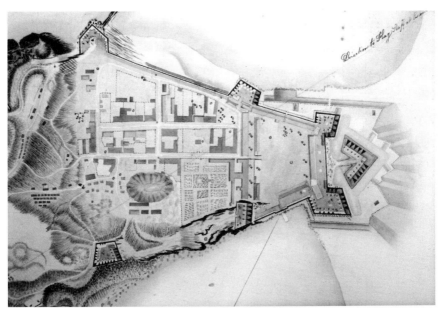

Plan of Fort Frederick, Trincomalee, 1829. (*TNA MPI 1/217*)

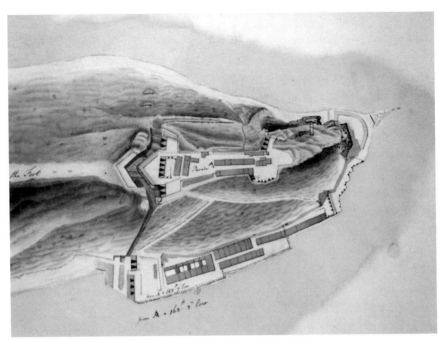

Plan of Fort Ostenburg, Trincomalee, 1829. (*TNA MPI 1/217*)

a curtain wall with a gate and two bastions, Enkhuysen and Holland Bastions, ran to where it met the high ground and cliffs, where further fortification was deemed unnecessary. On the north-west flank there was a shorter stretch of curtain wall as the high ground and cliffs were closer to the fort on this side. On the rising ground beyond the end of the curtain wall there was a trapezoidal-shaped redoubt for seventeen guns, four of which provided fire over the ground between the redoubt and the end of the curtain wall.

The VOC constructed Fort Ostenburg on a ridge overlooking the entrance to the inner harbour. Built at the seaward end of the ridge, the fort was cut off from the rear of the ridge by a front consisting of a bastion-shaped *redan* and two small wings. These wings were described at a later date by Captain William Dawson RE as being '*of trifling flanking power on a lower level*'.[1] The front and wings had embrasures for eight guns that defended the fort from attack on the landward side. Four guns were mounted centrally on a *cavalier* with two guns in each of the wings.

The Arrival of the British

In 1795, after the Netherlands had been overrun by the French Revolutionary forces, the British, fearing that the French would use Ceylon as a base for the

French navy and as a springboard for the invasion of India, took steps to occupy the coastal areas held by the Dutch. A force under the command of Colonel (later Major General) James Stuart arrived at Back Bay at Trincomalee on 1 August 1795. Initially the Dutch commander refused to capitulate but, after a short siege, Fort Frederick and Fort Ostenburg, the two forts defending Trincomalee, were surrendered.

The following February while British forces were being assembled for an invasion of the west coast of the island, with Colombo as the main objective, a certain Mr Hugh Cleghorn submitted a proposal for subverting the Swiss mercenary Regiment de Meuron which formed the bulk of the Dutch garrison. The regiment was ripe for subversion having not been paid for some months. Cleghorn negotiated the regiment's transfer to British service and, as a result, the British takeover of the Dutch fortresses was almost bloodless. Colombo fort and the forts at Jaffna, Mattara, Galle, Baticaloa and Trincomalee were quickly garrisoned by the British force, together with a number of the smaller fortified outposts in the interior also previously held by the Dutch.

Initially the captured Dutch possessions in Ceylon were administered by the Honourable East India Company (HEIC). However, due to inept and incompetent administration which resulted in a rebellion against an injudicious tax on fruit trees, the British Government was forced to take over the new colony in 1798. In an attempt to gain complete control of the island, the British became engaged in a war with the Kingdom of Kandy between 1803 and 1805. This war was followed by a further short war in 1815 which saw the deposing of the Kandyan ruler Sri Vikrame Rajasinghe. A third war between 1817 and 1818 saw the final crushing of the Kandyan nobility and the firm establishment of British rule.

In order to establish firm control over the local inhabitants the British took over all the forts previously garrisoned by the Dutch. The main coastal forts were Colombo and Galle, which were essentially fortified towns, while Jaffna, Batticaloa, Matara, Manaar, Negombo and Trincomalee were bastioned forts.

In a report on the condition of the forts by Colonel Sir John Murray in 1799 the defences of Colombo were described as being *'in a bad state. A considerable number of heavy gun carriages are not to be trusted.'* At Galle no guns were serviceable and Fort Frederick and Fort Ostenburg at Trincomalee were described as *'untenable'*.[2]

With the defeat of Napoleon in 1815 there was no longer an enemy in the Indian Ocean that could threaten Britain's hold on its possessions in India, the Straits Settlements, Mauritius and Ceylon. Fortifications and their maintenance, therefore, suffered in the ensuing years from a regime of financial stringency. However, war erupted once more with the kingdom of Kandy in 1818 so there was still a need to station small garrisons throughout the country to maintain law and order. These garrisons used the old Dutch forts as their bases and accommodation, but no attempt was made to keep them defensible against any attack other than by poorly armed local insurgents.

Apart from Colombo, Galle and Trincomalee only Jaffna was considered worth maintaining as a fortress as, unlike the other smaller Dutch forts, Jaffna was large, had been professionally built in the shape of a regular pentagon, and had a wet ditch, a good counterscarp and covered way all revetted in cut stone. The fort was armed with ninety guns, of which fifty-two were in the outworks.

In addition to the Dutch forts the British built a Martello tower and a number of small earthwork forts or stockades to assist in maintaining control over country seized from the kingdom of Kandy. The Martello tower, constructed of stone at Hambantota on the south coast about 1805-1806, was essentially a musketry tower, though it had a gun platform on top. The wall of the tower was vertical without a batter with a number of musketry loopholes, and the entrance to the tower was at first floor level. It was used to accommodate a garrison which guarded the nearby salt pans.

Most of the small forts built by the British were temporary structures constructed during the wars of 1803–05 and 1815 including Fort McDonald near Valimada, Fort King on the old road from Colombo to Kandy built in 1816, Fort McDowell at Matale built in 1803 and Fort Brownrigg. The last fort was situated some 25 miles (40kms) east of Hambantota and was somewhat more substantial than the others, being built of stone with two bastions. In 1813 it was described as a well-built modern fort '*by which date one bastion was ready to receive two guns*'.[3]

In 1811 a committee comprising Generals Brownrigg and Maitland and Admiral Hood RN had convened to consider the defences of Trincomalee Harbour. Lieutenant Colonel Bridges RE, previously the Commanding Royal Engineer in Ceylon, was summoned to advise the committee and he proposed the construction of three gun towers, two on the high ground overlooking Fort Ostenburg and one on Clappenburg Island. The two towers on the mainland were named after General Brownrigg, Quartermaster General and subsequently Governor of Ceylon, and Admiral Hood, members of the original committee.

By 1817 work had started on the two mainland towers but was stopped in April of that year when the wall of Admiral Hood's Tower, a square tower, had reached a height of 10 feet (3m) and the storeroom and tank were complete,

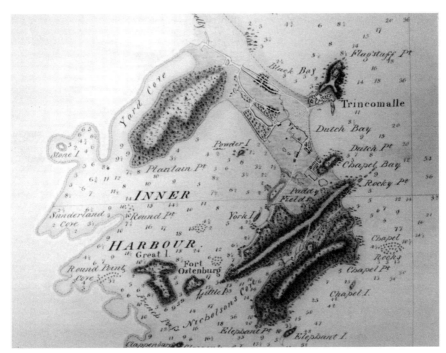

Map of Trincomalee Harbour 1806. (*Author's Collection*)

but the wall of General Brownrigg's Tower had only reached a height of 4 feet (1.2m). Despite urgent pleas on the part of the Commanding Royal Engineer, Lieutenant Colonel Watts, that all the materials needed to complete the towers had been assembled, they were never completed, nor work on the Clappenburg Island tower started.

By the late 1820s only piracy disturbed the peace and tranquillity of the Royal Navy's East Indies and China Station, and internally there was peace in Ceylon. In 1827 Captain Dawson RE produced a report for the governor of Ceylon on the fortifications of the colony. The report was produced only after much prompting by the governor, since Dawson was reluctant to carry out the work involved in the production of such a report. He felt it would take him away from his important work supervising the construction of the new road from Colombo to Kandy because of the immense amount of travel involved in preparing the report. In the end Dawson completed a survey of all the Dutch fortifications and produced an extensive report including plans of all the forts, sadly dying shortly after completing it.[4]

In Captain Dawson's view none of the existing fortifications could be considered to be defensible without considerable repair and improvement. Colombo he believed to be vulnerable because large parts of the water defences on the landward side could be controlled by an enemy force should it gain control of the sluices. The outline of the fort he considered to be inapplicable to mutual defence and badly, or not at all, defiladed, while the fort was without traverses or palisades. So his recommendation was, that rather than remodelling the fortifications, a substantial fort should be built at St Sebastian, a suburb of Colombo, which would cover the sluices and outlets of the inundation and could take in reverse an enemy's advance on the main fort.

Only the two forts at Trincomalee, Fort Frederick and Fort Ostenburg, and Jaffna Fort were considered by Dawson to be of use as defensive works. Galle Fort he believed to be too large, and if it was to continue in use as a fortification it would need to be reduced in size so as to be able to be held by the size of garrison likely to be stationed there. All the other smaller works at Manaar, Matara, Tangalle, Batticaloa, and Paltunpanne he dismissed as having been principally established for defence against 'Kandian Irruption and for revenue protection when the Interior was not in European possession'.[5]

Although Fort Frederick and Fort Ostenburg at Trincomalee were accepted by Dawson as worth garrisoning for the defence of the anchorage, both had significant drawbacks as defensive works. Fort Frederick's guns could not defend the inner harbour, the main anchorage, while Fort Ostenburg was overlooked from higher points on the ridge on which it was situated, and there was no fresh water other than rainwater that could be collected in cisterns.

Captain Dawson's view regarding the defences of Trincomalee was fully supported by Rear Admiral Sir Edward Owen, Commander-in-Chief HM Naval Forces in India, who wrote to Lord William Bentinck, the Governor General, on 31 October 1830 regarding 'the inadequacy of the defence at present situated for giving fit protection to the Naval Arsenal and other Establishments at Trincomalee', and recommended that a committee be set up to consider the whole matter of the siting of the dockyard and its defences.[6]

Most of the forts on the island remained garrisoned for the next decade, though as the country became more settled a number of the small forts were abandoned or had their usage changed. The fort at Tangalle became a provincial jail as early as 1827 and, in the same year, Kalutara became the Chief Secretary's country retreat. The garrison was withdrawn from the large fort at Batticaloa in 1836 and from the smaller fort at Ruwanwella, which had been built in 1817, three years earlier. Manaar, however, was still occupied in 1837.[7]

In 1842 the decision was taken that only the forts at Colombo, Galle, Jaffna and Trincomalee would be maintained, although at least one of the other forts, Fort McDowell at Matale, was still garrisoned in 1848 when it was unsuccessfully besieged during the Matale Rebellion of that year. In the same year Charles Pridham noted that the fort at Manaar was manned by Invalids.[8] Three other small forts, Tangalle, Matara and Hammenheil were also retained as prisons.

The Naval Base

As early as 1813 Captain Peter Pujet RN, Commissioner of the Royal Navy at Madras, recommended to the C-in-C East Indies and China Station that Trincomalee should be used as a re-fitting port for HM ships, and he selected Nicholson's Cove as a possible site for the naval base. Two years later in 1815, after Rear Admiral Sir Edward Pellew, had strongly endorsed Captain Pujet's recommendation of Trincomalee as a refitting base and his choice of Nicholson's Cove as its site, authority was given by the Admiralty for the establishment of the base. Work commenced on its construction and HMS *Arrogant* (ex-civilian ship *Adasier*) was berthed at Trincomalee as a hulk and storeship.

It would seem that the matter of the defence of the new base was not, initially, one of pressing importance as far as the Admiralty was concerned as in April 1846 Rear Admiral Thomas Cochrane RN wrote to Their Lordships complaining about the state of the defences at Trincomalee. His letter must

Main Gate, Trincomalee Royal Navy Dockyard c1895. (*Author's Collection*)

have struck a chord in the Colonial Office as later that year a report was made on the works recommended for the defence of the harbour. The total cost of the recommended defences came to £96,000, an astronomical sum at that time, so it is no surprise that the report '*led to no proceedings*'.[9]

However, the First Lord of the Admiralty was not prepared to let the matter rest and two years later (not an inordinate delay by Admiralty and Ordnance Board standards of the time) and in consequence of his previous representation in 1848 on the defenceless state of Trincomalee, a proposition was made from the Treasury for an expenditure of £36,000 on the most important works. The proposed works were to be:

a. A battery for thirteen guns on the water's edge at the extremity of Ostenburg Ridge.
b. Rebuilding the old Dutch battery on Elephant Point to mount eight guns.
c. A battery for ten guns on Little Sober Island.
d. A tower on Great Sober Island.
e. A battery on Plantain Point at the north end of the inner harbour.
f. Redoubts on Elephant Ridge and Chapel Hill.
g. A Martello tower on the extremity of Ostenburg Ridge.

Once again nothing came of the proposed works despite the reduction in the estimated cost. However, the outbreak of the Crimean War in 1853 would appear to have brought about a change of heart in both the Colonial Office and the Board of Ordnance, and steps were taken to mount guns in a battery on Ostenburg Point and one on Belfry Hill overlooking Nicholson's Cove. These batteries were essentially a temporary measure as the guns were without platforms, there were no magazines nearby, nor was there any cover for the men manning the guns.

The failure to carry out improvements to the defences which affected Colombo and Galle as well as Trincomalee was not, in fact, the responsibility of the Board of Ordnance. In 1845 the Master General of the Ordnance, General Sir Thomas Murray, stated:

'*The Works of Defence at Ceylon are not under the charge or control of the Ordnance. The Commander Royal Engineers on requisition from the Governor is authorized to make reports and to prepare Plans and Estimates for any Works or Repairs that may be deemed requisite, but the decision as to whose part of the proposed Works shall be sanctioned and the provision of*

installed as a temporary measure. However, the incoming Inspector General of Fortifications, Major General Sir Andrew Clarke, submitted a reduced scheme for Colombo which substituted four of the new 9.2-inch breech-loading (BL) guns for the 10-inch RMLs recommended by the Commission, and reduced the number of 9-inch RML guns from three to two.[16]

For Galle, considered to be the most exposed point of Ceylon, it was considered that the fort should be armed with the heaviest guns, so it was proposed that the Star, Eolus, Klippenburg and Triton Bastions should be remodelled to mount 10-inch 18 ton RML guns.[17]

The following year, 1881, a further commission was established to report on the defences of Ceylon. This recommended a garrison for the island of one infantry battalion, two batteries of artillery and a company of gun lascars, locally recruited personnel, to assist with the manning of the guns. The commission also recommended that Galle should be abandoned as a defended port as it was now used primarily by sailing ships.

As was the case in all colonies there was much debate with the Imperial government on the subject of the cost of maintaining the garrison. The debate was about the total amount to be contributed by the colony to the cost of its defence, and how much was the responsibility of the Imperial government. In 1883 an agreement was reached between the colonial and Imperial governments under which Ceylon was to pay Rs500,000 (£31,250) annually for five years from January 1884, with a review of that figure in 1889. In fact, the total colonial contribution had risen to Rs600,000 by 1888, of which Rs126,700 was for the construction and maintenance of the fortifications. The colonial contribution would continue to rise until in 1894. The total contribution was Rs1,394,500, or £87,156, a tripling in the size of the contribution over a period of only nine years.

A report produced by a Major Barker RE on the defences of Trincomalee recommended the occupation of Great Sober Island in Trincomalee harbour as an alternative to the scheme to construct a battery on Elephant Ridge recommended by the Inspector General of Fortifications. Major Barker's telling arguments included the fact that Great Sober Island could not be taken in reverse, was easily accessible from the dockyard and had ample space for barracks and stores out of range of enemy fire. His proposal was that a battery of four 10-inch RML guns should be built on Great Sober Island. He also proposed that Fort Ostenburg should be abandoned, but that a shielded battery for two 10-inch guns should be built on Ostenburg Point.[18]

The Panjdeh Incident

During the final years of the 1870s and the early 1880s tension grew between Britain and Russia as a result of Russia's continuing expansion into Central Asia. Matters came to a head in 1885 when a Russian force defeated an Afghan army in the Battle of Kishka, also known as the Panjdeh Incident. Seen by the British Government as a major threat to India, the Russian incursion was settled diplomatically, but, nevertheless, it had drawn the British Government's attention to the parlous state of the defences of British possessions in the Indian Ocean and the Far East. The Panjdeh Incident in March 1885 had been preceded two months earlier by the unannounced arrival in Singapore of a Russian naval squadron, the ships of which were armed with modern breech-loading guns superior in performance to the armament of Royal Navy warships.

By 1885 the defences of Trincomalee comprised:

Fort Ostenburgh	Regent's Battery	2 × 7-inch 6½-ton RML guns
	Half Moon Battery	1 × 9-inch 12-ton RML gun
	Ridge Battery	1 × 7-inch 6½-ton RML gun
	Belfry Hill	2 × 64-pdr RML guns
Fort Frederick	Flagstaff Battery	1 × 7-inch 6½-ton gun
	Eastern Battery	1 × 7-inch 6½-ton gun
	Portuguese Battery	1 × 7-inch 6½ -on gun
	Citadel Battery	1 × 7-inch 6½-ton gun
	Cavalier Battery	1 × 64-pdr RML gun
	Zeeburg Battery	1 × 64-pdr RML gun
	Amsterdam Battery	1 × 64-pdr RML gun
	Ostenburg Face Battery	1 × 64-pdr RML

Fear of Russia's plans for further expansion in the East led Prime Minister Gladstone to ask Parliament for a vote of £11 million for war preparations to pay for the Sudan expedition to rescue General Gordon, and for the modernization of the defences of ports and bases at home and overseas. In March 1885 this resulted in the approved armament for Trincomalee being:

4 × 10-inch 18-ton RML guns
3 × 9-inch 12-ton RML guns
4 × 7-inch 6½-ton RML guns
6 × 64-pdr 64 cwt RML guns

2 × 40-pdr RBL guns

2 × 20-pdr RBL guns

Three of the 10-inch guns were to be mounted in a new battery on Great Sober Island, with two 40-pdr RBL guns to cover the minefield. On Ostenburg Ridge a fourth 10-inch gun was to replace the two 7-inch guns in Ridge Battery, but the similar guns approved for Regent's Battery were to remain. The 9-inch RML gun at Half Moon Battery was to be removed as the emplacement was unsafe as the cliff on which it stood was becoming unstable. However, it was to remain in place until the 10-inch guns were mounted when the battery would be dismantled and the gun moved to Fort Frederick.

At Fort Frederick the 7-inch gun emplacements at Eastern Battery and Flagstaff Battery were to be remodelled to take 9-inch RML guns, and a new emplacement for a 9-inch gun, to be known as Western Battery, was to be constructed to the north of the citadel at a level of 100 feet (30m) above the low water mark.

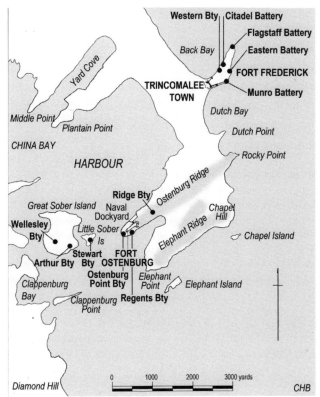

Map of Trincomalee defences, 1900.
(*Charles Blackwood*)

In 1886 a new report on the Defences of Ceylon was submitted to the Colonial Defence Committee. For Colombo the report recommended the construction of a battery at Galle Face to mount a 9.2-inch BL gun *en barbette*, with a second such gun mounted at Battenburg Battery and the two 7-inch RML guns at that battery to be removed and mounted in the new Galle Face Battery. A new battery was recommended for a site at Mutwal Point to be armed with two 9.2-inch BL guns and two 7-inch RML guns.

At Trincomalee, the new battery on Great Sober Island and the emplacement for a 9-inch gun at the Fort Frederick Western Battery were noted as being under construction, but apart from the mounting of the two additional 9-inch RML guns in Fort Frederick, the only other change in the armament was the installation of three modern 6-pdr QF guns in a battery on Ostenburg Point and the substitution of two similar guns for the older 40-pdr RBL guns on Great Sober Island where they defended the minefield.

As a result of the decision to make Trincomalee the Royal Navy station the importance of Colombo diminished and throughout the late 1880s work continued at Trincomalee to construct the emplacements for the heavier RML guns. By 1887 the emplacement for the 9-inch gun at the Western Battery in Fort Frederick was complete, followed in 1888 by the emplacement in the Eastern Battery, also in Fort Frederick, for a similar gun, and for a 7-inch 6½-ton gun on Portuguese Bastion. The following year a 9-inch RML gun was mounted in Flagstaff Battery and a 64-pdr 64cwt RML gun on Ostenburg Face Bastion, both in Fort Frederick, and two 7-inch 6½-ton RML guns in Regent's Battery in Fort Ostenburg. Cavalier Battery, for one 64-pdr 64cwt RML gun, was completed in 1890.

Breechloaders and Batteries

By 1890 most of the British coast defence forts were still armed with obsolete muzzle-loading guns. The 7-inch 6½-ton RML gun could only penetrate the armour of 2nd Class cruisers at 1,000 yards (920m), almost point-blank range, and all the RML guns had a very slow rate of fire which reduced their effectiveness as the speed of warships increased to 18 knots or more. However, by the early 1880s both the Royal Gun Factory and Sir William Armstrong's Elswick Ordnance Company were developing effective breech-loading guns in all calibres from 4-inch to 10-inch, together with a new hydro-pneumatic mounting to replace the old Moncrieff counter-weight carriage.

The promising development of these new guns in 1880 had led the Inspector General of Fortifications to recommend the new 9.2-inch BL guns for the defence of Colombo. These guns were capable of penetrating 12 inches (0.3m) of armour at 4,500 yards (4,150m), a much superior performance when compared with the armour penetration of the heavier RML guns. Lieutenant General Simmons recommended four of the new 9.2-inch BL guns, then under development, for Colombo, two to be mounted in a new battery at Mutwal Point, north of the harbour, one in a new battery at Galle Face, south of the harbour and the fourth on the old Battenburg Bastion position. These guns were to be supported by either one or two 7-inch 6½-ton or 64-pdr 64 cwt RML guns in the two new batteries, with a single 7-inch gun in Battenburg and Enkhuysen Batteries, and 7-inch 6½-ton RML guns in Klippenburg and Guard Batteries. The 9.2-inch guns were in place by 1892 mounted on hydro-pneumatic mountings (HP). However, despite the recommendation of new breech-loading guns for Colombo no such recommendation was made for the defences of Trincomalee and the older RML guns were to remain in place there.

The whole question of the defence of Ceylon was considered by the Colonial Defence Committee in 1892 when it was stated that any defence of the island turned upon the command of the sea and that the garrison allotted to Ceylon had been estimated on the assumption that that command would be retained. Therefore, under the conditions then existing, only a raid by cruisers should be considered and the question of defence resolved itself into the defence of Colombo and Trincomalee.[19] As a result it was finally decided that Galle should no longer be defended, though the detachment of the Volunteer Artillery at Galle, one officer and thirty Other Ranks, was retained in the Defence Scheme to man a battery of 9-pdr RML field guns.

In 1893 the threat of an attack on Trincomalee by torpedo boats was considered by the Local Joint Naval and Military Committee which concluded that an attack by such craft was unlikely due to the fact that potential enemy naval bases were located beyond the range of torpedo boats. However, there was a possible threat from Second Class torpedo boats carried by enemy cruisers, so an allocation of Defence Electric Lights (DELs) was approved. These lights were to be sited with one Fixed Beam (30°) light at Pujet's Wharf (dockyard), two more similar lights on Little Sober Island, and one Moving Beam at Flagstaff Point.[20]

Despite the decision to mount heavy breech-loading guns at Colombo, Trincomalee remained armed with RML guns until 1898 when a number of modern quick-firing guns were approved for both Fort Ostenburg and Fort Frederick. At Fort Ostenburg the two 7-inch RML guns at Regent's Battery were replaced by two 4.7-inch QF guns, and three 6-pdr QF guns were to be installed at Ostenburg Point to cover the minefield. At the same time three 4.7-inch QF guns were installed in Fort Frederick, one on Ostenburg Face Bastion, now re-named Munroe Battery, in place of the old 64-pdr RML gun, and two on Citadel Battery in place of the existing 7-inch RML.

The following year a Conference on Armaments considering the armament of the Colombo defences approved the removal of the two 7-inch RML guns from Galle Face battery in Colombo, and the mounting of two 6-inch BL guns of the latest type, which, in this instance, meant the new QF model. These new guns were to be mounted not in Galle Face Battery but in a new battery overlooking Mutwal Battery. Another 6-inch QF gun was to be added to Battenburg Battery and two were to be mounted at Flagstaff Battery. These last two guns were installed in November 1900. Approval was also given for the placing of four light quick-firing guns two at each of the entrances to Colombo Harbour. In 1902–1903 two 6-pdr QF guns and one Maxim machine gun were emplaced at the end of the South-West Breakwater, at the foot of the lighthouse.

At last, at Trincomalee, heavy breech-loading guns were to be mounted with one 9.2-inch BL gun to replace the two 10-inch RML guns of Ridge Battery on Ostenburg Ridge, and another single gun to replace one of the 10-inch RML guns at Arthur Battery on Great Sober Island. The other two

Flagstaff Battery, Colombo, under construction c.1900. (*Author's Collection*)

6-inch QF gun position at Arthur Battery on Great Sober Island, Trincomalee. (*Author*)

RML guns of that battery were to be removed at this time and two 6-inch QF guns substituted. There was also a proposal to mount two 12-pdr QF guns in a battery on Little Sober Island. A new battery for two 12-pdr and two 6-pdr QF guns was built on the island and named Stewart Battery and Ostenburg Point Battery was renamed French Battery, with a reduction in the number of guns from three to two.

By the turn of the century the international political situation in Europe was changing rapidly. The German Emperor's major warship-building programme aimed at equalling the number of battleships in the Royal Navy resulted in a naval race between Britain and Germany. To meet the German threat a defensive alliance was signed with Japan in 1902 which allowed the Admiralty to concentrate the major Royal Navy ships in European waters. The result of this policy, together with the construction of a large breakwater in Colombo harbour and of a large graving dock, the largest at that time between Malta and Hong Kong, meant a down-grading in the importance of Trincomalee. As a result, in 1904 the Admiralty announced that Trincomalee was to be abandoned as a naval dockyard and anchorage and in December 1904 the Army Council recommended the abandonment of Trincomalee as a defended port and the withdrawal of the garrison and armament.

A further result of the worsening relations between Britain and Germany was the decision by the Admiralty and the War Office to set up the Owen Committee in 1905.[21] As a result the armament approved for Colombo was now to be two batteries each of two 9.2-inch BL Mk X guns, one north of the harbour in the area of St Andrew's Church, close to Rockhouse Battery, with two 6-inch BL Mk VII guns at Rockhouse Battery. For the defence south of the harbour two 9.2-inch BL Mk X guns were to be emplaced in a new battery at the Pilot Station tower. All the existing armament at Colombo was now declared redundant, but the two older 9.2-inch guns at Battenburg Battery and Flagstaff Battery were to be retained until the new battery at the Pilot Station tower was operational and the Battenburg 6-inch gun was to be retained until the breakwater was completed. As it transpired, the Pilot Station Tower position proved to be unsuitable for a heavy gun battery, so an alternative site was selected at Galle Face behind the Green, near where the Taj Samudra Hotel now stands.

All three new batteries were sited almost at sea level and close to the commercial centre of Colombo, so there was a problem in finding suitable positions for the rangefinders and position finders to provide the fire control of the guns. This problem was overcome in a particularly imaginative way and one that was probably unique amongst all the defended ports in the Empire. As a disguise the towers were designed very much as civilian buildings with arched windows, balconies, verandahs and, in one case, a structure that resembled a small bell tower. The Flagstaff Battery Fire Control Tower, built in 1900, was 40 feet (12.3m) high, while the Rockhouse (Mutwal) 9.2-inch battery position finder tower was 36 feet (11m) high. The latter tower had elaborate arched windows with steel loopholed shutters disguised as louvres with a verandah around the base of the tower, and was sited on a rise to the rear of the battery behind a loopholed wall. The tallest tower was the Fire Control Post for Battenburg Battery which stood 46 feet (14m) high

Flagstaff Battery Command Post, Colombo. Sited to the rear of the battery it was designed to be mistaken for a civilian building. (*Author's Collection*)

on the Esplanade and housed an 18-foot (5.5m) Barr & Stroud rangefinder. The tower was completed in 1915.

The Galle Face battery was completed and operational in 1911. The design of the battery was unusual in that there were emplacements for a field gun and a machine gun on each flank of the battery. The new Rockhouse 9.2-inch battery was completed a year later behind the abandoned Mutwal Battery. The original location for the Rockhouse Battery proposed by the Owen Committee was the site of St Andrew's Church, but, needless to say, the elders of the kirk were not prepared to make way for a gun battery, so the alternate site of the old 6-inch gun battery site was selected, and the church found itself with two gun batteries sited immediately in front of the west end of the church. One can only assume that firing practices and church services did not coincide! At Battenburg Battery a second 6-inch BL Mk VII gun was added to the one already *in situ*, and the battery was renamed Mount Batten Battery.

The Royal Artillery garrison of the island had been maintained at a level of two garrison companies and a company of native gunners (gun lascars) for many years. In 1888 the Ceylon Artillery Volunteers had been formed as part of the Ceylon Defence Force, itself formed in 1881, and ten years later the company of gun lascars was formed into a new unit when it was combined with the Mauritius gun lascars to form the Ceylon-Mauritius Battalion RGA. However, this unit was abolished in 1907 and the Ceylon company disbanded when the RGA troops manning the Trincomalee defences were withdrawn. This left only the Ceylon Artillery Volunteers to assist the one remaining company of the RGA in manning the defences of Colombo.

The outbreak of the First World War in 1914 found Colombo as the only defended port in Ceylon, but during the war there was no call on its defences. The destruction of the German East Asia Squadron at the Battle of the Falkland Islands in December 1914 meant that there was no longer a threat to British interests in the Indian Ocean, other than an occasional solitary raider. However, the ever-increasing demands for manpower made by the Western Front meant that the there was a continuing reduction in the British personnel of the garrison. To replace these losses the Colombo Town Guard was formed in 1914, which included the Town Guard Artillery to assist with manning the coast defences. In 1918 the Ceylon Artillery Volunteers and the Town Guard Artillery were amalgamated to form the Ceylon Garrison Artillery as part of the Ceylon Defence Force, a mobilized section of which took over the role of garrison on the island and the manning of the coast defence batteries.

The Second World War and War with Japan

With Britain almost bankrupt after the end of the First World War, disarmament, or at least some form of arms limitation, seemed an attractive proposition to the government. The result was the acceptance of the proposals for a limitation on the sizes of the fleets of the major nations proposed by the United States at the naval disarmament conference in Washington called by President Harding's administration in 1921. The Washington Treaty effectively brought an end to the Royal Navy's 'Two Fleet' policy, and left Japan as the major naval power in the Far East. However, the Royal Navy plan was that in the event of war in the Far East – in other words with Japan – a battle fleet would be dispatched to defend Australia and New Zealand and British possessions in the Far East.

The new plan involved the construction of a new naval base at Singapore, but the Admiralty appreciated that a defended anchorage was also needed in the Indian Ocean. In 1923 the Admiralty announced that it was proposed to re-establish the Navy Yard at Trincomalee and move the headquarters of the East Indies Squadron from Bombay to Trincomalee. In the words of the Admiralty proposal document:

'Trincomalee is well-suited as a Naval anchorage for a moderate-sized fleet including capital ships. There is no other comparable anchorage on the coasts of India or Ceylon.'[22]

Indeed, the Admiralty went on to say:

'Trincomalee is the only port in British territory in the Indian Ocean that possesses the necessary strategical, physical, and economic requirements for a secondary repair port for capital ships in wartime. It is admirably suited to accommodate a floating dock capable of taking the largest class of men-of-war.'[23]

In 1924 a sub-committee of the Committee of Imperial Defence, the Committee on the Defence of Ports at Home and Abroad, considered the defences of both Trincomalee and Colombo. For Trincomalee the Technical Sub-committee recommended the installation of two 9.2-inch Mk X guns on 55° mountings at Fort Frederick; two 6-inch Mk VII guns on 45° mountings on Chapel Hill or Elephant Ridge and two 4.7-inch QF guns on Elephant Ridge. The new high angle mountings for both the 9.2-inch and 6-inch guns were, at that period, no more than a twinkle in the eyes of the gun designers.

For Colombo the recommended armament was for a single two-gun 9.2-inch battery and four 6-inch guns. The 9.2-inch battery to be reduced was the Rockhouse battery, while two 6-inch Mk VII guns on 45° mountings were to be installed in the Rockhouse 6-inch battery and the two 6-inch Mk VII guns on 15° mountings would remain at Battenburg Battery. The upgrading of the Rockhouse Battery with 45° mountings was required because the 9.2-inch guns of Galle Face Battery could not cover the area of water directly north of Colombo harbour.

In the event nothing came of the plans to develop the 55° mounting for the 9.2-inch BL coast defence guns; the economic climate of the late 1920s ensured that little was done to put into effect these recommendations. However, by 1935 the international political situation was more threatening with the rise of Hitler in Germany and Japan's withdrawal from the League of Nations in 1933. As a result, rearmament was in the air and now the 1924 recommendations for the rearming of Trincomalee were acted upon. Approval was given for the construction of the 9.2-inch battery at Trincomalee on Ostenburg Ridge on the Chapel Hill site with work on two mountings to commence in 1935–36 for completion in 1936–37. A site for a third mounting was selected in 1934 though it would be 1942 before that gun would be mounted.

Hood's Tower Battery, Trincomalee. A 6-inch Mk VII BL gun with a Second World War splinter shield fitted. The battery is now a museum. (*Author*)

In 1935 Major General Barron, the Inspector General of Fixed Defences, visited Ceylon as part of his tour of the defended ports in the Far East. He recommended that work start immediately on a 6-inch close defence battery at Trincomalee to be built on the site of the old nineteenth century Hood's Tower on Elephant Ridge. He considered this battery to be so important that he recommended that two guns should be mounted immediately on temporary platforms, with the permanent battery to be constructed later.[24] The haulage of the gun loads during mounting was done using elephants. However, the officer in charge of the operation did not recommend the future use of elephants for this task noting that they were *slow, moody, and not used to team work*.[25] The fact that they were not used to teamwork must refer to the particular elephants used for the mounting, as elephants were used in teams to pull heavy artillery in India.

Work on the permanent positions for the guns was commenced in July 1937 and the guns were mounted in October 1938 and were operational in February 1939. To enable the battery to fire by night, two 90cm 3° moveable beam DELs were also installed on Elephant Ridge, while two more, one 3° moveable beam and one 16° fixed beam light, were installed on Elephant Point. These were controlled from a direction station on Chapel Hill.

Defence of ports and harbours from air attack had been increasing in importance since the end of the First World War. Although it seemed that there was little imminent danger of an air attack on Trincomalee, in 1924 the naval base was allocated an approved armament of four two-gun sections of anti-aircraft guns, increased in 1937 to twelve guns, and one section of eight 0.303-inch Lewis anti-aircraft machine guns. However, in 1937 only two 3-inch AA guns were in position to defend the base, together with one LAA gun. These guns were manned by personnel of the 14 LAA Battery, a sub-unit of 6th Coast Regiment RA which had been dispatched to garrison Trincomalee, with the other two batteries of the regiment to man the coast defence guns. At Colombo there was a second section of two 3-inch AA guns manned by the 3rd LAA & SL Regiment, Ceylon Garrison Artillery, with a LAAMG detachment of eight 0.303-inch Lewis machine guns from the same regiment.

Interestingly, in 1939 serious consideration was given by both the War Office and the Admiralty to the stationing of the monitor HMS *Terror* at Trincomalee. The monitor, armed with two 15-inch guns, had been moored in Singapore as a floating battery until such time as the two 15-inch batteries being constructed at Singapore were complete. The proposal was that HMS *Terror* would again act as a floating battery anchored in China Bay and as an ammunition store and accommodation for naval personnel. In the event, however, the outbreak of war in September 1939 nullified this plan and the ship returned to the United Kingdom to be subsequently sunk in the Mediterranean off Libya by German aircraft in 1941.

The outbreak of war with Germany in September 1939 increased the importance of both Colombo and Trincomalee, the former as a commercial port and the latter as a naval anchorage. The Ceylon Defence Force was mobilised and detachments, each with two 6-inch BL guns, were sent to provide defences for the Cocos Keeling Islands and the Seychelles to protect them against possible German raiders. Steps were taken to improve the defences of both Colombo and Trincomalee and, in 1940, plans were accelerated for the installation of the 6-inch Mk XXIV guns at Rockhouse Battery at Colombo and the plans for the emplacements were modified in order to speed up their construction.

With the attack on Pearl Harbor and Malaya by Japan in December 1941 war now came close to Ceylon. Although there were plans to upgrade the Colombo guns with 35° mountings for the 9.2-inch BL guns and 45° mountings for the 6-inch BL guns, and a third 35° mounting for the Chapel Hill battery at Trincomalee, none had yet been completed. The Colombo 6-inch Mk XXIV guns were scheduled to come off the production line in May 1941 and the third 35° mounting for the third 9.2-inch BL gun for Trincomalee in September 1941, so the island faced any potential Japanese attack with its pre-war armament.[26]

For defence against air attack the island was in a parlous state with only the four out-dated 3-inch AA guns at Trincomalee. In December 1941 the Port Defence Committee of the Chiefs of Staff Committee noted that the approved armament for Colombo was sixteen HAA guns (3.7-inch) and twelve LAA guns (40mm) but none were in place. For Trincomalee the approved armament was twenty-four HAA guns and twelve LAA guns, of which total all but one LAA gun were still outstanding, though there were now four 3-inch 20cwt guns in place.[27]

It was clear to both the War Office and the Admiralty that immediate steps needed to be taken to provide an adequate anti-aircraft defence for Ceylon and in February two ships carrying the guns and personnel of HQ 1 AA Brigade RM, 1st AA Regiment RM with twenty-four 3.7-inch HAA guns, and 22 LAA Battery RM with sixteen 40mm LAA guns arrived in Colombo. These units were part of 1st Mobile Naval Base Defence Organisation RM (RMMNBDO) dispatched from the Middle East.

In February 1942 the anti-aircraft units were deployed as follows:

Colombo   One battery 1st HAA Regiment RM (8 × 3.7-inch HAA guns)
           14 AA Battery 6th Coast Regiment (4 × 3-inch AA guns)
           One troop 22 LAA Battery RM (8 × 40mm LAA guns)

Trincomalee   HQ 1AA Brigade RM
                       Two batteries 1st HAA Regiment RM (16 × 3.7-inch HAA guns)
                       22 LAA Battery RM less one troop (8 × 40mm LAA guns)

At Trincomalee the LAA battery was deployed for the defence of China Bay airfield.

Further anti-aircraft reinforcements in the form of 65th HAA Regiment RA with twenty-four guns and 43rd LAA Regiment RA and 55th LAA Regiment RA each with thirty-six guns arrived in March 1942.

The loss of Singapore to the Japanese meant that Ceylon was now in the front line of the war in the Far East. Although it is now clear that the Japanese never had any intention of invading the island, they were determined that any threat from a British fleet based there should be eliminated. At the end of March the Japanese sent a strong raiding force comprising six aircraft carriers into the Indian Ocean and aimed at striking at Colombo and Trincomalee. On 4 April the Japanese fleet was sighted by a RCAF Catalina operating out of Trincomalee, but despite the warning it transmitted before being shot down, the Japanese managed to attack Colombo on the following day virtually undetected. The Royal Navy armed merchant cruiser HMS *Hector* and the destroyer HMS *Tenedos* were sunk and twenty-seven RAF aircraft destroyed, most on the ground, for the Japanese loss of five aircraft, though British sources believed that total was actually eighteen.

Four days later, on 9 April, it was the turn of Trincomalee to be attacked by the Japanese fleet. Japanese aircraft attacked the harbour and the China Bay airfield causing severe damage, but lost eleven aircraft to RAF fighters and anti-aircraft fire. One Australian and two Royal Navy ships, the destroyer HMAS *Vampire*, the aircraft carrier HMS *Hermes* and the corvette HMS *Hollyhock*, were sunk in a second attack off Batticaloa.

The Japanese had failed to find the British fleet at anchor at Trincomalee but it seemed to Admiral Somerville that the anchorage was too vulnerable to further attack and he withdrew the fleet to Kilindini in East Africa. Nevertheless, the British authorities in London determined to increase the defences of both Colombo and Trincomalee against any possible further Japanese attack. The first priorities were to improve the anti-aircraft defences and to provide defences against submarine and torpedo boat attack. Anti-submarine and anti-torpedo boom defences had been provided at Trincomalee between Little Sober Island and Ostenburg Point, and between North End Head and Dockyard Shoal, prior to the outbreak of war, together with indicator loops and harbour defence Asdic.

Twin 6-pdr QF gun position on Clappenburg Point, Trincomalee. (*Author*)

To defend against motor torpedo boat attack four Twin 6-pdr 10cwt equipments were approved, two for Elephant Point, one for Elephant Island and one for Clappenburg Point. However, it would be 1943 before these guns were in place and operational, so, to provide some immediate defence, two 12-pdr 20cwt CD/AA guns and two 2-pdr anti-tank guns were installed at Elephant Point to cover the boom defences. Two Naval 4-inch BL guns were also provided for AMTB defence and these were mounted on Great Sober Island.

Additional close defence for the naval base was provided by the construction of a battery for two 6-inch BL guns on 15° mountings on Diamond Hill, on the opposite side of the harbour from Ostenburg Ridge. This battery, together with the AMTB battery on Clappenburg Point had the role of securing the southern arm of the harbour. To further improve the effectiveness of the close defence and AMTB batteries, a total of sixteen CASLs were installed with seven on Clappenburg Point to illuminate a new boom defence established between Clappenburg Point and Elephant Point.

To assist in the low-level air defence of the harbour single 40mm–Bofors LAA guns were mounted alongside the Twin 6-pdr QF equipments on Clappenburg Point, Elephant Point and Elephant Island. Two more similar guns defended Ostenburg Battery on Chapel Hill, together with an AA searchlight on the roof of No 4 CASL on Clappenburg Point and another on Elephant Island.

These guns were part of a total of forty-eight HAA guns and forty-eight LAA guns that defended Trincomalee in December 1942. A similar number of anti-aircraft guns defended Colombo city, with a further twenty HAA guns and nineteen LAA guns deployed to defend Ratamalana airfield and other vulnerable points on the outskirts of Colombo. In addition to these guns six of the modern 5.25-inch AA/CD guns were approved for Ceylon, three for the proposed Colpetty Battery at Colombo and three in a battery in Fort Frederick at Trincomalee. However, it would appear that these guns were never mounted.

By 1944 the coast defences of Ceylon were as follows:

Colombo

	Galle Face Battery	2 × 9.2-inch Mk X (35°) CB guns
		1 × 9.2-inch Mk X (15°) CB gun
	Rockhouse Battery	3 × 6-inch Mk XXIV (45°) CB guns
	Battenburg Battery	2 × 6-inch Mk VII (15°) CD guns
	Breakwater Batteries	2 × 75mm guns
		4 × Twin 6-pdr QF equipments
Trincomalee		
	Ostenburg Battery	3 × 9.2-inch Mk X (35°) CB guns
	Hood's Tower Battery	3 × 6-inch Mk VII (15°) CD guns
	Diamond Hill Battery	2 × 6-inch Mk VII (15°) CD guns
	Great Sober Island	2 × 4-inch BL Naval guns
	Clappenburg Point	1 × Twin 6-pdr QF equipment
	Elephant Point	2 × Twin 6-pdr QF equipments
	Elephant Island	1 × Twin 6-pdr QF equipment

In fact, after the April 1942 attacks on Colombo and Trincomalee no further attacks were made by the Japanese on Ceylon. By late 1944, after the installation of the third 35° mounting at Galle Face Battery, the decision was taken to place the Galle Face and Ostenburg 9.2-inch gun batteries in a state of care and maintenance. Defence of the two harbours was reduced to the four 6-inch gun batteries and two Twin 6-pdr QF equipments at each location, the East and Main Breakwater equipments at Colombo and the Clappenburg Point equipment and one of the two equipments at Elephant Point at Trincomalee.

In 1945 the defences of Colombo Harbour were reduced to just the anti-torpedo nets at each gate, while at Trincomalee the controlled minefields, boom patrol and searchlights were retained, together with the 6-inch guns and two Twin 6-pdr QF equipments and eight HAA guns. The anti-aircraft guns were retained as training guns. Two years later the 9.2-inch guns and the Twin 6-pdr equipments were all placed in a state of long-term care and preservation and in 1949 after Ceylon achieved Dominion status, the guns were taken over by the Ceylon Artillery, the new name of the old Ceylon Garrison Artillery. In 1962 the coast batteries of the Ceylon Artillery were finally disbanded.

Chapter Six

Mauritius

Located 700 miles (1,130km) east of Madagascar in the Indian Ocean, Mauritius, called in the past the 'Star and key of the Indian Ocean', is a volcanic island of some 790 square miles (1,040 sq kms) in area. The highest point on the island is the Piton de la Petite Rivière Noire at a height of 2,717 feet (828m), and the capital and main port is Port Louis on the north-western side of the island. The only other major centre of population with access to the sea is Mahébourg, previously known as Grand Port, which lies on the eastern side of the island.

The coast of Mauritius is almost totally surrounded by a coral reef through which there are twenty navigable gaps or passes on the east coast and twenty-five on the west coast. However, the main passes through the reef used by shipping are opposite Cannonier's Point north of Port Louis, opposite Port Louis itself and opposite Mahébourg and Flacq on the east coast. Offshore, to the north, there are three small, uninhabited islets of which only one, known to the British as Gunner's Quoin and so named because of its shape, is close to the coast.

The island was first settled in 1638 by the Dutch who named it in honour of Prince Maurice of Nassau, Stadtholder of the Netherlands. However, the settlement was a failure and the Dutch abandoned the island in 1710 and five years later, in 1715, the French took control and renamed the island Ile de France. The French colonization was more successful, and after a shaky start, a prosperous economy was developed based on the production of sugar.

During the Seven Years War, fought between 1754 and 1763, Mauritius was a base for French privateers and commerce raiders and during the Revolutionary and Napoleonic Wars (1793–1811) it was used as a base for French frigates preying on the ships of the British Honourable East India Company. The depredations of the French frigates and privateers forced the British Government, despite all their other worldwide commitments, to take action to eliminate the French forces operating from the island. In 1810 a squadron of four Royal Navy frigates blockaded the harbour of Grand Port, but despite capturing the fortified islet of Ile de la Passe, which controlled the entrance to the harbour, five French warships broke through the blockade.

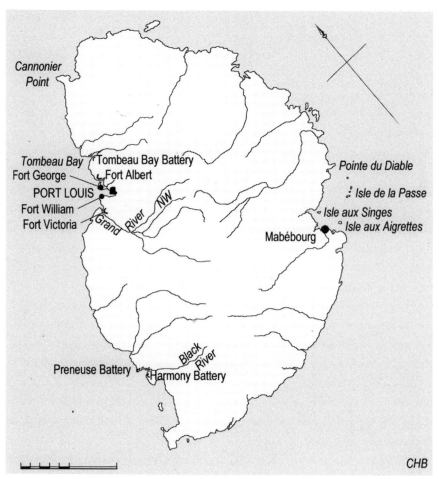

Map of Mauritius. (*Charles Blackwood*)

The resulting battle was the worst defeat for the Royal Navy during the entire period of the Revolutionary and Napoleonic Wars and is the only naval battle inscribed by Napoleon on the Arc de Triomphe in Paris.

In December 1810 a large British invasion force was dispatched to capture the Île de France, and this was successfully achieved with very few casualties on the British side. The name of the island was changed back to Mauritius by the British authorities and it remained a British colony until independence 158 years later in 1968.

The Early British Defences 1815–1840

While occupied by the French, the island was heavily fortified with major batteries defending Port Louis, the major town, and Grand Port, the major port on the east coast. In addition, in order to deter the blockading ships of the Royal Navy, batteries were established to protect many of the minor landing places and beaches around the island. In a report dated 6 December 1810 the British recorded a total of twenty-eight forts and batteries mounting, in theory, though probably not in practice, 176 guns and 31 mortars. However, in a further report of 1 March 1811 the total of mounted ordnance was believed to be only 24 guns and 3 mortars, with most of the smaller batteries reported as being either abandoned, destroyed, or 'out of repair'.[1]

Initially, the British Commander-in-Chief, General Sir John Abercromby, son of General Sir Ralph Abercromby who captured St Lucia, planned to maintain all the existing French batteries but, because of the uncertainty as to whether or not the island would be retained by the British on the conclusion of a peace with France, in a letter dated 9 January 1811, he instructed that:

'The uncertainty of this Island remaining annexed to the British Empire on the conclusion of a peace with France, no expense should be incurred in the Military department which is not indispensably necessary, either for the accommodation of the troops or the defence of the Island, and such buildings as it may be necessary to construct should not be of a solid, but of a temporary nature'.[2]

In fact, as a result of the Congress of Vienna held from 1814 to 1815, Mauritius remained in British hands, but politically and ethnically the island was permitted to maintain its essentially French character in view of the fact that the majority of the population comprised French settlers and Creoles (persons of mixed race) with a large slave labour force. When the French commandant, Decaen, signed the articles of surrender in 1810 the terms permitted the French settlers to retain their land, property, language and laws. However, the new British administration maintained a military garrison on the island.

The defences the British inherited comprised essentially the defences of Port Louis and batteries defending all the coves and bays where an enemy force could land. Most of the latter were small batteries, originally mounting two or three guns, but now disarmed and in a state of disrepair. The defences of Port Louis were considerably more substantial, with the main works of fortification on the Île aux Tonneliers, a headland on the northern side of the harbour, together with Fort Blanc, a masonry fort on the opposite headland. Additional batteries defended the entrance to Grand River North West to the south of Port Louis.

The Île aux Tonneliers was originally a small island situated at the entrance to Port Louis harbour and shaped like an apostrophe lying on its side. The French, from the very first, appreciated the tactical significance of the island for the defence of Port Louis and in 1741 it was joined to the mainland and fortified with a number of sea batteries. The British, therefore, inherited a strongly fortified position mounting over thirty guns, the largest of which were 36-pdr SB guns, in a number of batteries. The main French battery was the Batterie du Roy, subsequently known to the British as Royal Battery. Running along the shoreline from the Batterie du Roy was a line of retrenchments, with four *redans* and a *demi-bastion*, ending in another battery at the narrowest part of the island closest to where it joined the mainland. In addition, a short length of wall ran west to east from the retrenchment with a small *ravelin* half-way along the wall.

Fort Blanc, on the southern arm of the harbour, was an enclosed work of irregular shape and comprised three gun batteries and a mortar battery, all with earth parapets and revetments, two magazines, a shot furnace and barracks and stores. The armament of the fort in 1810 was fifteen guns, including four 36-pdr SB guns, and four 12-inch mortars. At the head of the harbour, close to the town there was a further bastion, the six-gun Batterie Fanfaron and a smaller earthwork battery shown on British maps as Channel Battery.

View of the French defences of Port Louis c.1860. (*Author's Collection*)

In 1815 the Commanding Royal Engineer, Lieutenant Colonel Mulcaster, suggested to the Inspector General of Fortifications in London that there should be improvements made to the existing coastal batteries and that a fortress should be erected on Petite Montagne, the hill overlooking Port Louis. General Mann accepted that some improvements should be made, including a small work or tower on both Petite Montagne and Morne de la Decouvert; improvements to the defences on Île aux Tonneliers and to Fort Blanc which guarded the entrance to Port Louis harbour and additional towers in place of repairing the existing redoubts and lines of defence which then defended the landward approach to Île aux Tonneliers.

Nothing came of these proposals because in the immediate years after Waterloo the defences of the island continued to be neglected as the British Government reduced the amount of money it allocated to defence matters, particularly in the colonies. Indeed, by 1821 in Mauritius the guns in all the defences had been dismounted and the works at Tombeau Bay, Souillac, Grand River North West, and Mahébourg had all been dismantled, although a small military detachment continued to occupy Île de la Passe. Only four guns remained mounted to defend the entrance to Port Louis harbour, two 24-pdr SB guns in Fort Blanc and two more in the battery on Île aux Tonneliers.

However, by 1825 the political scene on the island was changing dramatically. A resurgent France was beginning to adopt a more belligerent foreign policy and to the British authorities in Mauritius the nearby French possession of Réunion (formerly Île de Bourbon) appeared to constitute a potential threat. In addition, by 1824 the movement in England for the total abolition of slavery was beginning to gain momentum and in that year the Slave Trade Act was passed by Parliament.

It was obvious to the governor of the island, Sir Lowry Cole, that the complete abolition of slavery would have a devastating effect on the Mauritian economy and the fortunes of the many French plantation owners. It could possibly result in a rebellion of the pro-French settlers and slave owners which might be supported by the French from their nearby base on Réunion. So, in the same year that the Slave Trade Act was passed in Westminster, Sir Lowry Cole ordered a review of the island's defences to be carried out by the senior Royal Artillery and Royal Engineers officers on the island, Lieutenant Colonel Brough RA and Lieutenant Colonel Buchanan RE. In 1815 the total number of guns on the island was reported as being nearly 1,000, most of which were noted as being of foreign manufacture. However, by 1825 the only serviceable guns were seven 24-pdr, fifteen 18-pdr SB guns and nine 24-pdr carronades, all of English manufacture.

The recommendations made by the two senior Board of Ordnance officers in their report were that the defences should be primarily concentrated in seven locations: Île aux Tonneliers, Fort Blanc, Cannonier's Point and Grand River North West for the defence of Port Louis; Pointe du Diable and Île de la Passe for the defence of Mahébourg and Black River Bay. The report also proposed a fortress or citadel to be built at Port Louis and a number of coastal batteries and towers at strategic points around the coast at Grand River North West, Black River Bay, Mahébourg, and Tombeau Bay, the latter being locations where the French had previously built defences.

These recommendations wound their way somewhat dilatorily to the desk of the Inspector General of Fortifications in London. In 1829 the Board of Ordnance authorized the construction of a citadel on Petite Montagne and five Martello towers, on the understanding that the cost of construction would not exceed the original estimate of £32,000. One of the towers, the Cunningham Tower named after the commanding Royal Engineer at that time, was to be built on Île aux Tonneliers to protect the gorge of Royal Battery, one of the fortifications that defended Port Louis harbour. Of the other towers, two were to be built at the entrance to Grand River North West, just south of Port Louis, and two at Black River Bay where the towers were each to support two old two-gun batteries that were to be repaired and remodelled.

The Citadel

In order to ameliorate the hardship likely to be suffered as a result of the 1833 Act abolishing slavery within the British Empire, the British Government offered generous compensation to the French settlers. The offer of compensation went some way to reducing the financial impact of the abolition of slavery but, nevertheless, the British Government felt it necessary to press ahead with the improvement of the island's defences. The construction of the citadel in Port Louis was authorized on 8 August 1833, the year after new names had been given to Fort Blanc and Île aux Tonneliers which became Fort William and Fort George respectively.[3]

The role of the citadel was essentially that of a keep of last resort, a fortified place to which the garrison could retire if faced by an overwhelming enemy invasion force. However, it undoubtedly had the subsidiary role of overawing a rebellious population set on ousting the British authorities.

The cost of building the citadel was to be met from funds raised within the colony partly by the sale of some government buildings. It was also proposed that the construction costs should be kept to a minimum through the use

Interior of Fort Adelaide, looking towards the main gun platform facing due west. (*Author*)

of convict labour. Unfortunately for the new commanding Royal Engineer, Lieutenant Colonel Fyers, the use of convict labour proved to be illusory as the convicts were removed in January 1834, shortly after work on the citadel commenced, in order to repair damage to many buildings on the island which had been caused by a severe hurricane. In fact, the convicts never returned to work on the citadel and, as a result, masons and stonecutters had to be imported from Bombay so increasing the cost of construction. This necessitated a supplementary estimate of £13,269 15s 8d and, in the end, the cost of the citadel rose to a grand total of £45,268 15s 8d.

In a letter dated 19 July 1832 the Inspector General of Fortifications, Major General Sir Alexander Bryce, described the proposed citadel as follows:

'The work now submitted is an oblong redoubt having four 24-pdrs mounted in casemates in front overlooking the town – four mounted on traversing platforms on the rampart in the rear towards the ridge of Petite Montagne by which it is naturally commanded (and from which in laying out the work it must be carefully defiladed) and four 24-pdrs on traversing platforms in four short flanks constructed in the branches which connect the front and rear batteries and which will also bear upon the town and suburbs of Port Louis. The greater part of the branches are further flanked by loopholes; and in those parts which cannot be so seen, the escarpe is hors d'escalade; and

is provided with machicoulis *for the purpose of observing any attempt to attach a miner. The front and rear lines are flanked by arched* caponiers *for musketry; these lines are covered by counterscarps; but the branches from the narrowness of the ridge and the steepness of its sides cannot be covered and the* escarpe *is consequently exposed to cannonade; but at a distance of 1,500 or 1,600 yards. The work will contain a barrack for 1 field officer, 2 captains, 5 subalterns with a mess; and casemates for 192 men, commissariat stores for three months, tanks for 40,000 gallons of water, a magazine for 280 barrels of powder besides ordnance and barrack stores for the garrison.'[4]*

The citadel was built of black basalt rock and was sited on the ridge that dominated Port Louis at a height of 263 feet (90m) above sea level. The first stone was laid by the governor on 8 December 1835 and it was completed in 1840 with some small differences from the description given by Major General Bryce in 1832. There was accommodation for 208 Other Ranks and the magazine, when completed, only had a capacity for 240 barrels of powder; the cisterns held 38,500 gallons of water rather than the 40,000 as originally planned. In 1841 the armament was increased by the addition of four 24-pdr brass howitzers on wooden traversing platforms on the gun platform above the rear casemates, and by two brass 9-pdr field guns on common standing carriages on the gun platform above the front casemates.[5]

When completed the citadel was used as barrack accommodation for troops and with the withdrawal of the bulk of the British garrison at the end of the nineteenth century it fell into disuse and became dilapidated.

The Martello Towers

In 1825 the Brough and Buchanan report recommended the construction of a number of Martello towers of which five were subsequently built. Two towers were built on the shores of Black River Bay, each tower to support a battery, one at La Preneuse and the other at Pointe L'Harmonie at a cost of £3,000 for each tower. Nearer to Port Louis two more towers were authorized for the defence of Grand River North West, a potential landing place for an enemy force, at a similar estimated cost. Once again they were to be sited in the rear of batteries, in this case the old French Batterie Condé and the Batterie de L'Anjou. The fifth tower, to be named Cunningham Tower after the commanding Royal Engineer at that time, was to be built in the rear of Royal Battery to defend the gorge of the battery. There were plans for three other towers, two for the defence of Tombeau Bay at a cost of £5,000 each, and a third was to be sited on Île de la Passe at an estimated cost of £8,000. None of these towers were built, undoubtedly because of the high estimated cost of each tower.

The design of the towers was that of the standard English south coast towers built in 1805 to defend against a possible French invasion. Like the citadel, the towers were built of black basalt blocks with the thickest portion of the wall facing the sea and almost double the thickness of the rear wall. The front wall averaged 11 feet (3.38m) while the thickness of the rear averaged 6 feet (1.8m). The accommodation was on two levels,

L'Harmonie Martello tower at Black River Bay. (*Author*)

View of the harbour of Port Louis c.1830 showing the Cunningham Tower, and the flank of Royal Battery on the right of the picture. (*Author's Collection*)

with the accommodation for the personnel manning the tower on the first floor, and a magazine for thirty barrels of gunpowder and a cistern for 4,500 gallons of fresh water on the ground floor. Entrance to the tower was at first floor level by means of a removable ladder, and internally communication between the first floor, the gun platform, and the ground floor was also by means of ladders.

In 'A Statement of Barrack Buildings in Mauritius' dated 1838 the height of all five towers was given as 39 feet (12m) and the diameter as 43 feet (13.2m). However, in the event, the final dimensions differed from the original specification with the Cunningham Tower on Île aux Tonneliers shown as having a height of 35 feet (10.7m) on a plan and section dated 1833, while the La Preneuse tower at Black River Bay is shown on a plan and section of the same date as being only 30 feet (9.2m) high.[6]

The original armament of the Black River Bay towers was to have been two 24-pdr carronades on each tower, but this was changed to one 24-pdr SB gun and one 5½-inch iron SB howitzer on each. The Grand River North West towers, however, were always to have mounted a single heavy gun with a carronade as the subsidiary armament, though, as in the case of the Black River towers, this was changed to one 5½-inch iron howitzer. The Cunningham Tower, not having a coast defence role but sited to defend the gorge of the newly-named Fort George on Île aux Tonneliers, was to have been armed with three 24-pdr carronades but these were changed to howitzers when the tower was completed. Initially, there was no recommendation for traversing platforms for the guns and howitzers, but Lieutenant Colonel Cunningham believed these to be indispensable and they were subsequently provided. All were to have been mounted on teak carriages, but the decision was taken to mount all the armament on the new iron carriages and platforms. By 1862 this armament had been replaced by a single 8-inch SB shell gun.

At Black River Bay the towers each supported a battery mounting two 24-pdr SB guns on iron carriages and traversing platforms. The traversing platforms were mounted on basalt platforms on an earth *terreplein*. The guns were protected by an earth parapet with scarp and counterscarp constructed, like the towers, of black basalt blocks. Both batteries were provided with flanks to protect them from enfilade fire.

The Port Louis Harbour Defences

The Île aux Tonneliers defences, renamed Fort George in 1832, comprised the Royal Battery and Abercromby Battery; these were rearmed with five 24-

L'Harmonie two-gun battery today, with one of the Blomefield 24-pdr SB guns on an iron carriage and traversing slide still in position. (*Author*)

pdr SB guns mounted in Royal Battery and two similar guns in Abercromby Battery. Royal Battery was the original French elevated battery, open at the gorge but now supported by Cunningham Tower. It is difficult to identify Abercromby Battery, but it may well have been previously named Fort Cumberland, a battery at the end of the line of retrenchments nearest to where the causeway joined the mainland and shown on a chart of 1819.

Although open at the gorge opposite the causeway leading to Port Louis, Fort George was defended by a wall on the southern flank and a line of retrenchments on the western flank. In addition, there was a wall with a *demi-bastion* and a *redan* in the wall running west to east on the northern side of Royal Battery. The security of Royal Battery was further strengthened by a cut in the causeway crossed by a drawbridge. It is difficult to date these additional works, and some were certainly French in origin, but the wall protecting the northern side of the battery and that on the southern side appear to be British constructions resulting from the Brough and Buchanan report of 1825.

Fort Blanc, renamed Fort William in 1832, taking the name of the current King William IV, was also, originally, a French fortification and was described in 1832 as *'An enclosed work containing a Sea Battery not flanked having a low escarp and a wet ditch'*.[7] Entry to the fort was by means of a drawbridge over the wet ditch, and the armament of the fort as rebuilt by the British was five 24-pdr SB guns mounted on iron traversing platforms. There was also an adjoining mortar battery.

Under the French regime two other batteries defended the Trou Fanfaron or inner harbour. One was the Bastion Fanfaron, a masonry work, and the other a small earthwork battery named Caudan Battery. In 1811 the Bastion Fanfaron mounted three guns, while Caudan Battery mounted two guns, but both batteries were abandoned by the British almost immediately after taking possession of the island. Instead, the British relied on the two larger works, Forts George and William, to defend the harbour.

Cannonier's Point and the Île de la Passe

The other locations that the Brough and Buchanan report identified as being important for the defence of the island were Cannonier's Point, which controlled the entrance to Grand Baie at the very north of the island, and Île de la Passe, the islet that controlled the entrance through the reef to Mahébourg on the east coast.

The old French battery at Cannonier's Point was a large open earthwork battery with a small masonry magazine. The battery was defended in the gorge by a hexagonal-shaped masonry tower, sometimes referred to as a 'blockhouse'. When the island was captured in 1810 a British inventory showed the armament of the battery to be three 36-pdr SB guns, nine 24-pdrs and three 12-inch mortars. However, in March 1811 only five 24-pdr SB guns and one mortar were shown as mounted in the battery and ten years later the battery had been abandoned along with almost all the other old French defences.[8]

On the Île de la Passe, however, despite the views of Sir John Abercromby who believed that *'The post at Grand Port requires the greatest attention as it completely commands the best approach to the bay'*,[9] the two French batteries on the island had been permitted to fall into disrepair and had been disarmed. Prior to 1810 the French had manned a raised battery for nine heavy guns on the southern side of the isle and a smaller four-gun battery in the north-west

The French tower at Cannoniers Point. This hexagonal-shaped tower with its battery defended a pass in the reef into Grand Baie. (Andrew Clements).

corner. There was also a large masonry powder magazine, a masonry shot furnace and a small barrack building, all partially enclosed by a stone wall. Although disarmed, the importance of the site was given token recognition through the maintenance of a small garrison there.

By 1835 the battery at Cannonier's Point had been rearmed with four 24-pdr SB guns on iron traversing platforms in the battery, and three 24-pdr carronades mounted on the gun platform of the tower,[10] while on the Île de la Passe the raised battery was rearmed with five 24-pdr SB guns and a single 5½-inch howitzer.[11]

1841–1890

By 1848 the political situation in Europe was changing and the revolution of that year in France made the governor of Mauritius only too conscious of the parlous state of the island's defences. The governor, Major General Sir William Gomm KCB, was, as a soldier, only too aware of the deficiencies in the island's defences and he was also acutely aware of a strong French garrison on the nearby French island of Réunion, together with a large number of available steamships. Governor Gomm's predecessor had also realized that Mauritius was relatively undefended when two French Navy corvettes, the *L'Isere* and *Le Lancier* arrived in Port Louis in 1839. The unexpected arrival of the two French warships had caused the governor to reinforce the defences of the harbour by mounting two 24-pdr howitzers on Fanfaron bastion and four similar guns in the old Caudan Battery, both of which batteries had previously been abandoned and which he ordered to be reformed. In addition, as we have noted previously, four 24-pdr brass howitzers mounted on traversing platforms and two 9-pdr field pieces, were added to the armament of Fort Adelaide.

Sir William Gomm decided that work should be put in hand to improve the defences of Port Louis harbour by reinforcing the effectiveness of Fort George as a work of defence and repairing Fanfaron Bastion. In 1847 Lieutenant Colonel Blanshard RE, the Commanding Royal Engineer, described Fort George as *'an elevated battery open at the gorge but supported by a Martello tower commanding the terreplein of its rampart within musketry range'*, and steps had been taken to improve the armament by ordering sixteen 32-pdr SB guns and iron traversing platforms from the Royal Gun Factory and the Royal Carriage Department at Woolwich to replace the old 24-pdr guns.[12]

It was clear to Governor Gomm that Fort George should be rebuilt as the main defence of the harbour but, since it was dominated from the rear by Fanfaron Bastion, that work should be rebuilt as well. So, believing that it would take too long to apply to London for the appropriate financial authority from the Board of Ordnance, he gave instructions that work should commence on enclosing the gorge of Fort George, repairing Fanfaron Bastion and improving the old French lines. The gorge of Fort George was closed with a wall running along the south-west and south-east flanks and defended by a *caponier* on the south-east section of the wall. Improvements to Fanfaron Bastion included a parapet and Carnot wall to enclose the gorge, a *caponier* facing towards the town and a drawbridge over the canal. The cost of the work on Fanfaron Bastion alone came to £8,105 16s 3d, and here was where the trouble lay. Governor Gomm had expected the Board of Ordnance in London to appreciate the seriousness of the invasion threat but this was not the case.

In due course a letter from the Board of Ordnance arrived on the Governor's desk in reply to his request for authorization of the work currently under way. The letter curtly stated that with regard to the work commenced on the authorization of the Governor as a 'Special Service' without the authority of the Board of Ordnance, this work was to be discontinued *'except in so far as may be indispensably necessary for the security and preservation of any separate portion of the works which may have been already commenced'*. Despite this injunction, injunction, or perhaps as a result of the Governor's interpretation of it, Fanfaron Bastion was duly completed mounting eight heavy guns, six on rear pivots and two on front pivots, the latter on stone platforms.[13] In addition, a small battery for two guns outside the walls of Fanfaron Bastion was renewed.

Although the authorities in London were unwilling to authorize further expenditure on the defences of Port Louis, four years later, in 1852, there were further worries about a war in Europe whipped up by the British Press. However, this time the Secretary of State for War, the Duke of Newcastle (under-Lyme), was sufficiently impressed by the possible danger to Mauritius of a French invasion that he asked the Master General of the Ordnance to sanction reconstruction of Fort George at a total cost of £70,000.

The basic elements of the earlier plan to enclose the old Royal Battery within a pentagonal wall defended by four *caponiers* were retained, but a new plan divided the fort in two by the construction of an interior moat and *glacis* across the width of the fort. The interior moat and glacis were flanked at each end by two *cavaliers*, the North and South Cavaliers, which defended the rear of Royal Battery. On the left flank of the battery and adjoining the South Cavalier was a new battery, Channel Battery, and the magazine.

The gorge of Royal Battery was closed by casemated stores and tanks immediately behind the *glacis*, and between the stores and the battery *terreplein* was a soldiers' barrack building. In addition, three small *caponiers* were added on the western flank, including one in front of Royal Battery to defend the ditch on the side facing the sea and the breakwater, while a fourth projected from the casemated stores at the rear of Royal Battery. The Martello tower, Cunningham Tower, situated behind the new inner ditch and *glacis*, was retained.

A plan of Fort George dated 1862 shows that by that date positions for three howitzers had also been constructed at each end of the raised *terreplein* of Royal Battery and the armament of the fort was shown as:

Martello Tower	1 × 8-inch SB shell gun
Royal Battery Caponier	1 × 8-inch SB shell gun
South Cavalier	5 × 8-inch SB shell guns
Channel Battery	5 × 68-pdr SB guns
Royal Battery	6 × 68-pdr SB guns
	12 × 32-pdr SB guns[14]

By 1870 there had been additional remodelling of the fort with the construction of the East Cavalier and three *caponiers* (two large and one small) to defend the new *cavalier* and the flank walls of the fort. By this date Fort George was the major fortification defending Port Louis, as Fort William had been abandoned on the grounds that it was 'unhealthy'.[15] By 1878 there had been further changes in the armament of the fort as a result of the war scare in

Photograph of Port Louis Harbour with Fort George in the foreground c.1880. Royal Battery is shown still armed with smooth-bore guns, and two flanking smooth-bore howitzers can be seen in the foreground. (*National Army Museum*)

England caused by Russia's declaration of war on Turkey the previous year. This saw the mounting of four 7-inch rifled RBL guns, three of which were mounted in the North Cavalier and the fourth on Royal Battery. A further review of the fort's armament in that year by the newly formed Colonial Defence Committee recommended that four 7-inch RML guns should be mounted in the fort. Probably as a result of the remodelling of Fort George, the decision was taken to dismantle Fanfaron Bastion in 1877.[16]

Russian expansion eastwards in Asia continued to be seen by the British Government as a major threat to the British Empire. The strategic position of Mauritius as a coaling station meant that the defence of the island was reviewed by the War Office and the decision was taken that the island's defences should be concentrated around the capital, Port Louis. By 1877 many of the older defences were in a poor state of repair and at Port Louis Fanfaron Bastion had been dismantled and the old Fort Cumberland, or Abercromby Battery, was in ruins. It was decided that these works and the other older defences at Black River Bay, Mahébourg, and Cannonier's Point should be given up and they were finally abandoned in 1884. Therefore the armament of Fort George was reviewed which led to a further remodelling of the fort, the rearming of Fort William, the decision to build a new battery on the coast just north of Fort George and new batteries at the mouth of Grand River North West and Tombeau Bay.

In 1880 the defences of the harbour were reinforced with the provision of a submarine minefield comprising four loops containing twenty-four ground mines for the entrance channel to the harbour. A locally recruited Royal Engineers submarine mining company was formed and a submarine mining establishment constructed adjacent to Fort George. The 'observing chamber' for the minefield was constructed on the South Cavalier of Fort George, and two 7-inch RBL guns were installed in the fort to cover the newly installed controlled minefield with fire.

Two years later, in 1882, the *terreplein* of Fort George was modified to mount four 10-inch 18-ton RML guns, two 64-pdr RML guns, and three 7-inch 7-ton RML guns with a fourth 7-inch gun being mounted on the North Cavalier. However, only four years later the armament was changed again when two of the new 9.2-inch BL Mk 1 guns on hydro-pneumatic (HP) mountings were installed on Royal Battery in place of two of the 10-inch RML guns. At the same time it would appear that the unhealthy nature of Fort William had been overcome and the fort was remodelled to mount a single 9.2-inch BL HP gun, similar to the two guns mounted in Fort George,

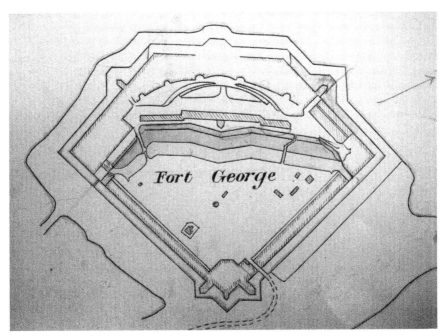

Plan of Fort George c.1890 (*TNA WO 78/7894*)

and two 7-inch RBL guns. An 'unclimbable' fence 8 feet (2.5m) high was constructed as an obstacle in the ditch surrounding the fort.

As well as rearming the older Forts George and William, three new batteries were built: Albert Battery, which was sited a short distance north of Fort George at Roche Noire Point in order to protect the right flank of Fort George; Tombeau Point Battery to defend Tombeau Bay, a possible enemy landing point north of Port Louis; and Fort Victoria, on the site of the old French Condé Battery, to defend the entrance to Grand River North West. These batteries comprised concrete gun emplacements and magazines built into an earth *glacis* with another *glacis* and a ditch at the rear defending the gorge. This was a design for gun batteries coming into fashion at this time incorporating what is now known as the Twydall profile.

Albert Battery was the largest of the three new batteries mounting two 10-inch 18-ton and two 64–pdr RML guns. The battery consisted of a front *glacis* standing 23 feet (7.07m) high at the front parapet, into which were sunk the four gun positions, the 10-inch gun positions in the centre with a position for a 64–pdr gun on each flank. The rear *glacis* stood 18 feet (5.5m) high at its highest point, with the main magazine for the battery beneath it. A second, smaller, magazine was situated under the front *glacis* between the two 10-inch gun positions. There was also a flanking gallery with musketry embrasures which enabled the face of the rear *glacis* to be covered by musketry fire. Two 0.303-inch (0.77mm) Maxim machine guns on parapet mountings were provided for the close defence of the battery. The battery was surrounded by a ditch with an iron fence 7 feet (2.15m) high.

Fort Victoria and Tombeau Point Battery were smaller than Albert Battery, each mounting two 10-inch 18-ton and one 64-pdr RML guns. Both batteries were built to a similar design to that of Albert Battery with the gun positions sunk into the front *glacis*, but in the case of these two batteries there was no rear *glacis*, both being open at the gorge which was secured simply by a steel fence. In the rear of Fort Victoria there was one of the old Martello towers that had been disarmed in 1880. The two magazines for the fort were sited beneath the *glacis*, one between the two 10-inch gun positions and the other between the left hand 10-inch gun position and the position for the 64-pdr gun. The battery at Tombeau Point was built to the same design with a similar armament, but had a flanking gallery, smaller than the Albert Battery gallery, covering the rear of the battery. As with Albert Battery, both Fort Victoria and Tombeau Point Battery were armed with Maxim machine guns for local defence.

The Advent of the Breech-loaders 1891–1918

In the last decade of the nineteenth century further changes were made to both Fort George and Fort William. In 1895 the War Office decided on yet another major remodelling of Fort George which entailed filling in the internal ditch, levelling the internal *glacis* and mounting two 6-inch BL HP guns. One of these guns was mounted in the right flank 7-inch RML position on the North Cavalier, while a new gun position was constructed for the second gun on the left flank of the 9.2-inch guns. Accommodation for the garrison was built along the inner walls running between the North and East Cavaliers and the East and South Cavaliers. Surprisingly, it would appear that the Cunningham Tower was not demolished at this time. Four Defence Electric Lights (DELs) were installed, three at Fort George and one at Fort William.

The Fort George searchlights were 90cm lamps and were placed one outside the northern corner of the fort and one in the south-east *caponier* of Royal Battery. The third, a fixed beam emplacement, was sited some distance south of the fort on the foreshore of the harbour. The Fort William searchlight was also a fixed beam light and was on the foreshore outside the fort and opposite the Fort George fixed beam emplacement so that the whole of the entrance to the harbour could be illuminated.

Fort George c.1990. The positions for the three 6-inch BL guns can be seen clearly in the foreground of the photograph. (*Philippe La Hausse de Louvière*)

The year 1898 saw further changes in the armament of the two forts with the removal of the 7-inch RBL guns in Fort George which defended the controlled minefield and the substitution of three 6-pdr QF guns on cone mountings with shields. These guns remained until 1904 when they were moved to Fort William. In 1902 the right flank 64-pdr RML was removed and the 6-inch BL Mk VI gun on a hydro-pneumatic mounting, which had been installed in Albert Battery some years previously in place of one of the 10-inch RML guns, replaced it. In the same year a practice battery comprising four 3-pdr QF Nordenfelt guns was installed in the fort, these in turn being replaced by 5-inch BL guns.

Fort Victoria and Albert Battery were both remodelled in 1902–03 to enable them each to mount two 4.7-inch QF guns on Mark III mountings. The remodelling involved the dismounting of the old 10-inch RML guns and construction of new gun positions, shell and cartridge stores, and telephone communications. The removal of the large RML guns was always something of a problem and at Fort Victoria the problem of removing the 10-inch RML guns each weighing 18 tons was solved by burying one gun in its emplacement which the Royal Engineers had to fill in in order to build a retaining wall. The second gun was buried in the *terreplein* of the fort and the engineers adopted a rather innovative method of dismounting the two guns. Each gun was dismounted by firing a practice shell at full charge with the gun run back, the buffer disconnected and the stop plates removed. The platform was then removed and the gun and carriage buried. At the same time the 6-pdr QF gun was removed.

After the rearmament of the defences of Port Louis with powerful breech-loading guns there was a need to improve the fire control of the batteries. Previously depression rangefinders mounted close to the guns had been considered adequate for the engagement of targets up to 3,000 yards (2,700m), but now the new guns were effective to ranges in excess of 9,000 yards (8,300m). The answer to this problem for the heavier 6-inch and 9.2-inch guns was the Watkin position-finder which enabled a remote observer to calculate the range and bearing to a target vessel and fire the guns of the battery remotely. At Port Louis six position-finding cells and a fire control position were constructed on Priest's Peak, a hill overlooking and slightly to the rear of Fort Adelaide. For the 4.7-inch QF guns, installed to deal with fast moving torpedo boats, automatic sights were provided, together with Barr & Stroud Mark III rangefinders.

As we have seen the Owen Committee in 1905 brought about a rationalization of the coast artillery, but the changes resulting from the recommendations of the committee were only partially carried out in Mauritius where the older 9.2-inch BL HP guns remained *in situ* until the end of the First World War. In 1907 the Committee on the Armaments of Defended Ports Abroad approved the mounting of two 6-inch BL Mk VII guns in Fort George's Royal Battery, together with a 9.2-inch BL Mk X gun, also in Fort George. These were modern guns with a maximum range of 12,000 yards (11,076m) for the 6-inch guns and 15,500 yards (14,300m) for the 9.2-inch gun.

The 6-inch guns were installed in 1910, one in the old 7-inch RML No 2 gun position (where a 6-inch Mk VI BL HP gun had previously been installed), and the other in a new gun position immediately to its left. With these guns emplaced the 9.2-inch BL HP gun in Fort William was considered surplus to requirements but was retained as 'mounted reserve' – that is as a spare should the 9.2-inch gun in Fort George become unserviceable. It was at this time also that the 6-pdr QF guns in Fort William became a practice battery and the 6-inch Mk VI BL HP gun was removed and a moveable armament of two 5-inch BL howitzers substituted.

The Anglo-Japanese Alliance of 1902, renewed in 1905 and 1911, changed the strategic outlook in the Far East, and by 1912 the defence of Port Louis harbour became the responsibility simply of Fort George, with no armament mounted in Fort Victoria and Albert Battery, as the 4.7-inch QF guns had been removed.[17] Tombeau Point Battery had been previously disarmed when the RML guns were removed from Fort Victoria and Albert Battery but, unlike these batteries, it had not been rearmed with QF guns at that time.[18]

The defences of Port Louis had been mobilized between 18 November 1904 and 31 January 1905 during the Russo-Japanese War when there was a fear that the port might be attacked by ships of the Russian Baltic Fleet on its way to its destruction at the battle of Tsushima. The defences were mobilized once again in 1914 with the outbreak of the First World War, but the only immediate improvements made to the defences were in the form of field defences. Four blockhouses sited to defend the flanks of Fort George were constructed by converting existing buildings. Two Chinese-owned storehouses and an old police station were commandeered and part of the old Fort Cumberland on Île aux Tonneliers was reconstructed. Positions for two 4.7-inch QF Mk I guns on field travelling carriages were built in front of Fort Adelaide.[19] During the war there was also an upgrading of the DELs.

With the Japanese as allies in the First World War and the German Navy's East Asia Squadron destroyed at the Battle of the Falklands in December 1914 there was little threat to Mauritius. As a result, 56 Company RGA was withdrawn and a new unit, the Mauritius Volunteer Artillery, was formed to man the fixed defences, together with the Mauritius company of the Hong Kong & Singapore RGA. However, in 1917 Port Louis was reduced to the status of an undefended port and in 1918 the Mauritius company of the Hong Kong & Singapore RGA was disbanded.

The Second World War

In the period between the wars little was done to improve the defences of Port Louis. The obsolete 9.2-inch BL HP guns in Fort George and Fort William were scrapped and the defence of the fort now rested with the two 6-inch BL Mk VII guns that were all that remained of the armament of Fort George. One significant addition to the fort in 1932 was the installation of a Barr & Stroud 18-foot (5.5m) rangefinder on the *terreplein* of Royal Battery between the two 9.2-inch gun positions. However, with the outbreak of the Second World War, the evacuation of the BEF from France in 1940 and the increasingly belligerent attitude of Japan, the defence of Mauritius became a much higher priority for the War Office. Nevertheless, with the requirement for guns for the defence of Britain there were few available for Mauritius. As late as February 1941 the two guns were noted in the Chief of Staff Committee's Review of Fixed Defences at Defended Ports at Home and Abroad under '*Further commitments*

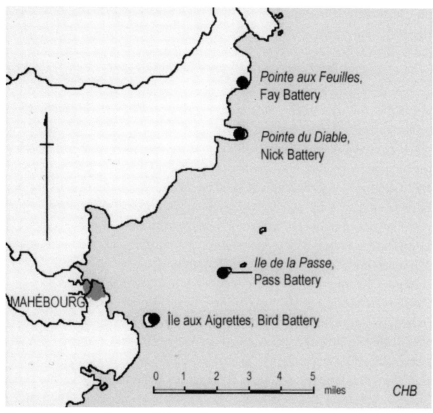

Map of Mahébourg Defences 1942–43. (*Charles Blackwood*)

(priority not yet allotted)'.[20] This quickly changed with the entry of Japan into the war and the loss of Singapore resulted in the defence of the island moving to the top of the priority list.

It was clear to the British planners in 1942, as it was to their counterparts 130 years earlier, that it was not possible to defend all the possible landing places around the coast of Mauritius. Instead, the decision was taken to defend the main harbour at Port Louis and the smaller port of Mahébourg. At Port Louis it was decided to replace the existing 6-inch BL Mk VII guns on 15° mountings with two 6-inch BL Mk XXIV guns on 45° mountings which would increase the range of the guns considerably. The new guns were to be mounted in Royal Battery in the old 9.2-inch gun positions once these had been modified to take the new guns, and a new BOP was constructed on Signal Hill. This would enable the 6-inch guns currently in position to remain in operation while the new gun positions were being prepared.

Meanwhile the reserve 6-inch BL Mk VII gun, which had been moved from Vacoas to Fort George in October 1939, was moved to the island of Rodrigues, the old French Île Bourbon to the west of Mauritius, in May 1941 with a 90cm 3° Coast Artillery Searchlight (CASL) (the new designation of the old Defence Electric Lights), to provide the defence for Port Mathurin. The gun and searchlight, together with a 57-mm gun on a recoil mounting (probably a 6-pdr Hotchkiss QF gun), were manned by a party comprising one officer, four RA gunners and thirty men of the Mauritius Territorial Force and were known as the Mauritius Anti-Raider Battery.

To provide close defence of Port Louis harbour in 1942 two 12-pdr QF guns were mounted near the old searchlight directing post until two Twin 6-pdr QF equipment positions were built, one on the right flank of Royal Battery, and one on the foreshore in front of the fort. However, only one equipment was eventually installed in late 1944. Four more CASLs were mounted in Fort George. These were fixed-beam lights that provided increased illumination of the entrance to the harbour in front of the proposed Twin 6-pdr equipment positions.

The defence of Mahébourg was provided, initially, by an emergency battery on Île aux Aigrettes, a small island just off Mahébourg where a battery of two 6-inch BL Mk VII naval guns on PIII mountings was established. This battery was named, unsurprisingly, Bird Battery and in addition to the guns it

6-inch BL Naval gun in its emergency battery position on Île aux Aigrettes. (*Author*)

was equipped with two 90cm 3° CASL fighting lights. The magazine for the guns and the other battery buildings were simple brick-built structures, all sited above ground. Further defence was provided by a battery of two 12-pdr QF guns on Île de la Passe (Île de la Passe Battery), guarding the entrance to the harbour through the reef. The new gun positions were built into the *terreplein* of the old French battery and a small circular fire control post was sited close to the gun positions.

Another battery, Nick Battery, also of two 12-pdr QF guns, was installed behind the old Franco-British battery position at Pointe du Diable and the battery command post was built on the summit overlooking Nick Battery. Illumination for the two 12-pdr batteries was provided by four CASLs on Île de la Passe. These lights were one 90cm 3° fighting light and three fixed beam lights, two 90cm 45° lights and one 90cm 30° light.

While work was continuing to construct the new gun positions on Royal battery, the decision was taken to build a battery at Pointe aux Feuilles, north of Mahébourg to defend the northern passage through the reef at Grand River South East. The new battery was to be named Fay Battery and was to be a more permanent battery rather than an emergency battery since it was to be armed with the 6-inch BL Mk VII guns on 15° mountings that were to be removed from Fort George when the new Mk XXIV guns were emplaced. These older guns, unlike the naval 6-inch guns, required deep pits for their

Nick Battery Command Post, Pointe du Diable. (*Author*)

mountings, and the battery was provided with a standard underground magazine and concrete accommodation buildings and a generator house. The battery observation post was on the hill behind the battery and two searchlight positions on the shore line for 90cm 3° fighting lights. The first gun was installed in 1943 and the second in 1944.[21]

Work continued on the new gun positions in Royal Battery in Fort George and in 1943 the War Office decreed that all new 6-inch and 9.2-inch batteries should consist of three guns rather than just two, so work commenced on a third 6-inch gun position in Royal Battery, between the two old 6-inch-gun positions. For fire control the position-finding cell on Priest's Peak continued to be used as well as the rangefinder installed in 1932. However, by 1944 two radars had been installed, one, a Radar No.1 Mk II, on Signal Hill and the other, a Radar No.2 Mk I, in Royal Battery.

From 1918, when the Mauritius Volunteer Artillery was disbanded, until the start of the Second World War in 1939, the fixed defences of Mauritius were manned by personnel of 25 Heavy Battery RA and 43 Fortress Company RE. However, in 1935 the Mauritius Territorial Force was established to reinforce the infantry garrison on the island. With the decision to erect the emergency batteries for the defence of Mahébourg and Vieux Grand Port it became necessary to raise a new coast defence regiment, the Mauritius Coast Regiment, Mauritius Artillery (MA), to man the guns. With the withdrawal of 25 Coast Battery RA in 1943 the manning of the guns was taken over by the new regiment with 1 Coast Battery MA manning the guns of Fort George and

Mauritius Coast Regiment, Mauritius Artillery c.1944. (*Author's Collection*)

personnel of 2 Coast Battery MA manning Bird Battery on Île aux Aigrettes. The latter battery was formed by white Mauritians who had previously formed X Battery MA and who had manned the Diego Garcia Anti-Raider Battery. The battery at Pointe aux Feuilles was manned by personnel of 3 Coast Battery MA.

By late 1945 the second twin 6-pdr QF equipment at Fort George had not been mounted nor the third 6-inch gun on the 45° mounting. All the Grand Port guns had been dismounted and were stored in Port Louis, together with the 6-inch gun that had been used to defend Port Mathurin on Rodriguez.[22] All the guns mounted at the end of the war remained on the island until the end of coast artillery in the British Army in 1956.

Chapter Seven

Ascension Island

The Early Years: 1815–1840

Ascension Island lies in the middle of the South Atlantic Ocean between Angola and Brazil. A volcanic outcrop rising 10,000 feet (3,030m) above the seabed, the island has been a British possession and now a British Dependent Territory for 193 years. It was named in 1503 by Afonso d'Albuquerque, the Portuguese navigator who was the second sailor to sight the island. Geologically it is a rocky peak of purely volcanic origin, with forty-four distinct craters, all 'dormant' (i.e. not 'extinct').

Ascension has an area of 35 square miles (90.3 sq kms) and is largely barren with only sparse vegetation. The highest point is Green Mountain at some 2,817 feet (866m) above sea level and, on its upper slopes, there is lush vegetation in contrast to the volcanic clinker of the rest of the island. Ascension has had no indigenous population, only a military garrison and then

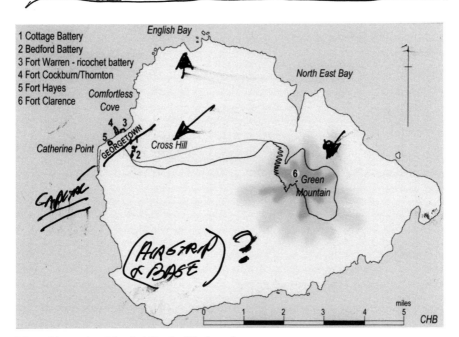

Map of Ascension Island. (*Charles Blackwood*)

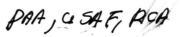

employees of various civil and military organisations resident in Georgetown, the only settlement.

No nation claimed this barren outcrop until 1815 when Admiral Cockburn RN, the British admiral responsible for conveying Napoleon Bonaparte to exile on the island of St Helena, sent two sloops-of-war, HMS *Peruvian* and HMS *Zenobia*, to claim the island and garrison it in order to prevent it being used by any other nation or group to rescue Napoleon. As a result, Ascension Island is unique in that for over 100 years it was garrisoned by the Royal Navy and was initially administered as a ship, HMS *Ascension*, described as a stone sloop-of-war of the smaller class. Subsequently, it became a tender, firstly to HMS *Flora*, a store ship based at Georgetown, before becoming the receiving ship at Cape Town, and then, at the end of the nineteenth century, to HMS *Cormorant*, the receiving ship at Gibraltar.

For the first fifteen years of the island's occupation by the Royal Navy the small garrison lived in makeshift accommodation close to the beach in an area named 'Regent Square'. Little attempt was made to adequately defend the settlement and the initial defences comprised two guns sited to cover the main anchorage. One, an 18-pdr SB gun, was mounted on a stone platform at Tartar Steps, the main landing place, and the other on top of a nearby limekiln. Subsequently the guns were mounted on the low headland that overlooked the roadstead beside Tartar Steps.

In 1819 a garrison of Royal Marines under the command of a Major Robert Campbell was dispatched to garrison Ascension and some improvements to the living conditions were made by his successor Lieutenant Colonel Edward Nicholls RM. However, the only improvement to the defences made during this period was the establishment of a small battery on the headland which overlooked Clarence Bay and the anchorage. This was to become the future site of Fort Cockburn. It would seem that the two original guns were moved to the site at this time, and at the same time a semaphore mast and lookout was established on Cross Hill, in communication with the settlement at Regent Square, and a carronade was installed on Weather Hill to act as an alarm gun.

However, it was the arrival in 1827 of the third Royal Marine commandant, Captain William Bate, that resulted in major improvements in all aspects of the living conditions and defences of Ascension. The Admiralty had decided that Ascension Island would be a suitable victualing base for the West Africa Squadron which had been tasked with establishing a blockade to prevent the transportation of slaves to the Americas. By 1829 the garrison of the island comprised four officers and ninety Marines, together with an African population of servants and Kroomen (Africans employed by the Royal Navy) totalling forty-seven men, fourteen women and twenty-two children. There was also a British civil establishment of a surgeon, an assistant surgeon, an attendant storekeeper and an attendant (cooper).[1] Bate asked the Admiralty to send out an engineer officer to report on the island and in 1829 Captain Henry Brandreth RE was dispatched to Ascension with instructions to draw up plans to improve the living conditions, water supply, and defences.

When Captain Brandreth arrived on the island he described the settlement on Ascension, now known as Georgetown and locally as 'The Garrison', as follows:

'The population at the period of my arrival consisted of about 140 Europeans, principally of the Royal Marine Corps, and seventy-six Africans, making a total of about 220 persons, including military and civil officers, a few white women (the wives of NCOs and privates and some black women and children. A small town or rather village had grown up near the roadstead, which on my arrival consisted of a collection of miserable tenements, with walls put together without lime, and harbouring vermin; roofs of canvas or shingle and floors of sandstone or tarras. The hospital......consisted of four rooms.....and the Africans occupied wretched hovels dark and filthy. A victualing store, a tank and a small stone tenement for the officers were the only buildings that redeemed the settlement from the appearance of an African village.'[2]

The only defensive work Captain Brandreth found was a single position on a projecting piece of land, about 70 feet (21.5m) above the sea overlooking the roadstead. According to Brandreth:

'The anchorage was defended by a few guns....without any breastwork or other cover and in the rear, on a higher elevation, a building with a canvas roof was occupied as a powder magazine.'[3]

In 1829 this position was referred to as Fort Cockburn and the guns were mounted on wooden naval carriages and, as Brandreth described, were without a parapet or even platforms. The guns mounted in this position were four 18-pdr SB guns, two 12-pdr SB guns, one 32-pdr carronade and one 12-pdr carronade.

Brandreth drew up plans for a water supply to feed Georgetown from Green Mountain and for a number of new buildings including a barracks for the Marines, quarters for the officers, a hospital and a storehouse. For

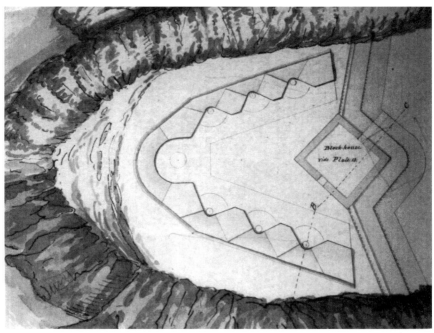

Captain Brandreth's original plan for Fort Cockburn, later re-named Fort Thornton. (*TNA MR 1/1771*)

the defences he proposed rebuilding Fort Cockburn into an enclosed work mounting five guns with a defensible blockhouse for thirty-five men in the rear of the fort and building a Martello tower mounting two guns at Pyramid Point to defend Comfort Cove (now known as Comfortless Cove). In addition, a second Martello tower, a second enclosed work similar to Fort Cockburn and a half-moon battery for two guns were also to be built. The half-moon battery was to be built on Goat Hill, on the right flank of Clarence Bay.

In the event the remodelled Fort Cockburn was the only one of Brandreth's proposed defensive works to be built. When completed it differed from his original plan with the number of guns increased from five to seven and the blockhouse built to the rear of the fort rather than as an integral part of it. Work on Fort Cockburn was authorized in 1832 and appears to have started in 1833. The work was carried out by the Royal Marines of the garrison, and additional Marines, chosen because of their trades and skills, including an officer's party of the Royal Marine Artillery, were sent to the island to augment the garrison. These reinforcements included masons and in May 1835 Captain Bate's log recorded that the masons were preparing stone for the inverted arches of the blockhouse. On 30 May 1835 Captain Bate reported in his log that there was 'a party at gun drill in Fort Cockburn'.[4] These additional

Marines, totalling one sergeant, three corporals and eighty-six Marines, had returned to England by the end of August 1835.

As previously mentioned, when it was completed Fort Cockburn differed from Captain Brandreth's original design. As a result of moving the blockhouse to the ground behind the fort, it was possible to extend the rear of the fort to mount two additional guns, so in its final form the fort mounted seven 24-pdr SB guns on traversing platforms. The two additional guns in the rear of the fort were mounted 3 feet (0.9m) below the level of the other guns. Two guns provided flanking fire to the landing place; two covered Long Beach and Clarence Bay; and the three at front of the fort covered the anchorage and the roadstead. The fort was sunk into the volcanic headland with only a low parapet wall above the level of the ground.

Behind the fort stood the blockhouse approximately 38 feet (11.6m) square and 22 feet (6.75m) high. It was essentially a musketry tower and no provision was made to mount guns on top of it. The lower floor of the blockhouse comprised four rooms: a magazine with a vaulted bomb-proof ceiling; a store; a small room, possibly to accommodate an officer or senior NCO; and an entrance hall with a staircase to the upper floor. Part of the lower floor was provided with musketry loopholes to cover the entrance with fire. The upper floor was open-plan with a line of musketry loopholes along all four walls and a further staircase that led to the roof level. This gave access to a walkway and an overhanging machicolation built on all four sides of the blockhouse roof.

View over the naval buildings to Fort Thornton and the blockhouse. (*TNA ADM 195/2*)

Captain Brandreth visited Ascension briefly for a second time in 1835 when his ship stopped there on his return journey from St Helena to England. In an article he wrote published in the *Royal Geographical Society Journal* in the same year entitled *Communications on the Island of Ascension* he paid tribute to the energy and initiative of Captain Bate and mentioned *'a small enclosed work for the defence of the roadstead'* that had been completed in addition to Fort Cockburn under the supervision of Lieutenant M'Arthur of the Royal Marine Artillery.[5] This was sometimes referred to as a 'richochet battery' and was situated at sea level on the right flank of Fort Cockburn. The battery, known as Fort Warren, appears to have mounted two guns and was surrounded by a stone wall. At the rear in one corner of the battery there was a small stone magazine with a barrel-shaped roof.

After the death of Napoleon in 1821 the value of Ascension to the Admiralty lay primarily in its use as a victualing station for the Royal Navy West Africa Squadron that was involved in the suppression of the West Africa slave trade. Steps were taken to establish a farm on Green Mountain to provide fresh vegetables for the garrison and visiting ships, and there was also a small herd of cattle. However, the main source of fresh meat was provided by the Green turtle that used Ascension to breed on and the garrison built holding ponds to maintain a supply of live turtles after the breeding season was over.

In the years after Captain Brandreth's second visit to the island in 1835 there were further improvements in the garrison's living conditions, and in the defences despite the death in post from influenza of Captain Bate in 1838. A barracks and a recreation building for the seamen and Marines and a separate quarantine ward for the hospital were built. In the 1840s work started on building a church and a large naval storehouse. A small battery for two 24-pdr SB guns was established on the lower slopes of Cross Hill, near Bate's Cottage, the commandant's house. This was the battery known as Fort Murdoch or Murdoch's Battery.

A Period of Stagnation: 1841–1882

Ascension continued as the base for the Royal Navy West Africa Squadron until 1865 when the base for the squadron was moved to Cape Town. Throughout most of this period the Royal Navy ships continued their war against the slave traders and Ascension continued to provide water, fresh vegetables and later, with the advent of steam power in the Royal Navy, the island took on an additional role as a coaling station. The hospital on the island provided medical care for the ships' crews on patrol off the notoriously unhealthy West African coast. In 1841 HMS *Tortoise* was sent to Ascension as guard ship and store ship, and a coal hulk, the *Independencia*, which seems to have been a captured slaver, was anchored at Georgetown in 1857. It was at this time that Admiralty policy regarding the command of the island changed and the captain of the store ship based at Georgetown became the governor with the senior Royal Marine officer the commandant. The *Shipping Gazette & Sydney General Trade List* for 21 May 1844 reported that:

> '*The Tortoise is fitting out at Chatham as a guard and store ship for the Island of Ascension. From the position of this island, in the South Atlantic, and its great importance as a midway station between Madeira and the Cape of Good Hope, and as a rendez-vous for ships of war and the South American station, the Government has been induced to put their establishment at that place on a different footing than hitherto. A naval officer is to be governor and a Marine officer the commandant*'.

HMS *Tortoise* was replaced by HMS *Maender*, an old sailing frigate that acted as a coal store and store ship until 1859, being finally wrecked in a storm in 1870. In 1865 HMS *Flora* arrived at Ascension to act as store ship and remained there until 1871 when it was ordered to Cape Town to act as receiving ship there. It was at this time that Ascension Island officially became a tender to HMS *Flora* and remained so until being transferred as tender to HMS *Cormorant* at Gibraltar in 1891.

Between 1840 and the opening of the Suez Canal in 1869 work continued to improve the living conditions and the defences on the island. The foundation stone of a church had been laid in 1843 and the church was completed in 1847. In 1848 a second storey was added to the Marine barracks and a sanatorium was built high on Green Mountain. The defences of the island were also improved and in 1849 three 24-pdr SB guns were placed in a newly constructed battery on Goat Hill, subsequently renamed Hayes Hill and the battery Hayes Hill Battery, to cover the southern portion of the anchorage. This new work was built by the simple expedient of excavating the clinker on top of the hill and constructing three gun positions. At the same time the two 24-pdr SB guns in the battery known as Fort Murdoch, near the governor's lodge on Cross Hill, were replaced with newer guns of the same type. It seems likely that it was about this time that Fort Cockburn was renamed Fort Thornton, apparently after Henry Thornton, a leading abolitionist of the slave trade.

A new 'fort', Fort Clarence, had also been established on Green Mountain around the Royal Marine farm on the mountain. This 'fort' was actually just a 'position of last resort' to which the personnel of the garrison and their families would withdraw should an enemy force manage to land and occupy Georgetown, and it simply comprised a number of gun positions covering the approaches to the farm. These guns were protected by sandbags and included a 32-pdr SB gun on a traversing platform; an 18-pdr SB gun; two 18-pdr carronades; three 12-pdr brass field howitzers; and three 6-pdr brass field guns. A number of small magazines, each simply a hole in the ground covered over with an earth roof, were established close to each gun position. It also appears that the small stone barracks on the mountain, built to accommodate twelve or fourteen men, may have been fortified as a form of 'keep' as it is this building which is referred to as 'Fort Clarence' on a map dated 1852.

However, the abolition of slavery in the United States at the end of the Civil War in 1865, and the opening of the Suez Canal in 1869 meant that the importance of Ascension as a supply and coaling station was considerably reduced. The number of ships stopping at Ascension dropped dramatically from some 500 to a mere 50 ships a year after the opening of the Suez Canal and the island's strategic importance was, therefore, much diminished.

In 1866 the population of the island was reduced from 442 men, women and children to approximately 360, and in 1873 a report showed the garrison had been dramatically reduced in size to consist of one Commander RN, one Gunner 2nd Class, two assistant surgeons, one assistant paymaster-in-charge, twenty-four petty officers and seamen, one pensioner cook, and one corporal and ten privates of the Royal Marine Light Infantry. There were also twenty-four Kroomen, but the report did not include the numbers of women and children. In addition to HMS *Flora*, the guard ship, there was also the steam tug *African*, the mooring vessel *Swift*, and a water tank vessel.

In 1871 the Royal Navy moved HMS *Flora* to Simonstown in Cape Province because of the lifting of the anti-slavery blockade of the West African coast. The Admiralty therefore carried out a further review of the importance of Ascension, but decided that the island should still be maintained as a coaling station, together with St Helena.

Three years later, in 1874, Captain J.W. East RM arrived on Ascension for a three-year tour of duty as commandant and immediately described the defences of the island in a report. His report is evidence that some attempt had been made in the preceding years to modernize some of the armament of the batteries. To the rear and just above Fort Warren, on the lower slopes of Cross Hill, a new two-gun battery had been established mounting one 10-inch 84cwt SB shell gun and one 68-pdr 95cwt SB gun, with a second 68-pdr SB gun mounted on top of Cross Hill. Despite these new guns

Captain East found that since the reduction of the Ascension establishment all the defences had been totally neglected, but he considered this to be of little consequence as he believed the guns would be utterly useless against any ship armed with modern artillery. However, there was some improvement in the effectiveness of the island's defences when the three 24-pdr SB guns on Hayes Hill (formerly Goat Hill) were replaced by three more powerful 68-pdr SB guns.

In January 1880 Commodore Frederick Richards RN inspected Ascension and reported on the state of the island's defences. He found that *'the batteries are unarmed, at present the old guns have been removed and the four 64-pdr MLR [sic] guns sent out in 1878 are not yet in position. I have directed Captain Roe to mount these guns without delay. The guns will be distributed as follows:*

Murdoch's Battery	*2*
Fort Warren	*1*
Hayes Hill Battery	*1*

These guns are too small to keep the enemy's cruisers out of range.'[6]

The following year a second report made it clear that the four guns had now been mounted. Fort Warren had a masonry platform with a wooden deck and the gun mounted; Murdoch's Battery had a concrete platform, also with a

Murdoch Battery 64-pdr 71 cwt (Palliser Conversion) RML gun on a wooden garrison carriage. This is one of the guns mounted in 1874. (*TNA ADM 195/2*)

wooden deck and two guns mounted; and the gun on Hayes Hill was protected by casks filled with cement and formed into a revetment. There were five magazines in use holding gunpowder, shells and small arms ammunition. There were magazines situated, one behind Hayes Hill and one behind Fort Warren. The magazine in Fort Thornton was in use together with the Blockhouse magazine, and the 'Billiard Room' magazine. None of these were considered to be bomb-proof.[7]

By 1881 there had been a further increase in the island's armament with the arrival of a fifth 64-pdr RML gun which was mounted in Fort Warren. These five guns were of two types, three 64-pdr 71cwt guns (converted from 8-inch SB shell guns) and two more modern 64-pdr 64cwt guns all mounted on old wooden truck carriages, and the carriages at Fort Murdoch were on wooden ground platforms.[8] A small laboratory building was also built in Georgetown close to Long Beach and used for shell filling.

In the same year, as a result of the Carnarvon Commission on the defence of coaling stations and a report by a Lieutenant Colonel Phillips RE, the Commanding Royal Engineer on St Helena, consideration was given to the rearming of Ascension. Unusually, the matter was considered by the War Office rather than the Admiralty, and the Inspector General of Fortifications in a Memorandum dated 9 April 1881 recommended a new armament of five 10-inch 18-ton RML guns and four 64-pdr RML guns. The 10-inch guns were to be mounted in a remodelled Fort Thornton, two mounted *en barbette*, and three behind iron shields. The distribution of the 64-pdr guns was to have been one at Fort Warren, two at Murdoch's Battery, where there was to be a thickening of the parapet, and one in a small redoubt on the top of Cross Hill. The Memorandum also recommended that the Green Mountain water supply should be defended by a number of musketry breastworks on the road to the Sanatorium, supported by six light field guns. This proposal was subsequently modified to two 10-inch RML guns to be mounted *en barbette* at Hay's Hill Battery on Hay's Hill and three similar guns behind iron shields at Fort Thornton.

The total cost of these new guns and the works in which they were to be emplaced came to an estimated cost of £54,000, so perhaps it is not surprising that the Admiralty felt that the rearming of Ascension's defences could not be justified in view of the island's declining strategic value, and nothing came of this proposal. However, because of the poor condition of the numerous magazines on the island authority was given for the construction of a modern magazine at the base of Hayes Hill.

The Rearming of Ascension 1883–1922

Despite the reduction in the size of the garrison the Admiralty continued to maintain Ascension as a coaling station. There had, however, been considerable debate not only in the War Office and the Admiralty, but also in Parliament, regarding the respective values of Ascension Island and St Helena as coaling stations. The Admiralty view was that Ascension was closer than St Helena to the trade route and should therefore be retained as a coaling station as well as St Helena. Both were, therefore, retained, St Helena as a major coaling station, and Ascension as a second-class coaling station.

Despite its status as a second-class coaling station, a further report on the defences of Ascension in 1882 by Colonel Phillips RE recommended that the island should be rearmed with 10-inch RML guns. Fort Thornton was to have two such guns, with two more on Bates's Point and two on Hayes Hill. Once again nothing came of this recommendation.

In 1887 a further report for the Admiralty proposed yet another change in the armament of the island's batteries. On this occasion Fort Thornton was to be rearmed with one 7-inch 6½-ton RML gun and one of the newer 64-pdr 64cwt Mk III RML guns, with two of the older 64-pdr 71cwt guns placed on Hayes Hill. A second 7-inch RML gun and another 64-pdr 64cwt Mk III gun were proposed for what was now called Cottage Battery, behind the old Fort Warren, while a third old model 64-pdr RML gun was to be emplaced on Traveller's Hill. The *pièce de resistance* of the new armament was to have been a single 6-inch BL gun to be installed on the summit of Cross Hill. The 71cwt guns already on the island remained mounted on old wooden truck carriages while the two more modern 64cwt guns were to be fitted with iron carriages and slides.[9]

Captain Napier, the commandant, reported that the magazine at the base of Hayes Hill was under construction, and that the guns currently on the island were the three 64-pdr 71cwt RML guns (Palliser conversions from 8-inch SB shell guns) and two more modern 64-pdr 64cwt RML guns. One 64-pdr was mounted on Hayes Hill.

The following year, 1888, the Admiralty took the decision to send two 6-inch BL guns to the island, but the problem was that these guns were not immediately available. They were, however, included in the plans for the distribution of the new armament. These guns were to be mounted on Vavasseur central pivot mountings and the guns were to be allocated as follows:

Fort Thornton	1 × 6-inch BL MK IV gun
	3 × 64-pdr RML Mk III guns
	1 × Nordenfelt machine gun
Hayes Hill	2 × 64-pdr RML Mk III guns
	1 × Nordenfelt machine gun
Cottage Battery	2 × 7-inch RML Mk I guns
Cross Hill	1 × 6in BL Mk IV gun

In addition, Captain Napier requested permission from the Admiralty to retain two of the 64-pdr guns already on the island, one Mk I, and one Mk II, one to be mounted on Red Hill and one on Traveller's Hill. The Admiralty agreed the retention of these guns as a temporary measure until two more Mk III guns could be shipped to Ascension so that all the 64-pdr guns would then fire the same charge.[10] In the following year Napier also proposed that a 4-inch BL gun and two Gardner machine guns, weapons held in reserve for Royal Navy ships operating in the area, should be transferred to the Island's establishment but, after some correspondence, this was not agreed the Admiralty.

The War Office was responsible for supplying the 6-inch BL guns but these modern weapons were in short supply as were the mountings for the 64-pdr guns. In a Minute dated 12 November 1888 the War Office informed the Admiralty that it was unable to provide either 6-inch BL guns and mountings or the garrison mountings for the 7-inch RML guns required by the Admiralty for Ascension. The War Office Minute stated: *'The supply of these guns and mountings must wait until more pressing demands from other stations have been complied with.'*[11]

Since it would obviously be some time before the 6-inch BL guns would become available the Admiralty decided to send out two 7-inch RML guns as a temporary measure. These were naval guns, but as the War Office was still unable to provide garrison mountings for them, the Admiralty decided to provide naval mountings adapted for land service. In March 1889 two 7-inch 6½-ton Mk I RML guns and naval mountings together with five 64-pdr Mk III RML guns were dispatched to Ascension. The latter guns were to replace the 64cwt and older 71cwt guns. Five common wood carriages for the 64-pdr guns and the mountings for the 7-inch RML guns were shipped to Ascension aboard HMS *Wye* in September 1889. The wood carriages were only to be used until Garrison Central Pivot parapet mountings could be provided by the Royal Carriage Department.[12]

Cottage Battery (formerly Murdoch's Battery) today showing the two 7-inch 6½-ton Mk I RML guns on Sea Service slides adapted for Land Service. (*Author*)

The RML guns were mounted according to the new plan with the 7-inch guns being mounted on the cinder ground at Cottage Battery without a parapet and using old cannons as pivots and with stone racers. By mounting them in this fashion it enabled the guns to be used should an emergency arise before the arrival of the central pivot mountings. Plans were drawn up to mount the two guns behind a 6 foot (1.89m) high parapet of either concrete or stone, but nothing came of this plan.

The 6-inch BL guns were eventually ordered in February 1890 for delivery in 1891. The plan then changed again and it was decided to mount these two guns in a new battery to be named Bedford Battery on Cross Hill just above Cottage Battery. The Admiralty Works Department decided that a proper concrete emplacement should be provided for each gun with an underground magazine between the two gun positions. In May 1893 two 6-inch Mk III BL guns were issued by Woolwich Arsenal and were shipped to Ascension on the store ship HMS *Wye* and were installed in 1894.

In the mid-1880s the Eastern Telegraph Company planned to lay an undersea telegraph cable between South Africa and England using Ascension Island as one of the cable stations. Suddenly Ascension was strategically important once again and, in view of its new importance, the Admiralty reviewed the defences. The War Office was asked to send a Royal Engineers officer to report on how the island should be defended. In September 1896

Lieutenant Colonel J.F. Lewis RE arrived and he produced a detailed report that provides a full description of the island's forts and batteries at that time.[13] On arrival Lewis discovered that the Admiralty had recently sent two 6-inch Quick-firing (QF) guns and two 4.7-inch QF guns to Ascension, but these guns had not been mounted.

Lieutenant Colonel Lewis found that the two 6-inch Mk III BL guns in Bedford Battery were mounted, but there was still work to be completed on the magazine for the No 2 emplacement. Fort Thornton he described as '*a small well-built battery that is disarmed*', and he found that Hayes Hill Battery had also been dismantled. Lewis felt that the blockhouse at the rear of Fort Thornton was very conspicuous. As regards Cottage Battery with its two 7-inch RML guns, Lewis found that it had no proper ammunition service, the sweep plates, which were laid on wood, were bent and unfastened, and the guns were neither accurate or long-ranging. He dismissed this position saying: '*I would not recommend anything whatever being done with this battery.*' A new magazine below Hayes Hill he described as being '*of modern construction but not now shell-proof*'. Hayes Hill Battery was briefly described thus: '*The gorge of the work is closed with a parapet but mainly to prevent the entrances to the ammunition stores being visible from outside. It covers Number 3 emplacement but not the others.*'[14]

Colonel Lewis considered that the threats to Ascension were a bombardment of Georgetown from the sea, or possibly, though more unlikely, a bombardment combined with a beach landing by a raiding force, followed by an overland attack on Georgetown. He considered that Bedford Battery, although retired 1,000 yards (930m) from the sea, was admirably sited at a height of 305 feet (92m) to provide plunging fire on any attacking ships. So, having one battery set back from the coastline Colonel Lewis believed that the approved armament still to be mounted, two 6-inch QF and two 4.7-inch QF guns, should be sited forward of Bedford Battery so as to obtain the maximum range to the westward. Therefore, he recommended the reconstruction of both Fort Thornton and the Hayes Hill battery, and the construction of a lightly armed redoubt on the site of the Admiralty signal station on the top of Cross Hill.

At Fort Thornton he recommended that one 6-inch QF gun should be mounted with an arc of fire from Comfortless Cove to Hayes Hill, with four 1-inch Nordenfelt (4-barrel) machine guns to sweep the beach to the right and left and to the rear to deal with any beach landing or land attack. The armament proposed for Hayes Hill, was one 6-inch QF, two 4.7-inch QF guns and two 1-inch Nordenfelt (4-barrel) machine guns. The arc of fire for the

Fort Hayes viewed from Cottage Battery with the old Royal Marine barracks in the foreground. (*Author*)

Interior of Fort Hayes looking towards the 6-inch QF gun position upper right. (*Author*)

Interior of Fort Thornton as it is today, looking towards the rear of the fort and the magazine constructed by cutting down the old blockhouse. (*Author*)

6-inch gun was to be from Pyramid Point to Payne Point, while one of the 4.7-inch guns was to fire due westwards round into Clarence Bay, and the other from the north-west round to Payne Point and inland. Fire control for the two forts was to be provided by a 'sighting station' to the left of Bedford Battery.

His recommendation for the 'conspicuous' blockhouse was that it should be cut down to half its height, roofed with concrete and earthed up as much as possible around the base. It would then act as a store for the Nordenfelt ammunition and provide a shelter for the garrison.

The proposed redoubt was to have had a light parapet, shelter and water tank, and the armament was to have been four Nordenfelt (4-barrel) rifle-calibre machine guns. The proposed sighting station was to have been built above and to the left of Bedford Battery, and to have been manned by the commandant, two orderlies and a signalman at a total cost of £200. The estimated total cost of these works came to £14,171, including some £4,000 for work to improve the capability of the coaling ships. In fact, neither the redoubt nor the sighting station were subsequently constructed.

Spurred on, no doubt, by the imminent arrival of the cable from South Africa, which actually arrived on the island in 1899, the Admiralty accepted most of Colonel Lewis's recommendations, though they baulked at the construction of the redoubt on the summit of Cross Hill. They did, however, authorize the replacement of the 6-inch BL guns of Bedford Battery with two more efficient 6-inch BL Converted (BLC) guns. These latter guns had a different breech-block that permitted faster operation and so a greater rate of fire. Fort Thornton was enlarged to include the cut-down blockhouse and, when completed, there were positions in the fort for four 3-pdr QF guns in place of the Nordenfelt machine guns suggested by Lewis. Hayes Hill Battery was also rebuilt internally with new gun positions for the modern quick-firing guns sunk into the clinker so that no parapet was visible from seawards, and renamed Fort Hayes, together with two depression range finder (DRF) positions and a crew shelter. Additional Royal Marines were sent out from England to assist with the mounting of the guns.

A further inspection of the island's defences was made by Vice-Admiral Sir Robert Harris who visited when returning to England from South Africa where he had been the Commander-in-Chief Cape of Good Hope and West Coast of Africa Station in early 1901. Admiral Harris commented that the substitution of the 6-inch BLC guns for the old BL guns at Bedford Battery, and the mounting of the 4.7-inch QF and 3-pdr QF guns had greatly improved the sea defence of the island. A further recommendation was that 5,000 War Office Pattern II sandbags (tarred) should be provided and filled with volcanic dust. These were to be placed on the seaward faces of the two forts to reduce the effect of enemy shellfire hitting the surrounding rock.

There was considerable debate about the construction of the sighting station which Lewis considered important. In his view the DRF positions were too close to the guns and were affected by the concussion when the guns fired, requiring recalibration each time, and were also difficult to sight because of the smoke and dust. In 1901, after Admiral Harris's inspection, the decision was taken to build a central range-finding station close to Bedford Battery to contain three range-finders, one for each battery. The estimated cost was £640 and the proposed smaller 'sighting station' was abandoned, as was the idea of linking all three batteries by telephone, probably on the grounds of economy. The reconstruction of the forts was complete by 1903.

Ascension's strategic importance having increased with the arrival of the cable from South America, the island had now become one of the communication hubs of the British Empire and continued as such throughout the First World War. In January 1915 the garrison was reinforced by thirty Marines of the Royal Marine Mobile Force and that year the Admiralty sent out a radio station and signal personnel. The station was a spark transmitting and receiving station designed to communicate with Royal Navy ships, and six masts, each 300 feet (92m) high, were erected on what is now called

Wireless Plain behind Cross Hill. However, the initial fears of an attack by German warships was dispelled with the destruction of the German East Asia Squadron at the Battle of the Falklands in December 1914, and the forts and batteries saw no action during the war.

Once the Armistice had been signed in November 1918 the garrison was gradually reduced and in 1921, as a result of Treasury budget cuts, the Admiralty decided to withdraw all personnel. Fort Thornton, Fort Hayes and Bedford Battery were disarmed, the guns dismounted and rendered unserviceable and the island administration handed over to the Eastern Telegraph Company. This remained the situation until the outbreak of the Second World War in September 1939.

The Second World War 1939–1945

Throughout the 1920s and 1930s Ascension slumbered peacefully, populated only by the employees of the Eastern Telegraph Company which in 1934 changed its name to Cable & Wireless Ltd (now Cable & Wireless Plc), and the only works carried out on the island were such as to improve the lot of the company staff. The outbreak of the Second World War in 1939 found Ascension completely disarmed and at the mercy of German raiders. The cable station was still a vital link in the network of British Empire communications but there was no garrison. The superintendent of the cable station immediately set about forming a local Home Guard detachment under his command. A small quantity of small arms was sent from England and the detachment eventually comprised one officer and forty-three other ranks armed with three 0.303-inch Lewis light machine guns (LMGs), an assortment of rifles and four Thompson sub-machine guns. One NCO was sent from St Helena to train the new force, now known as the Ascension Volunteer Defence Force.

In 1940 personnel of the Royal Navy Civilian Shore Wireless Service arrived on the island to set up a HF/DF station monitoring German naval wireless traffic at a site known as Benin City. It was one of three stations, the others being at Freetown in Sierra Leone and on St Helena, each connected to the cable station in their location. If a signal was picked up from a German U-boat or surface vessel a Flash signal was sent by cable to the other stations giving frequency and bearing, thus enabling cross bearings on the signal to be obtained.

The British Government, the Admiralty and the War Office were all too aware that Ascension, despite its importance as a communications hub, could not be defended against attacks by German surface raiders or, and this was more likely, attacks by U-boats. To remedy this situation the Admiralty offered two 5.5-inch BL guns that had been removed from HMS *Hood* during the ship's refit in 1935 and stored in Malta. These guns were shipped to Ascension with ninety-five rounds of ammunition for each gun. They were fitted with coast defence shields and mounted in the old Bedford Battery position. To man the guns the War Office sent out a small detachment of the Royal Artillery consisting of one officer and forty-two other ranks.

In 1941 these guns opened fire on the German submarine *U-124* when it surfaced off Georgetown. The U-boat, commanded by Kapitänleutnant Jochen Mohr, was carrying over a hundred survivors of German merchant ships that had been resupplying U-boats in the Atlantic and had been sunk by the Royal Navy. On his voyage back to France, Mohr, in an attempt to convince the British that the U-boats were still active, attempted a diversion by shelling the cable station on Ascension. Return fire from the Ascension guns forced *U-124* to crash-dive, and this was the only occasion the guns were fired at an enemy target.

In early 1942, with America now in the war, there was a requirement to establish an air link between America and North Africa to facilitate the delivery of aircraft to the Middle East through West Africa. Ascension was an obvious choice for the construction of an airfield, and in March 1942 a convoy arrived off Georgetown carrying the personnel and equipment of Task Force 4612

Bedford Battery, showing the two 5.5-inch BL guns (ex-HMS Hood) mounted during the Second World War. (*Author*)

comprising 38th US Combat Engineer Regiment and Battery A of the 426th Coast Artillery (AA) (Separate) Battalion. A Signals Air Warning detachment, a station hospital and other administrative personnel were included, making a total of 63 officers and 1,432 enlisted men. The complement of Battery A comprised six officers and 148 enlisted men to man the twelve light anti-aircraft (LAA) guns of the battery. The provision of the LAA guns does make one wonder if the Department of Defense in Washington were really aware of the actual location of the island!

The Royal Artillery detachment manning the 5.5-inch guns was withdrawn to the United Kingdom in May 1942 and the personnel of Battery A took over the responsibility for the guns. In August 1942 the airfield was completed and became operational and preparations were underway for the withdrawal of the engineers and Battery A, and their replacement by a new unit, Composite Force 8012. This latter formation comprised HQ and HQ Company, two rifle companies of the 3rd Battalion 91st US Infantry Regiment and Battery B and 2 Platoon Battery C of the 28th Coast Artillery Battalion (Separate). The 2nd Platoon of Battery C was a coast artillery searchlight platoon equipped with five portable 60cm coast artillery searchlights.

On its arrival on Ascension Island Battery B took over the manning of the British 5.5-inch BL guns and established their own guns – four 155-mm M1918 M1 GPF field guns of First World War vintage and French design – on a site on Catherine Point adjacent to the old Fort Hayes. Gun positions were dug in the cinder and magazines constructed to the rear of the gun positions. The magazines were made 'bomb-proof' by using timber and railway lines from the disused buildings of the English Bay Company, that operated in English Bay between 1923 and 1931 extracting guano from the island.

The battery plotting room on Catherine Point was just a pit covered by timbers and the battery commander's station was on top of a small timber tower. Primary and secondary fire control stations were established on Cat Hill and Cross Hill respectively, but later a longer base line was established from Cross Hill to Pyramid Point. The searchlights of 2 Platoon were sited at 2,000-yard (1,846m) intervals along the west coast of the island.

The island benefited considerably from the arrival of the American force with the construction of roads in particular. The problem of the provision of fresh vegetables for the garrison was overcome with typical American ingenuity by establishing a large hydroponics farm. Hydroponics, the growing of terrestrial plants in a nutrient solution in order to provide fresh vegetables, had already been successfully used on Wake Island where, like Ascension, there was no topsoil.

When Battery A of the 426th Coast Artillery (AA) Battalion departed Ascension it would appear that at least some of the LAA guns were left on the island. There is documentary evidence that in 1943 the US commander requested that the Ascension Volunteer Defence Force take over the equipment.[15]

Battery B carried out regular target practice with their guns, but never fired them in anger while on Ascension, and by early 1944 the battery was reduced in numbers and finally de-activated in October 1944. The American 155mm guns were removed but the 5.5-inch guns of Bedford Battery were retained in a state of care and maintenance, although no troops remained on the island.

By May 1947 the last US Army personnel had left Ascension and the island was back in the hands of Cable & Wireless Ltd. In 1953 the Royal Navy frigate HMS *Sparrow* arrived and removed all the remaining ammunition from the magazines, so ending the history of the coast defences of Ascension Island.

In 1956 coast artillery in the British Army was disbanded, and even when the Falklands War with Argentina erupted in 1982 and the island became a base supplying the Royal Navy task force assembled to retake the islands, no attempt was made to provide the island with any form of ground defence.

Chapter Eight

Singapore

The Founding of Singapore

Singapore, an island approximately the size of the Isle of Wight, lies at the tip of the Malay Peninsula. The island, together with more than sixty smaller islands, forms the modern Republic of Singapore. The main island is some 25 miles (40 kms) in length and 14 miles (22 kms) at its greatest breadth, with an area of 272 square miles (716 sq kms). To the north it is separated from the mainland of Malaysia by the Strait of Johore. There is a natural harbour on the south side of the island and deep water in the Strait of Johore.

Off the southern extremity of Singapore lies the island of Blakang Mati, today known as Sentosa Island, a teardrop-shaped island some 2½ (4 kms) long (4 kms) and 800 yards (740m) wide in average breadth. The highest point on Blakang Mati is Mount Serapong at the eastern end of the island which stands some 300 feet (92m) high. Between Blakang Mati and Singapore Island there is a channel with a minimum depth of six fathoms which forms a large natural harbour originally known as New Harbour.

The ending of the war with Napoleon reactivated the old rivalry between the British Honourable East India Company (HEIC) and the Dutch Vereenigde Oostindische Compagnie, or Dutch East India Company (VOC). The war with France and Batavia, the French-occupied Netherlands, having ended in 1814 with the Convention of London signed between Viscount Castlereagh for the British Government and Hendrik Fagel for the Dutch Government. Under the terms of the Convention all the colonial possessions as they were on 1 January 1803 that were taken by the British from the Dutch in the late war were returned to the Dutch with the exception of the Cape of Good Hope and a number of South American settlements that were to become British Guiana.

Also returned to Dutch rule two years later in 1816 was the port of Malacca on the Malay Peninsula. Malacca had been seized by the HEIC in 1798 when the Company realized that a base was needed close to the Strait of Malacca to enable the Company's ships to replenish their stores and water, and to counter

Dutch control over the strait. Such a staging post would prevent the Dutch from interfering with the Company's China trade and ensure safe passage for HEIC ships through the Malacca Strait.

Aware of the need for a new base after the return of Malacca, Sir Stamford Raffles, the ambitious young Resident at Fort Marlborough at Bencoolen, the Company's only trading post in Sumatra, proposed to the Governor General in Calcutta that he should seek a suitable site for a new base close to the narrowest part of the Malacca Strait, with Singapura, Banka, or the Riau-Lingga Islands being the most likely suitable locations.

Raffles, who had previously been interpreter for Lord Minto, the Governor General and Governor of Java, before becoming Resident at Fort Marlborough, which he considered to be a career demotion, assembled a small fleet of ships at Penang in January 1819 and, together with Major William Farquhar, who was the Resident at Malacca until its return to the Dutch, sailed for the Malacca Strait. Raffles had to select a spot that was not currently occupied or under the influence of the Dutch East India Company, and it is clear that he had already identified the ancient port of Singapura as being the most suitable location for the new HEIC trading post and base.

Despite a somewhat complicated political situation regarding the sovereignty of Singapura, Raffles landed on the island where the Temenggong, a semi-royal official of the Sultanate of Riau, was in charge. With the position of the Sultan of Riau in dispute between two brothers, Raffles and the Temenggong summoned the brother currently resident in Riau, the Tenkku Hussain, to Singapura and Raffles, entirely on his own authority, installed Tenkku Hussain as Sultan of Riau. Having done this, Raffles promptly signed an agreement with the new sultan which permitted the HEIC to establish a settlement on the island and in return the new sultan and the Temenggong were to receive a monthly allowance.

Raffles left Major Farquhar as the new Resident, and Singapore, as it was now called, officially became a dependency of Fort Marlborough rather than of Penang. All this was much to the anger of the VOC authorities and Major Farquhar was given strict instructions by Raffles to fortify Singapore in case of a Dutch attack. In his instructions he directed that:

'I have no hesitation in conveying to you my authority for constructing the following works.... On the hill overlooking the Settlement, and commanding it and a considerable portion of the anchorage, a small fort or a commodious blockhouse....Capable of mounting eight or ten 12-pounders and of containing a magazine of brick or stone, together with a barrack for *the permanent residence of thirty European Artillery and or the temporary accommodation of the rest of the garrison in case of emergency. Along the coast in the vicinity of the Settlement one or two strong batteries for the protection of the shipping and at Sandy Point* [Tanjong Katong] *a redoubt and to the east of it a strong battery for the same purpose…. These defences, together with a Martello tower on Deep Water Point, which it is my intention to recommend to the Supreme Government, will in my judgment render the Settlement capable of maintaining a good defence.*[1]

It is not possible to establish accurately when the first defence works were built in the new settlement, now known as Singapore. When Raffles returned on his way back to England in 1822 little seems to have been done to construct the defences as he had instructed. However, there are reports of a battery to the north of the entrance to the Singapore River which appears to have been armed with six guns. Probably, this was essentially a temporary earthwork fortification built in 1820 by Captain Ralfe of the Bengal Artillery who was in command of the artillery garrison. By 1827 this battery at what had become known as Scandal Point had become decayed though it was retained as a saluting battery until 1851 when the sea wall along the Esplanade was built.

A Captain Lake of the Madras Engineers was sent from Penang in 1827 to report on the fortifications required to provide an adequate defence for Singapore. Lake drew up an elaborate plan of defence including defences of the harbour, St George's Island (Blakang Mati), and Sandy Point (Tanjong Katong), and a keep of last resort to which the garrison could retire in an emergency. Although some work started on Captain Lake's scheme, the newly appointed Governor General in Calcutta, Lieutenant General Lord William Bentinck, ordered all work to stop as part of a series of cost-cutting measures. The only work to be completed was a redoubt and battery at the mouth of the Singapore River which was named Fort Fullerton in 1826 in honour of Robert Fullerton, the first governor of the Straits Settlements.

No further work was carried out on the defences although another review was carried out in 1844 by Captain Samuel Best, also of the Madras Engineers. Best accepted Lake's earlier proposals for batteries to defend the shoreline and recommended five additional batteries for the defence of New Harbour. No attempt was made to implement Captain Best's report, though it is interesting to note that the sites he selected for the defence of New Harbour would subsequently feature in all later plans for the defence of Singapore.

In 1851 the matter of Singapore's defences resurfaced and the Governor General in Calcutta took the opportunity of stating the level of attack he

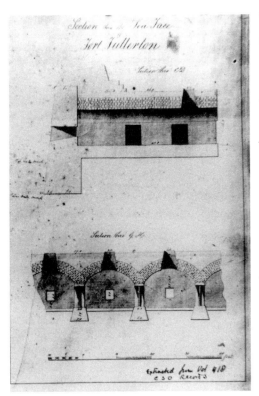

Section of a plan of Fort Fullerton, Singapore, 1843. (*Author's Collection*)

believed the island might be subjected to. His view was that *'The defences of the settlements [Singapore, Penang, and Malacca] should be calculated only for the repulse of privateering attacks, or for the resistance against assault in the temporary absence of men-of-war and steamers from the port.'* The Governor General went on to instruct that *'The defences should be limited to two Batteries of four heavy guns each, with one Battery for the Back Bay* [New Harbour] *if it shall be considered absolutely necessary.'*[2]

The tradition of not acting upon an engineer's report continued and no action was taken to improve the island's fortifications for the next ten years, though the armament of Fort Fullerton was improved by the provision of eight 8-inch SB guns. In 1853 Captain Henry Yule of the Bengal Engineers was sent to Singapore to produce yet another report on the defences considered necessary. Yule recommended changes to Fort Fullerton and changes to the sites of two batteries previously authorized but not constructed. The report was approved the following year when Britain and France were engaged in the war against Russia in the Crimea.

The two new batteries were to be built one on the lower slopes of Mount Palmer and the other on the forward slope of Mount Faber. Yule also recommended that a battery for two 13-inch mortars be built on the summit of Mount Faber. The armament of Singapore before the completion of Lake's Battery, the new battery on Mount Palmer, was:

Fort Fullerton	3 × 56-pdr 98cwt SB guns
	2 × 32-pdr 63cwt SB guns
Mount Faber Battery	2 × 56-pdr 98cwt SB guns

Much to the satisfaction of the government in Calcutta the construction of Lake's Battery and the changes to Fort Fullerton were carried out at a minimal charge to public funds as the work was done by convict labour.

Since Raffles first suggested the requirement for a keep of last resort, or place of refuge for the white population, there had been proposals for such a fortification and considerable debate as to which of the numerous hills on the island would be the most suitable site. Despite all the discussion nothing was done until 1854 when serious rioting occurred involving elements of the now numerous Chinese population. In April 1856 Governor Blundell wrote to the government of India urging construction of a place of refuge for the European population and garrison and suggesting Pearl's Hill as the best site.

As we have seen from previous chapters the military solution to this problem at this time was to construct a citadel, such as Fort Adelaide in Port Louis on Mauritius. Shortly after receipt of the governor's letter the Calcutta government authorized the construction of a citadel on Pearl's Hill, but subsequently refused to approve the design submitted.

However, the outbreak of the Indian Mutiny in 1857 increased the pressure for a secure refuge for the European population. The new Chief Engineer of the Public Works Department, Captain George Collyer, rejected Pearl's Hill as being too small in area and instead recommended to Governor Blundell that the best site was Government Hill, where a citadel would not only act as a refuge, but the guns could defend the town and harbour. Despite Governor Blundell's continued preference for Pearl's Hill, the Calcutta government accepted Captain Collyer's revised plan.

The government also took the view that, in view of the rapid commercial development of Singapore, steps should be taken to improve the island's defences and Collyer produced a second and even more extensive plan which included batteries for the defence of New Harbour and Sandy Point [Tanjong Katong] and a new battery for Mount Palmer. He also proposed batteries on Mount Serapong and at Rimau Point on Blakang Mati; on Pulau Brani; and at the foot of Mount Palmer. This plan was also opposed by Governor Blundell on the grounds of expense and because he was firmly of the belief that the security of the town and harbour lay in the ships of the Royal Navy. He did, however, authorize work to commence on the construction of the citadel on Government Hill and a further reconstruction of Fort Fullerton.

The citadel was completed in 1861 and named Fort Canning. It comprised the main fort, the walls of which followed the irregular outline of the top of the hill, and a battery, South Battery, situated 30 feet (8.5m) below the level of the main fort with its gorge closed by the parapet wall of the fort.

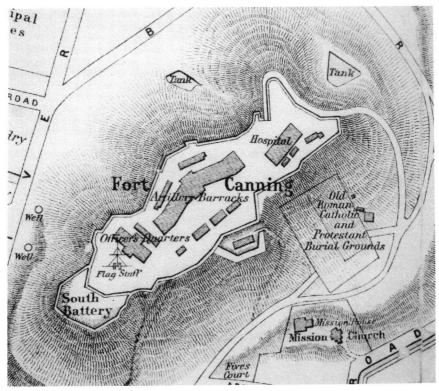

Plan of Fort Canning, Singapore, c.1865. (*TNA WO 78/2420*)

By 1869 the existing defences of Singapore comprised:

Fort Canning	8 × 8-inch SB shell guns
Fort Canning South Battery	7 × 68-pdr 95cwt SB guns
	2 × 13-inch mortars
Fort Fullerton	9 × 68-pdr 95cwt SB guns
	1 × 13-inch mortar
Mount Palmer Battery	5 × 56-pdr 98cwt SB guns
Mount Faber Battery	2 × 56-pdr 98cwt SB guns
Mount Faber Mortar Battery	2 × 13-inch mortars

There was, however, a considerable shortage of gunners to man these guns with only forty-seven European artillerymen and twenty-one Ordnance lascars on the strength of the garrison. This seems to indicate that Singapore still remained a low priority as far as the Indian Government was concerned. Indeed, the state of the fortifications in 1864 was probably best described by John Cameron FRGS, who visited Singapore that year. In his book *'Our*

Tropical Possessions in Malayan India', published the following year, he describes a visit to the batteries on Mount Faber as follows:

> *'On top of this hill are two mortars, and lower down is a battery for two 56-pounder guns, with barracks attached forming part of the far-famed fortifications of Singapore. It is difficult to say whether the two gaping mortars on the top of the hill, or the two lonely guns below convey the greatest feeling of desolation and decay. The very sepoys that guard the latter – for they don't man them – seem touched with the melancholy of neglect.'[3]*

Cameron also noted that not a single heavy gun mounted on any of the forts was capable of firing inland.

In the late 1850s, as Singapore's prosperity increased, so there arose opposition to the manner in which the island was governed from India. The citizens of Singapore were of the opinion that the Indian Government regarded the settlement as a useful 'cash-cow' and protested strongly against any attempt to remove the town's free-port status. In 1858 the Imperial government decided to transfer Singapore to Imperial rule, though it would be another nine years before the settlement became a Crown Colony.

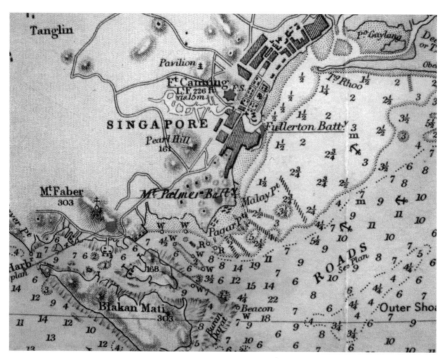

Map of Singapore Defences c.1860. (*Author's Collection*)

Prior to the transfer of the Straits Settlements to Imperial rule the Governor of Hong Kong, Sir Hercules Robinson, was asked by the Secretary of State for the Colonies, the Duke of Newcastle, to chair a committee to report on the state of defences of the new Crown Colony. The committee concluded that while the western approaches to New Harbour were relatively secure, the eastern entrance was undefended. To add to that it appeared that as a result of the commercial expansion of Singapore, Fort Fullerton was now in the centre of the town and useless as a work of defence since, as a battery *à fleur d'eau*, shipping at anchor in the harbour would mask its fire.

The committee proposed the construction of a fort at Tanjong Katong where a fort had been previously proposed on a number of occasions. The previous proposals had always been opposed by the authorities of the time on the grounds that it was too far from the town to be easily defended. The Robinson committee believed that the construction of a fort at Tanjong Katong could be funded by the sale of Fort Fullerton but, although the demolition of Fort Fullerton was authorized, the Tanjong Katong fort remained just a proposal.[4]

In 1867, when control of the settlement passed to the Colonial Office, a spotlight was focused on the new colony and in 1868 the Colonial Office reviewed the strength of the garrison. The Robinson Committee, having been of the opinion that the role of the garrison was essentially one of maintaining

South Battery, Fort Canning c.1880. The photograph shows two of the 68-pdr 95-cwt SB guns with an associated magazine. (*TNA CO 1069/484*)

public order, had recommended that it could be reduced to two batteries of European gunners and six companies of the newly-formed Ceylon Infantry Regiment. Acting on this the War Office withdrew one of the two Madras Native Infantry regiments that comprised the infantry garrison at that time.[5]

Rifled Guns and the Russian 'Scares' of 1877 and 1885

The advent of rifled guns in the mid-nineteenth century made all smooth-bore guns obsolete at a stroke. The rifled guns with longer barrels had higher muzzle- velocities and were, therefore, capable of penetrating a greater thickness of armour plate. The problem for the British Army and the Royal Navy was that the British arms manufacturers had not, in the late 1860s and early 1870s, managed to develop effective breech-loading guns, though a number of Continental manufacturers were producing such guns, particularly Krupp of Essen.

This technological change in artillery had the effect of making the armament and fortifications of Singapore obsolete, but at the same time the unification of Germany and Russia's expansion into Central Asia meant that the potential threat to prosperous Singapore was increasing. In 1869 the new Secretary of State for War consulted the Deputy Director of Works and Fortifications, Colonel William Drummond Jervois RE, on the defences of Singapore. Jervois could see no external threat to the colony beyond a naval attack by a single cruiser or raider.[6]

Jervois' recommendations included the abandonment of both Fort Fullerton and the Mount Palmer battery with reliance to be placed on Royal Navy ships based in Singapore. These proposals were strongly opposed by the governor, Sir Harry Ord, who did not believe that the Admiralty would provide a warship for the permanent defence of Singapore and, therefore, felt that coastal batteries must still be retained. Nevertheless, by 1871 the garrison of the colony had been reduced still further to one infantry regiment and one battery of artillery. The armament of the forts and batteries in 1871 comprised:

Fort Fullerton	9 × 68-pdr 95cwt SB guns
Mount Palmer Battery	5 × 56-pdr 98cwt SB guns
Mount Faber Battery	2 × 68-pdr 95cwt SB guns
Mount Faber Mortar Battery	2 × 13-inch Mortars
Fort Canning	8 × 8-inch SB shell guns
	3 × 13-inch mortars
Fort Canning South Battery	7 × 68-pdr 95cwt SB guns[7]

Four years after the reduction of the garrison, in 1873, the General Officer Commanding Troops in China, Major General Whitfield, reported to the War Office that in his opinion the forts and batteries in Singapore were incapable of withstanding the fire of modern naval guns, and that the existing fortifications should be rebuilt and new batteries constructed in order to provide an effective defence for the town and harbour.[8]

Two years later Sir William Jervois left the War Office to take up the post of Governor of the Straits Settlements Crown Colony. Perhaps unsurprisingly his appointment as governor appears to have changed his view on the state of the colony's defences. In the following year, 1876, he presented a report to the Colonial Office that contrasted radically with his earlier opinion. He dismissed the existing defences as weak and insignificant and Fort Canning as being only suitable as a defence work for the town after a redistribution of its existing armament. He also dismissed the batteries on Mount Faber and Mount Palmer as having no merit as defence works and, indeed, it would seem that the Mount Faber Battery was, in fact, in a ruinous condition at this date.

Jervois' plan was to build new forts and batteries capable of mounting the new, large muzzle-loading rifled guns now in service in the British Army. He proposed two new works on Blakang Mati for the defence of New Harbour, one on Mount Serapong and the other on Mount Siloso, defending the eastern and western approaches to the harbour respectively. There was also to be a new fort on the summit of Mount Palmer armed with four 11-inch 25-ton RML guns, and the battery on Mount Faber was to be rebuilt. The Mount Serapong fort was to be armed with ten 11-inch 25-ton RML guns, with six similar guns in the battery on Mount Siloso.

Once again there was a proposal for a battery at Tanjong Katong where Jervois proposed that a battery armed with five 11-inch guns should be built to defend the eastern approach to New Harbour. The overall cost of the Jervois plan was estimated at £130,000 which, he mischievously noted in a dig at the Royal Navy, was less than the cost of one ironclad turret warship.[9]

There was every likelihood that Jervois' report would have remained pigeon-holed in the Colonial Office had not the European political situation erupted as a result of Russia declaring war on Turkey in 1877. The Ottoman government's attempt to suppress nationalist revolts in the Balkans brought about the persecution of many of its Christian subjects and resulted in bringing Russia to their aid. The war was ended by the Treaty of San Stefano in 1878 which gave Russia unrestricted right of passage for its Black Sea Fleet through the Dardanelles and into the Mediterranean. The British Government refused to recognize the treaty and warned Russia that there would be war between the two countries if the offending clause was not withdrawn.

As we have seen in previous chapters this Russian 'scare' brought about an immediate review of the defences of the Royal Navy's coaling stations around the world, and Singapore, with trade estimated at £78 million passing through the port annually, was allocated ten 7-inch 7-ton RML guns and six 64-pdr RML guns. Eight of the 7-inch guns were destined for the two new batteries to be built on Blakang Mati, five to arm the battery on Mount Siloso and three for the battery on Mount Serapong. The remaining two guns were to be placed in the existing battery on Mount Palmer until the new battery on the summit was completed. The 64-pdr guns were to be distributed at the discretion of the military authorities on the island.[10]

The newly formed Colonial Defence Committee also authorized the construction of a self-defensible battery at Tanjong Katong and a battery for two 64-pdr RML guns at Teregeh Point on Pulau Brani. Mines were also to be laid to protect the harbour and the Royal Navy was requested to provide a warship and two 'flat-iron' gunboats of the *Comet* class, a request that the Admiralty felt it was unable to accede to.

Although six of the new guns and half the ammunition was dispatched in June 1878 on a sailing vessel, with the remainder to follow by steamer, it would be a matter of months before the guns arrived in Singapore. In the interim the War Office ordered that the seven serviceable 68-pdr SB guns in

64-pdr Mk III RML gun at Fort Palmer c.1880. (*Author's Collection*)

the existing batteries were to be distributed to the new batteries, and the guns removed from the South Battery at Fort Canning were to be replaced with those 8-inch SB shell guns from the main fort that were serviceable, so as to be able to meet any civil disturbance in the town.[11] In the event, the Local Defence Committee decided that only three of the 68-pdr SB guns were to be re-mounted in the Mount Palmer battery and the two 56-pdr SB guns already there would be left in place.

By August 1878 work was in progress to construct the new batteries on Mount Serapong and Mount Siloso on Blakang Mati, and by early 1879 the land for the self-defensible battery at Tanjong Katong and the new battery on Mount Palmer had been purchased. However, in the same year in London the Secretary of State for the Colonies, Lord Carnarvon, set up a commission to report on the defence arrangements for all the colonies. The Carnarvon Commission heard evidence from the governors and local defence committees of each colony, and also sent an officer, Colonel William Crossman RE, previously an Assistant Director of Fortifications and Works at the War Office and currently the officer in charge of submarine mining, to Singapore and Hong Kong to inspect and report on the defences of those two colonies.

By the time Colonel Crossman arrived in Singapore the construction of the new batteries had been completed and the batteries armed with 7-inch 6½-ton RML guns rather than the 7-ton guns originally specified. These and the 64-pdr guns were the only guns available at that time. A further change was a proposal from the War Office that heavier guns should be mounted in the Mount Siloso and Mount Palmer batteries; the suggested armament for those two sites was now three 10-inch 18-ton RML guns and two 64-pdr guns.[12] The second battery on Blakang Mati, known as Blakang Mati East, was to be armed with four 7-inch 6½-ton RML guns.

Crossman reviewed the defences and recommended three new batteries and a sea fort, together with some improvements to the existing batteries. The sea fort was to be similar to the recently completed Spitbank Fort in the Solent and was to be armed with five 10-inch 18-ton RML guns. This was a particularly expensive proposal which ultimately did not meet with favour in either the Colonial Office or the War Office.

The new batteries suggested by Colonel Crossman were: one on the southern shore of Blakang Mati 900 yards (830m) from Mount Serapong, a position originally suggested by Captain McCallum RE the Government Engineer; a battery at Pasir Panjang, near Berlayer Point opposite Mount Siloso; and a battery on the dock wall at Tanjong Pagar or, if this site was not approved, then the existing battery on Mount Palmer was to be remodelled.

All three batteries were to be armed with 10-inch RML guns. For the defence of Singapore Town Crossman recommended that a number of infantry redoubts should be built to defend the area between Mount Faber and Fort Canning and that Fort Canning should be rearmed with four 64-pdr RML guns and the smooth-bore armament retained.

The total cost of Colonel Crossman's review was estimated at approximately £148,000 if the battery at Tanjong Pagar was to be included. Reconstruction of the Tanjong Katong Battery to mount 10-inch RML guns and the plan for a sea fort added a further £144,000, so it is no wonder that both the War Office and the Colonial Office baulked at such a cost. Negotiations on the financial responsibility for Singapore's defences continued until 1885 when the Colonial Office finally accepted financial responsibility for the fortifications and the War Office similarly accepted responsibility for the submarine minefields.

The Russian occupation of the Central Asia oasis of Panjdeh in 1885 raised fears in Singapore of a possible attack by the Russian Pacific Fleet. Such fears arose because in 1882 the existing defences were stated to comprise only the earthwork batteries on Mount Siloso and at Blakang Mati East and two masonry and earthwork forts, Fort Palmer and Fort Tanjong Katong. The Carnarvon Commission had, in the same year, recommended that the armament of the colony should be ten 10-inch 18-ton guns, three 7-inch 6½-ton guns, seven 64-pdr guns and a number of 40-pdr 'guns of position', all rifled muzzle-loading guns. However, the Inspector General of Fortifications submitted his own proposal that the latest 9.2-inch breech-loading guns on hydro-pneumatic mountings should be substituted for the 10-inch RML guns.

Acting on a request from the Colonial Office, the War Office reviewed the existing defences of Singapore yet again and authorized the construction of a new battery on Blakang Mati using the site of an existing infantry redoubt on Mount Serapong. Improvements to the existing batteries were also authorized to enable them to mount more modern, larger guns. In addition, the War Office approved the dispatch of the following guns to the colony:

2 × 10-inch Mk I BL guns
7 × 9.2-inch Mk IV BL guns
8 × 7-inch 6½-ton RML guns
7 × 64-pdr Mk III RML guns[13]

These new breech-loading guns were, however, still under development at this time. Indeed, the 9.2-inch Mk I BL gun was not to be approved for service until 1881 and even then, proved not to be a successful weapon, being superseded by the Mark IV gun in 1889.

Despite the fact that the fears generated by the Panjdeh Incident had subsided, the citizens of Singapore were still very firmly of the view that the port's defences were inadequate. This view was strongly reinforced in January 1885 when a Russian squadron of four warships, three armoured cruisers and a sloop, arrived unexpectedly in Singapore in transit to join the Russian Pacific Fleet. The four ships between them mounted a total of fourteen 8-inch and twenty-nine 6-inch BL guns – a greater number of guns than were mounted in the Singapore defences, and all more modern.

As none of the heavy breech-loading guns were available at this time from either the Royal Gun Factory or from Armstrong's Elswick factory in Newcastle, the War Office had to look elsewhere for such guns to assuage the demands of Singapore. In May 1885 four Armstrong 8-inch BL guns were purchased in China from the Viceroy of Canton and two of these guns were eventually mounted in Fort Tanjong Katong and two in the new battery on Mount Serapong on Blakang Mati.[14] For various reasons, including delay in shipping the guns and modifying the batteries in which they were to be mounted, the guns were not installed until 1890.

An additional defensive measure authorized by the War Office was the provision of two submarine minefields for the defence of New Harbour, as previously recommended by Colonel Jervois. The minefields were sited to protect the two entrances to New Harbour and, in order to ensure that they provided an effective form of defence, a number of the new 6-pdr QF guns were provided to cover the minefields by fire and prevent an enemy force lifting or destroying the mines.

In 1887 the approved armament of the forts and batteries in Singapore comprised:

Fort Pasir Panjang	2 × 9.2-inch BL guns
	2 × 7-inch RML guns
Fort Siloso	1 × 9.2-inch BL gun
	4 × 7-inch RML guns
Fort Connaught (formerly Blakang Mati East)	2 × 9.2-inch BL guns
	3 × 7-inch RML guns
Mount Palmer	2 × 10-inch RML guns
Fort Tanjong Katong	2 × 8-inch BL guns
Fort Serapong	2 × 8-inch BL guns
Teregeh Point Battery	2 × 64-pdr RML guns
Minefield Defence	6 × 6-pdr QF guns

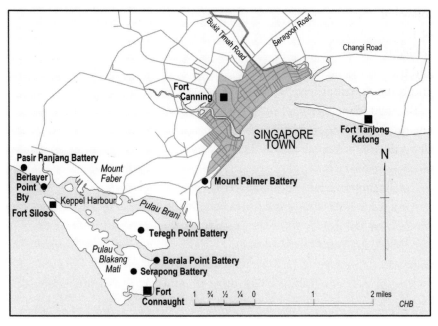

Map of the defences of Singapore 1890. (*Charles Blackwood*)

In the late 1880s, while work was in progress to rearm the defences of Singapore, an increasingly acrimonious argument developed between the Straits Settlement legislature and the Colonial Office in London over the financial contribution to be made by the colony towards the cost of its defence and the maintenance of the Imperial garrison. During the years of peace after the Crimean War the aim of the Treasury in London was to keep the War Office's share of the British budget as small as possible. The Army was to garrison the colonies while the Royal Navy was to be maintained as the country's principal arm of defence. As a result, all colonies were expected to make a contribution to the upkeep of the Imperial forces stationed there, and to the cost of the construction of such fortifications as were deemed essential.

In the 1860s the contribution to be made by Singapore had been set at £50,000 per annum, but in 1889 the principle on which a colony's contribution would be based was settled by the Chancellor of the Exchequer and the Secretary of State for the Colonies on the basis that the Royal Navy would provide the main defence while each colony was to be responsible for the fortifications. As a result, Singapore's contribution was raised in 1890 from £50,000 to £100,000 per annum. There was immediate uproar in Singapore at this huge rise in the Imperial Contribution and this brought about a reduction to £70,000 per annum in 1894, though the sum was raised to £80,000 in the following year, and to £120,000 in 1898. At this all the Unofficial members of the Legislative Council resigned in protest. The matter was never finally settled to the satisfaction of the colony's taxpayers as Singapore was booming and the colony was seen by the government in London to be rich and able to afford the contribution.

By 1890 it was quite clear that rifled muzzle-loading guns were obsolete and quite unable to cope with the more heavily armoured and faster warships that were now part of most foreign fleets. The War Office now acted to replace all the remaining RML guns in the fixed defences with the modern 6-inch, 4.7-inch, and 12-pdr quick-firing guns.

Two years later, in 1892, the two 10-inch BL guns for Fort Palmer were finally installed in the rebuilt fort and by the mid-1890s the heavier 9.2-inch Mk IV BL guns had been mounted in the modified Fort Pasir Panjang, Fort Siloso and the Blakang Mati East Battery, now renamed Fort Connaught. In addition, Fort Pasir Panjang received four more guns, becoming a six-gun battery with two 6-inch QF and two 6-pdr QF guns. Four years later, in 1896, approval was given for the four 7-inch RML guns at Fort Siloso to be removed and replaced with two 12-pdr QF and two 6-inch QF guns, the former mounted in 1899 and the latter the following year. Additional 12-pdr

6-inch QF gun at Fort Pasir, Panjang. This original gun is displayed in one of the Labrador Battery gun positions with a replica gun crew. (*Author*)

QF guns were provided in 1897 in a new battery for two guns at Silingsing Point on Pulau Brani. This battery was to reinforce the defence of the eastern entrance to New Harbour and counter any attempt by enemy torpedo boats to enter the harbour.

While these improvements in Singapore's defences were being approved and constructed, the fort at Tanjong Katong was declared redundant, partly on the grounds that it was too isolated to be defended, and also because of the sandy ground on which it was built meant that the rangefinders had to be re-calibrated after each salvo. The fort was eventually evacuated in 1901, having lately been used as a training camp for the Singapore Artillery Volunteers.

The Owen Committee and the First World War

In 1905 the Owen Committee estimated that the form of attack that Singapore was most likely to be subject to would be a raiding attack by a single armoured cruiser. The Owen Committee recommended that the latest mark of the 9.2-inch BL gun, the Mark X, on a *barbette* mounting should be sent to the colony This gun had a greater range and faster rate of fire when compared to the older Mark IV gun on a hydro-pneumatic mounting which was currently mounted in the fortifications.

Between 1905 and 1908 further reviews of Singapore's fixed defences resulted in approval for a new battery on the high ground above Silingsing Point on Pulau Brani for two 6-inch QF guns which had previously been mounted at Fort Connaught where they had been installed in place of the 7-inch RML guns. The 6-inch QF guns were to replace the two 12-pdr QF guns presently mounted at the nearby lower battery.

In 1908 a new battery was approved for Mount Imbeah on Blakang Mati to be armed with a modern 9.2-inch Mk X gun. The construction of this battery was part of the rearmament of the Singapore defences resulting from the Owen Committee's recommendations, with the modern gun replacing the old Mark IV gun mounted at Fort Siloso. At the same time Fort Pasir Panjang and Fort Palmer were disarmed, and the two 6-inch QF guns at Fort Siloso were moved to a new site adjacent to the fort to become the examination battery for the Western Examination Anchorage which lay to the west of Blakang Mati. Silingsing Battery was designated the examination battery for the Eastern Examination Anchorage and was operational in 1910/1911.

The Owen Committee recommendations for Singapore had been implemented by 1913 and the fixed defences had been reduced to six forts and batteries armed with modern guns. These were:

Fort Connaught	1 × 9.2-inch Mk X BL gun on Mk V (15°) mounting
Mount Imbeah Battery	1 × 9.2-inch Mk X BL gun on Mk V (15°) mounting
Mount Serapong Spur Battery	1 × 9.2-inch Mk X BL gun on Mk V (15°) mounting
Fort Serapong	2 × 9.2-inch Mk X BL guns on Mk V (15°) mountings
Fort Siloso	2 × 6-inch Mk II QF guns on Mk II pedestals
Silingsing Battery	2 × 6-inch Mk II QF guns on Mk II pedestals

For the general defence of the colony six 6-inch BL howitzers and twelve 15-pdr BLC field guns were provided and the old 9-pdr and 7-pdr RML guns withdrawn. The size of the garrison was increased with the addition of a second company of the Royal Garrison Artillery, while the Royal Engineers were made up to a full fortress company.

In 1914 the First World War broke out, but Singapore was to be little affected. The garrison of the colony comprised one British and one Indian infantry battalion and two companies of the Royal Garrison Artillery. Almost immediately after the outbreak of war the British battalion was ordered back

Mount Serapong Battery 9.2-inch Mk X BL gun on a Mk V *barbette* mounting. The photograph shows the gun crew at action stations c.1935. (*Courtesy of Sentosa Leisure Group*)

to Britain, together with a number of men of the garrison artillery, with four of the 6-inch howitzers and six of the 15-pdr BLC field guns from the garrison's moveable artillery.

The only occasion on which war came close to Singapore was when the German light cruiser SMS *Emden* raided Georgetown on Penang Island, sinking a Russian light cruiser and a French destroyer. However, the most serious event occurred in February 1915 when the Indian garrison battalion, the 5th Light Infantry, mutinied. The mutiny was subsequently quashed, but not without serious loss of life, twelve officers and forty-two Other Ranks of the garrison being killed as well as fifty-nine mutineers. The 5th Light Infantry was transferred to the Cameroons and replaced by the 4th Battalion Shropshire Light Infantry (TF) from Rangoon.

The Armistice in November 1918 and the cessation of fighting brought about a return to peacetime establishments and routine, and Singapore sank back to being the military backwater it had been before the outbreak of war.

Building the Naval Base and the Second World War

With the end of the First World War it was clear that Japan was now a rising military power in the Far East. Throughout the war Japan, although honouring the Anglo–Japanese Alliance and declaring war on Germany in 1914, had an ambivalent attitude to Germany. The Japanese Army had been modelled and trained by the German Army, and the army's sympathy was for the Germans, particularly in view of the fact that for some time Germany appeared to be the winning side. In November 1914 Japan occupied the German-administered enclave of Qingdao and, despite a specific assurance to China by Japan that the country had no designs on acquiring Chinese territory at the end of the war, Japan presented China with the infamous 'Twenty-one Demands' aimed at increasing Japan's influence in China. If accepted by China these demands would have given Japan control of the Chinese army, navy, police, and finance.

Although Japan attempted to keep the matter secret, details soon leaked out and British diplomatic pressure forced Japan to drop the Demands. This British diplomatic success in fact resulted in a reduction in British popularity in Japan and a loss of British influence with the Japanese Government.

The increase in the size of both the United States and Japanese navies during the war and the acute post-war financial crisis faced by Britain meant that it was no longer possible for the Royal Navy to maintain its pre-war 'two-power' standard, that is a navy equivalent in size to the next two largest world navies. It was clear that it was no longer possible for the Royal Navy to maintain fleets in home waters, the Mediterranean and the Far East, nor, indeed, was it believed necessary to do so. Rather the British fleet was to be held in European waters, with the ability to reinforce the Far East as and when required.

While such a policy was obviously attractive to the Royal Navy's political masters, it did not take into account that such a policy required a naval base with full facilities to maintain the fleet if sent to the Far East. The question was should such a base be built and, if so, where? Having accepted that a base was necessary four ports were considered, Colombo, Sydney, Hong Kong and Singapore. The Committee of Imperial Defence eventually settled on Singapore as the most central of the four to defend Burma, Malaya and Hong Kong. In June 1921 the British Government accepted the Committee of Imperial Defence's recommendation that Singapore should be the base for any main fleet which might be sent in the event of war in the Far East or the Pacific.

This decision was to be dramatically affected by the Washington Naval Treaty of the same year. This treaty was aimed at preventing another naval arms race akin to that before the late war. For Great Britain the conference had disastrous consequences, limiting both the tonnage and the construction of battleships and aircraft carriers and also the sizes of other warships. The treaty formally put an end to the Royal Navy's 'two-power' policy and also prohibited the construction of new military bases in the Pacific region, though this did not affect the construction of the new naval base at Singapore.

After considerable discussion and inspection of potential sites on Singapore Island, the Admiralty settled on the anchorage in the Johore Strait as the most suitable location for the new base. With deep water and sheltered from direct fire from an attacking fleet, together with land on which to build the facilities – though hindered by the Causeway between the island and the mainland – it appeared to offer the most advantages. The site selected was Sungei Sembawang where a huge graving dock and oil storage facilities were to be built. The Oversea Defence Committee proposed a total of fourteen guns for the defence of the island and the new base, four 15-inch BL guns, six 9.2-inch BL guns, two 6-inch BL guns, and four 4.7-inch QF guns. In addition, the four 6-inch QF guns already emplaced as the examination batteries and for the defence of New Harbour, now renamed Keppel Harbour, and the two similar guns defending the western side of the island were to be retained.

The 15-inch BL guns, the largest coast defence guns to be used by the British Army, were recommended on the grounds that, while in European waters the Admiralty believed there was no threat from an enemy battle fleet, in the Far East the threat came from the battleships of the Japanese fleet.

The original plans were for a base to support a fleet of seven battleships and ancillary vessels and this entailed the construction of a very large number of docks, wharves, graving docks and a fuel storage area. Added to this were all the other buildings required for such a base, offices, married quarters, storehouses, magazines and a hospital. Needless to say, in a time of great economic stringency the plan did not meet the Treasury's approval.

The Admiralty plan was therefore reduced to a more practical level based on a smaller fleet being sent to Singapore. In the new plan there was to be a single graving dock and a floating dock, with a reduced number of wharves. The cost of this scheme was estimated at £15 million without taking into account the fuel for the fleet or the cost of the fixed defences.

Despite the reduction in the size of the Admiralty's plan, work on building the base proceeded slowly. In 1919 a near-bankrupt British Government had instructed the armed forces to draft their future budget estimates on the assumption that Britain would not be engaged in a major war during the next ten years. This limited the amount of money available for the construction of the Singapore base, and the future of the base was placed in jeopardy in 1924 when the newly-elected Labour government ordered all work on the base to be stopped, with the Prime Minister, Ramsey Macdonald, describing it as 'a wild and wanton scheme'.[15] However, the Labour government was short-lived and fell in November of the same year, and the in-coming Conservative government quickly reversed the decision to stop work on the base.

The Wall Street financial crash of 1929 and the similar fall on the London Stock Exchange enabled the second Labour government to convene the London Naval Disarmament Conference at which the British delegation offered to reduce the number of cruisers in the Royal Navy and suspend work on the Singapore base. The result of the Conference was the London Naval Treaty signed by the representatives of Great Britain, France, Italy, Japan and the United States.

The impact of the Great Depression forced Japan to look towards China as a market for its manufactured goods, and the Japanese Army staged a number of 'incidents' in the early 1930s in order to provide a suitable excuse for the takeover of the commodity-rich Chinese province of Manchuria. The Japanese occupation of Manchuria was condemned by the League of Nations which demanded Japan's withdrawal from Manchuria and this, in turn, led to Japan withdrawing from the League of Nations in 1933.

Despite the decision to suspend work on the defences of the naval base, some work had continued and this accelerated in 1933 after the Japanese action in China and its formal renunciation of the Washington Naval Treaty in 1934.

This action clearly indicated to the British Government that Japan now posed a major threat to British interests in the Far East, therefore construction of the base at Singapore was now vitally important. Work now continued apace and the base was finally operational in 1939, but not fully completed until 1941 at a cost of £60 million.

With the decision taken to complete the base, the question now was how was it to be defended? In 1923 the Oversea Defence Committee had recommended four 15-inch BL guns to counter an attack by battleships, however the Admiralty argued that the recommended armament, even with the 15-inch guns, was inadequate to repel an attack by a fleet of six battleships, the total number of such ships in the Japanese fleet at that date, two of which were armed with 16-inch guns. The Admiralty view was that to meet such an attack the fixed defences of Singapore needed to be armed with six 15-inch guns, four mounted on the eastern side of the island and two in the west.

The following year, 1924 and six years after the formation of the Royal Air Force, the Air Ministry, seeking to maintain the Royal Air Force as an independent air arm, saw in the defence of Singapore a role that would strengthen its position and therefore objected to any heavy fixed armament being installed for the defence of the base. Instead the Air Ministry proposed that the main defence of the colony should be provided by aircraft. The Army and the Royal Navy were not prepared to accept that guns should be replaced by aircraft, particularly since a suitable anti-shipping strike aircraft for the role was still under development.

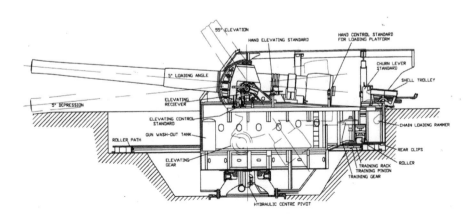

Section drawing of a 15-inch Mk I BL gun as mounted in Johore and Buona Vista Batteries. (*Author's Collection*)

The 'Guns versus Planes' debate raged in Whitehall for the next two years, but it was the fact that the Air Ministry would not agree to aircraft being permanently stationed in Singapore that swung the decision to install heavy guns. The compromise accepted was that three 15-inch BL guns were approved, two to be sited on the east coast near Changi village, with the third on Blakang Mati. However, before any more large-calibre guns were authorized there was to be a re-examination of the whole matter of the substitution of aircraft for the balance of the 15-inch guns in the light of aircraft development during the intervening period.[16]

In October 1925 the Singapore sub-committee of the Committee of Imperial Defence agreed proposals for the medium, light and anti-aircraft defences, but instructed the Air Staff to produce their scheme for aircraft to replace the heavy armament in greater detail. Only minor changes to the original plan were accepted with the substitution of two 6-inch Mk VII BL guns for the two 4.7-inch QF guns at Changi Point, and eight Twin 6-pdr QF equipments in place of eighteen 2-pdr Pom-pom guns as the anti-coastal motor boat armament.

By 1933 the Army General Staff being firmly of the view that any threat to Singapore would be from the south, the approved armament was now:

3 × 15-inch BL guns
6 × 9.2-inch Mk X BL guns on 35° mountings in two three-gun batteries
6 × 6-inch BL guns on 15° mountings in three two-gun batteries
2 × 6-inch BL guns on 45° mountings in one two-gun battery
24 × 3-inch AA guns
10 × Defence Electric Lights

The 35° mountings of the guns of the two three-gun 9.2-inch BL batteries would give the guns a maximum range of 29,000 yards (26,770m). One of the two batteries would be a new one to be built on Pulau Tekong Besar to defend the eastern entrance to the Strait of Johore, with the other three guns, also on Mark VII (35°) mountings, replacing the older gun in a rebuilt Fort Connaught.

As was the case with other defended ports, Singapore was subject to a number of inspections and reports. In 1927 the War Office sent a commission headed by Lieutenant General Sir Webb Gillman, the Director Royal Artillery, to inspect the defences and make recommendations for the number and location of the fixed defence batteries. The Gillman Commission recommended an increase in the number of 15-inch guns from three to four with two mounted near Changi and two on Blakang Mati. In addition, three 6-inch gun batteries were recommended for the eastern entrance on Pulau Tekong Besar, Pulau Tekong Kechil and Pulau Ubin, all undeveloped islands. An additional 6-inch gun battery that had been proposed to defend Calder Passage, a narrow passage between Pulau Tekong Besar and the Johore mainland, was not recommended.

The decision having been taken to divide the installation of the 15-inch guns into two phases, with three guns to be manufactured in Phase I, it was decided not to mount a single gun on Blakang Mati as it had become clear that the position selected would not allow the gun to cover an area near the western entrance and the gun would be in too prominent a position. It was decided that the third gun should be installed in a new position at Buona Vista on the main island west of Singapore Town.

General Gillman was followed eight years later, in 1935, by Major General F.W. Barron, Inspector of Fixed Defences at the War Office, who was instructed to report on whether the siting of Singapore's fixed defences was effective in view of their role. In his report General Barron rejected the siting of the single gun at Buona Vista, believing that a single-gun battery was of little value and, instead, proposed that the gun should be mounted at the Changi site, making that a three-gun battery.

General Barron accepted the siting of the existing batteries but he, together with the War Office, had concerns regarding the defences of Keppel Harbour where the floating dock was anchored and major fuel storage facilities were sited on the harbour shore. Because of this he recommended three more 6-inch close defence batteries, each of two guns, one in the old Fort Pasir Panjang, another on Mount Serapong and the third at Beting Kusah south east of Changi village.

The GOC Malaya, Major General Ernest Lewin, disagreed with General Barron's proposal to move the Buona Vista gun to Changi, recommending instead that an additional gun should be added to the Buona Vista battery. Since only three 15-inch guns had been approved there was no money available in the War Office budget for the additional gun. However, the problem was solved by a gift of £500,000 from the Sultan of Johore to celebrate King George V's Silver Jubilee. The Committee of Imperial Defence decided that £400,000 should be allocated to completing the two 15-inch batteries with a total of five guns, two at Buona Vista Battery and three at the battery at Changi now named Johore Battery in honour of the Sultan.

15-inch Mk I BL gun at Johore Battery 1939. (*Author's Collection*)

To provide the fire control for the 15-inch guns the largest rangefinder in the world, the Barr & Stroud 100-foot (30m) rangefinder, was transferred from its experimental site at Portsmouth to Singapore. This rangefinder was accurate to within 17 yards (15.6m) at 31,000 yards (28,615m).

By 1936 the fixed defences of Singapore, completed or under construction, were placed in two Fire Commands:

Faber (West) Fire Command

Buona Vista Battery	2 × 15-inch Mk I BL guns on Mk II (45°) mountings
Fort Connaught	3 × 9.2-inch Mk X BL guns on Mk VII (35°) mountings
Labrador Battery	2 × 6-inch Mk VII BL guns on Central Pivot Mk II (15°) mountings
Silingsing Battery	2 × 6-inch Mk VII BL guns on Central Pivot Mk II (15°) mountings
Fort Siloso	2 × 6-inch Mk VII BL guns on Central Pivot Mk II (15°) mountings
Pasir Laba Battery	2 × 6-inch Mk VII BL guns on Central Pivot Mk II (15°) mountings
Serapong Spur Battery	2 × 6-inch Mk VII BL guns on Central Pivot Mk II (15°) mountings

Changi (East) Fire Command

Johore Battery	2 × 15-inch Mk I BL guns on Mk II (45°) mountings
	1 × 15-inch Mk I BL gun on Mk I (55°) mounting
Tekong Besar Battery	3 × 9.2-inch Mk X BL guns on Mk VII (35°) mountings
Changi Battery	2 × 6-inch Mk VII BL guns on Central Pivot Mk II (15°) mountings
Beting Kusah Battery	2 × 6-inch Mk VII BL guns on Central Pivot Mk II (15°) mountings
Pengerang Battery	2 × 6-inch Mk VII BL guns on Central Pivot Mk II (15°) mountings
Sphinx Battery (Pulau Tekong)	2 × 6-inch Mk XXIV BL guns on Mk V (45°) mountings[17]

For defence against motor torpedo boats eighteen Twin 6-pdr QF equipments were approved, seven for the outer defences of the main harbour; four to defend the inner harbour; and seven for the defence of Keppel Harbour. Although the gun positions and director towers were completed by 1940 none of the equipments had been delivered. By early 1942 only ten of the eighteen equipments had been installed, with older 12-pdr QF guns mounted in the newly-constructed Twin 6-pdr equipment positions at Siloso Point and Ladang.

The anti-aircraft defence of the island had gradually improved and by 1937 the approved number of guns had risen from twenty-four to seventy-two.

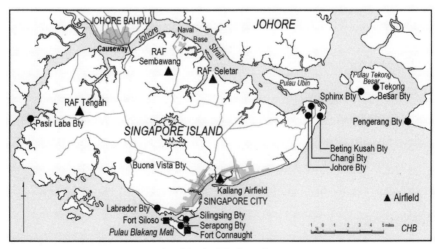

Map of Singapore Defences 1939. (*Charles Blackwood*)

However, this number was never achieved by the time war came to Singapore since Britain and other theatres of war had priority for the production of anti-aircraft and other guns. In February 1941 the anti-aircraft defences of Singapore comprised two 4.5-inch HAA guns on static mountings and forty-one 3.7-inch HAA guns, of which fourteen were trailer-mounted. There were also twenty old 3-inch AA guns and sixteen 40-mm LAA guns for point defence.

War Against Japan and the Battle for Singapore

In 1941 the fixed defences of Singapore were manned by men of the Royal Artillery and the Hong Kong and Singapore Royal Artillery, the latter unit comprising Indian personnel. The artillery units manning the fixed defences were 7th Coast Regiment RA manning the guns of Faber Fire Command, and 9th Coast Regiment RA manning the guns of Changi Fire Command. Both units had batteries of the Hong Kong and Singapore RA under their command. The beach defences, the pillboxes and the 18-pdr QF guns of the moveable artillery were the responsibility of 16th Defence Regiment RA.

The two Fire Commands were manned by personnel of the following batteries:

<u>7th Coast Regiment RA</u>

11 Coast Battery RA	Fort Connaught
	Serapong Battery
	Berhala Reping AMTB Battery
	Pulau Hantu AMTB Battery
31 Coast Battery RA	Buona Vista Battery
	Batu Berlayer AMTB Battery
5 Battery HKSRA	Silingsing Battery
	Oso (Siloso Point) AMTB Battery
7 Battery HKSRA	Labrador Battery
	Pasir Laba Battery

<u>11th Coast Regiment RA</u>

7 Coast Battery RA	Johore Battery
	Beting Kusah Battery
22 Coast Battery	Tekong Besar Battery
	Sphinx Battery

	Ladang AMTB Battery
	Pulau Sehajat AMTB Battery
32 Coast Battery	Pengerang Battery
	Changi Battery
	Calder Harbour AMTB Battery
	Tanjong Johore AMTB Battery

The whole concept of the siting of the fixed defences in 1942 was to defend the island and the naval base from attack by sea, because in the 1930s an attack from the north was considered to be unlikely due to the nature of the country which was believed to be impassable to major troop movements.

When originally mounted the majority of the guns had a reasonable traverse though, in a number of cases, this traverse was limited owing to the construction of concrete overhead cover designed to protect the guns from air attack. In the case of Johore Battery only the two guns on Mark II mountings were capable of firing on Johore Bahru and the Causeway linking the mainland with Singapore Island, as the gun on the Mark I mounting had a limited traverse of 180°. In addition, the effectiveness of the guns of Buona Vista Battery was limited since they were unable to fully traverse as they were fitted with gun stops to prevent the gun from interfering with electric and hydraulic cabling. To remove the gun stops meant disconnecting the cables and thus affecting the power traverse and hydraulic loading of the guns.

To add to these restrictions, since the role of the 15-inch guns was considered to be anti-shipping, the ammunition provided was entirely armour-piercing. Belatedly the Army authorities on the island realized the requirement for high-explosive and shrapnel shells, but these had still not been delivered when the island fell to the Japanese. Even the 9.2-inch and 6-inch guns were restricted in the amount of high–explosive ammunition with a total of twenty-five rounds for each 9.2-inch gun and fifty rounds for each 6-inch gun.

War came to Malaya and Singapore on 8 December 1941 when Japanese troops landed in southern Siam (Thailand) on the border with the Federated Malay States. The Japanese quickly overcame the British forces defending the Jitra Line and pushed on down the west coast, while further landings at Kota Bahru on the east coast forced the British to evacuate the airfields at Alor Star and Butterworth, the latter opposite Penang Island. The Japanese advance moved inexorably and speedily towards Singapore driving the British before them. Spearheaded by tanks, the Japanese thrust along the few roads and, except for a brief stand on the Johore Line at Gemas, the British were unable to hold back the invaders.

Threatened by a further Japanese advance along the west coast road, the British and Australian forces were forced to fall back on 'Fortress Singapore'. 'Fortress' was undoubtedly a misnomer as far as Singapore was concerned. Always afraid of a possible attack by the powerful Japanese battle fleet, the British planners had assumed that an attack would come on the southern side of the island, so the possible landing places for a Japanese invading force were defended by barbed wire, searchlights, pillboxes and mobile artillery.

In contrast the northern shore was virtually undefended despite requests from Brigadier Ivan Simpson, sent to Singapore in June 1941 to take up the post of Chief Engineer Malaya Command. He had received verbal instructions *'to install the most modern types of defences throughout Malaya, including Singapore Island, and to bring all existing defences up-to-date, specifically against possible beach landings and against tank and air attack'.*[18] Lieutenant General Percival was not, however, receptive to Brigadier Simpson's suggestions believing that *'Defences are bad for morale – for both troops and civilians'.*[19] This was the situation until 23 January 1942 when General Percival gave orders for defences to be prepared on the north shore, sadly much too late.

The loss of the airfields and the sinking of the Royal Navy ships HMS *Prince of Wales* and HMS *Repulse* gave the Japanese complete control of the air and sea, and ultimately this was to seal the fate of the island. This was not immediately clear to General Wavell, the C-in-C American-British-Dutch Australian Command (ABDACOM), who expected Singapore to hold out for two months, but in the event, the Japanese captured the island in two weeks.

General Percival's plan for the defence of Singapore was based on his view that he had to deploy his forces to prevent an enemy landing anywhere on the island, and so it was necessary to defend all 72 miles (120 kms) of coastline. He divided the island into three defensive areas: Northern, Western and Southern. The Northern area included the coast east of the Causeway to Changi Point, including the island of Pulau Ubin. The Western area comprised the coast westwards from the Causeway to the Jurong River in the south-west, and the Southern area comprised the city of Singapore, Pulau Tekong Besar and the southern islands.

General Wavell believed that the Japanese assault on the island would come from the north-west, but Percival, lacking air reconnaissance and other intelligence, was deceived by Japanese troop movements on Pulau Ubin designed as a feint attack and was of the opinion that the assault would come from the north-east. For that reason, he deployed III Indian Corps with five infantry brigades to defend the area east of the Causeway, with his two Australian brigades and another Indian brigade holding the area west of the

Causeway. This mis-appreciation of the Japanese commander's intentions was further compounded by the allocation of the bulk of the field artillery in support of III Indian Corps. The Southern area was garrisoned by two Malay infantry brigades, elements of the Straits Settlements Volunteers and troops of the fixed defences, while two more Indian infantry brigades were retained centrally as the Command reserve.

When war came to Singapore on 6 January 1942 it was the fixed defences that took the first blow when Blakang Mati was heavily bombed, causing damage to Fort Connaught and Serapong Spur Battery. This was a sign of things to come as most of the guns of the fixed defences were sited outside the protection of the island's anti-aircraft defences and so were to suffer from enemy air attack. The only batteries to be provided, initially, with any form of active air defence were Buona Vista and Johore Batteries which were defended from low-level attack by a small number of 40-mm LAA guns.

Between 4 and 8 February the main action was a heavy Japanese bombardment, together with limited British counter-bombardment fire in which the guns of Johore, Tekong Besar and Sphinx Batteries took part.

On the night of 8/9 February the 5th and 18th Japanese Divisions crossed the Johore Strait west of the Causeway as General Wavell had predicted, with diversionary troop movements east of the Causeway which continued to distract General Percival from realizing the direction of the main attack. The defenders east of the Causeway were the 22 and 27 Australian Infantry Brigades that held an extended front intersected with mangrove swamps and deep creeks, which made the area very difficult to defend. The Australians were supported by one of the 6-inch guns of Pasir Laba Battery. Only No 1 gun could engage the Japanese crossing the Strait as prior to the enemy attack part of the concrete shelter built to defend the gun from air attack had been removed. This gun fired some forty rounds but the No 2 gun, still enclosed in its concrete shelter which limited its traverse, was unable to engage. With daylight on 9 February the battery was attacked by Japanese aircraft and both guns put out of action.

During the early hours of 9 February Johore, Tekong Besar and Sphinx Batteries continued to engage the Japanese forces assembled east of the Causeway. Unfortunately, most of the larger calibre ammunition was armour-piercing so, though having a certain psychological effect, actually caused little damage.

On 10 February the Japanese 5th and 18th Divisions advanced on an axis towards Pasir Panjang and Bukit Timah where the British had established a makeshift defence line. On the night of 10/11 February the Japanese smashed

Sphinx Battery in 1937, showing one of the 6-inch Mk XXIV on a Central Pivot Mk V mounting with splinter shield. (*Author's Collection*)

through the line threatening the guns of Buona Vista Battery. The battery having been prepared for demolition the previous day, the guns were destroyed by their gun crews and the battery abandoned in the early hours of 11 February.

On the afternoon of the same day the Imperial Guards Division crossed the Strait just east of the Causeway and landed unopposed as 27 Australian Brigade was in the process of withdrawing from its positions. The Japanese divisions now aimed to split the defending forces and capture the high ground overlooking the city and, equally important, the reservoirs providing the island's water supply.

In the south-west corner of the island 44 Indian Infantry Brigade had been holding defensive positions and was now ordered to make a stand on the so-called 'Kranji-Jurong Line' in conjunction with the remnants of 22 Australian Brigade. This line was really only a line on the map and any chance of holding it disappeared when the commander of 22 Brigade misinterpreted General Percival's preparatory warning order regarding the holding of a 'last ditch' perimeter around the city and withdrew prematurely to the proposed perimeter, leaving a section of the Kranji-Jurong Line undefended.

Throughout 11 February the guns of the fixed defences capable of bearing on the enemy continued to engage. The guns of Changi Fire Command continued to fire on targets on the mainland, while the guns of Faber Fire Command, less Buona Vista Battery, concentrated on the Jurong River position and the village of Ulu Pandan.

The battle reached its climax on 12 February when last-ditch counter-attacks were made, unsuccessfully, against Japanese forces attacking Bukit Timah. The guns of the fixed defences assisted by engaging Japanese units forming up on Tengah airfield and Bukit Timah where the Japanese attack was spearheaded by two battalions of tanks. Johore Battery fired on targets in the Bukit Timah area before the guns were destroyed to avoid them falling into Japanese hands and Tekong Besar and Sphinx Batteries continued to shell targets on the mainland.

The occupation of the final 'last ditch' perimeter was a clear indication that Singapore was about to fall. The establishment of this final defence line involved the loss of the main store dumps, including stocks of ammunition and rations, together with the abandonment of the fixed defences and the loss of the – albeit limited – fire support provided by these guns.

Throughout 13 February the guns of Fort Connaught and Fort Siloso on Blakang Mati continued to shell targets on the west coast road, while Labrador Battery, the only battery on the western side of the main island supported the 1st Malay Regiment (1 Malay) in their valiant attempt to hold Pasir Panjang ridge. Holding hastily constructed positions and some pillboxes on the coast road, 1 Malay was the only major unit between the Japanese and the southern flank of the new perimeter.

At 1400 hours Japanese counter-battery fire seriously damaged one gun, the observation post and the magazine of Labrador Battery, and 1 Malay were unable to hold the determined Japanese attack. As a result, orders were given for the guns of Labrador Battery to be destroyed and the battery abandoned. The battery personnel withdrew to Faber Fire Command and, as a consequence of their withdrawal, the AMTB batteries at Berlayer Point and Pulau Hantau were also destroyed by their gun crews and abandoned.

On the eastern side of the island the 6-inch guns of Sphinx Battery remained in action, supported by the 12-pdr QF gun of Ladang AMTB Battery throughout 13 February, but the following day saw the end for the remaining guns of the fixed defences. A false report of Japanese forces landing on Blakang Mati resulted in the guns of Fort Siloso being destroyed by their crews at 0600 hours, followed soon after by the guns of Fort Connaught. The destruction of the guns of Serapong Spur followed at midday. Twelve hours later all the operational guns of the remaining batteries had been destroyed.

With the island's water supply now in the hands of the Japanese, a shortage of ammunition and heavy damage to the city including many civilian casualties, General Percival requested permission from General Wavell to surrender to General Yamashita, the commander of the Japanese forces. The surrender occurred at 1715 hours on 15 February 1942.

The Post-War Defences

For the remainder of the war the Japanese made little use of the captured guns other than to remove them for scrap. They found only four guns in working order or in a condition that permitted them to be repaired. These were one of the 15-inch guns at Buona Vista Battery, two 6-inch guns, one from Beting Kusah Battery and one from Labrador Battery, and the 12-pdr gun from Oso AMTB Battery at Siloso Point. Attempts had been made to destroy the gun at Buona Vista but these failed and the gun was still operable, though the mechanical loading system had been destroyed.

Although the Japanese refurbished these four guns, little use was made of them as it appears they were never fired because there were no gun crews with the knowledge of how to do so. However, this would seem to be an unlikely explanation as the 6-inch guns and the 12-pdr QF gun were of designs familiar to the Japanese.

When the British recaptured Singapore after the surrender of Japan in August 1945 Colonel F.W. Rice was sent from the War Office to Singapore and Hong Kong to examine what remained of the defences, evaluate their potential future use, and make recommendations on the future defence requirements of the two colonies.

12-pdr QF gun at Oso Battery on Siloso Point. In 1941 a 12-pdr QF gun was mounted in the empty Twin 6-pdr QF gun position. The gun illustrated is a modern replica. (*Author*)

Having inspected the remains of the fixed defences at Singapore he confirmed that '*every gun of the original twenty-four batteries in Singapore is out of action for reasons varying from complete disintegration, as in the case of Tekong Besar No 2 gun, to the deficiency of minor parts, as in the case of No 2 gun at Buona Vista Battery.*'[20] Colonel Rice did recommend that the heavy guns salvaged by the Japanese as being serviceable should be repaired and placed in a state of care and maintenance. All the other batteries were declared obsolete and were not to be repaired.

Although Colonel Rice made recommendations regarding the future defences of Singapore nothing was done immediately other than the installation of the two remaining serviceable 6-inch guns in Fort Siloso, but without rangefinders, transmitting and receiving dials, gun telescopes, or telephones. Nor was any fire control equipment provided, so to all intents and purposes the guns were useless for anything but simple gun drills.

In December 1947 the Chiefs of Staff Committee considered the defences of Singapore and the Admiralty representative made it clear that to protect the naval base it would be necessary to have defences at both entrances to the Strait of Johore. The only immediate result of this meeting was the transfer of a Twin 6-pdr QF equipment from Colombo to Singapore where it was mounted in the old Oso Battery position at Siloso Point.

In 1950 the two guns that had been recovered at the end of the war and mounted at Fort Siloso were replaced with two modern 6-inch Mk XXIV BL guns, while a third gun was retained in the fort in reserve and for training. In the same year two more Twin 6-pdr QF equipments arrived from Haifa, one being mounted at Batu Berlayer Point opposite Fort Siloso and the other at Berhala Reping on Blakang Mati.

However, with the development of guided missiles the days of coast artillery were coming to an end. Although radar was now the main means of range finding, by 1951 the Chiefs of Staff Committee decreed that the role of coast artillery should be limited to support of the Examination Service, what was termed Anti-Small Battle Unit defence, and closure of straits.[21] This was the beginning of the demise of coast defence generally and on 17 February the Minister of Defence, Sir Walter Monckton, announced in the House of Commons that, in the light of modern weapon development, there was no longer any justification in maintaining coastal artillery and it was to be disbanded. On 31 December 1956 coast artillery in Britain and overseas ceased to exist.

Chapter Nine

Hong Kong

The Early Years

'Fragrant Harbour' and 'Barren Rock' are two descriptions that have been used to refer to Hong Kong, a rocky island lying off the south coast of China at the entrance to the Pearl River delta, and which strategically controls the sea approach to Canton (Guangzhou).

Hong Kong island has an area of approximately 30 square miles (79 sq kms) and has two ranges of high hills divided by a narrow pass known as the Wong Nai Chung Gap. The western range includes Mount Davis, 874 feet (269m) high and five other peaks all over 1,300 feet (400m) high. The eastern range includes Jardine's Lookout at 1,400 feet (433m) high overlooking Wong Nai Chung Gap, and seven other peaks over 1,000 feet (312m) high. Between the island and the Chinese mainland there is one of the best natural harbours in the Far East.

Hong Kong island was acquired by the British under the Treaty of Nanking at the end of the First Anglo-Chinese (Opium) War in 1842, and an additional 2½ square miles (7 sq kms) of the Chinese mainland, including the settlement of Kowloon, was added in 1860 under the Convention of Peking on the conclusion of the Third Anglo-Chinese (Opium) War. The north shore of Hong Kong island and the mainland shoreline at Kowloon form a magnificent natural harbour easily secured at its western and eastern ends.

Hong Kong was not the important commercial port that Prime Minister Palmerston had expected would be ceded to Great Britain as a result of the successful war of 1839–1842, *'a barren island with hardly a house on it'* was his description of the new addition to the growing British Empire. Although the Honourable East India Company (HEIC) used Macao as a base for its China trade, the magnificent harbour at Hong Kong had its use as an alternative harbour to retire to when there was trouble with the Chinese authorities. The Royal Navy also appreciated the value of Hong Kong as a base for the ships of the China Squadron.

After 1842 the small settlement quickly developed into the town of Victoria but, initially, no attempt was made to fortify the town as the British

Fort Victoria, Kowloon, 1843. This was an old Chinese fort reconstructed by the British when the Kowloon Peninsula was occupied, but rebuilt by the British in the Chinese style. (*Author's Collection*)

Government's view was that Hong Kong was to be held 'in pawn' until the government's objectives in China were achieved by formal treaty. However, in his book *The Account of the Chinese War*, published in 1844, Lieutenant John Ochterlony of the Madras Engineers mentioned a battery on Kellett's Island manned by a detachment of Madras Artillery. Although probably a temporary battery when first established, this battery would appear to be the first defensive structure to be built in Hong Kong.

By 1847 the defences had been considerably strengthened by the construction of three further batteries: Royal Battery on the shoreline just east of the present cathedral in the centre of the town; Wellington Battery, also on the shoreline and east of Royal Battery; and Murray Battery, for six smooth-bore guns and three mortars, set back on higher ground west of the cathedral and close to the present Government House.

In 1853 war clouds were forming on the horizon as Russia and the Ottoman Empire clashed over the rights of Christian minorities in the Holy Land. Britain and France, fearing the expansion of Russian influence in the Mediterranean supported the Ottomans and declared war on Russia in 1854. Although the bulk of the fighting during the war was largely in the Crimea

Murray Battery, Hong Kong Island. The photograph appears to have been taken in the early 1900s when the approved armament of the battery was a single 64-pdr RML gun seen in the far left of the photograph. The second gun appears to be a 40-pdr RBL gun on a travelling carriage. (*Courtesy of the Hong Kong Museum*)

and the Baltic, the British authorities were conscious of a potential threat towards Hong Kong from the Russian Siberian flotilla.

In 1854 the defences of Hong Kong comprised the four original batteries and a new battery at West Point. On Kellett's Island the battery was armed with three 32-pdr SB guns and guarded the eastern entrance to the harbour, while Wellington Battery mounted nine 32-pdrs, some of which covered the eastern entrance to the harbour with the others covering the anchorage. Murray Battery, standing back from the shoreline was armed with six 24-pdr SB guns covering the town and anchorage, and three 10-inch mortars. Royal Battery, with nine 32-pdr SB guns, covered the anchorage, but the western approach to the harbour remained undefended.

In order to defend the western entrance a house and garden at West Point, Mr Edgar's bungalow, described as having 'a commanding position' was leased for the construction of a temporary battery for ten 32-pdr SB guns, with an emplacement *a fleur d'eau* for two 8-inch iron howitzers on travelling carriages. Additional support for the batteries was provided by arming with ten 32-pdr SB guns the old 74-gun third rate ship-of-the-line HMS *Hercules* which had been disarmed and moored in the harbour to act as a hospital ship.

It is likely that these batteries were temporary constructions since, as late as 1862, batteries built on the newly occupied Kowloon side were described as being *'revetted with commissariat casks, embrasures with Jones Patent Gabions'* and on the Hong Kong side *'Jones Patent Gabions were used throughout'*.[1]

In the event no attempt was made by the Russians to threaten Hong Kong and the Royal Artillery contribution to the garrison was maintained at a single company assisted by a company of Gun Lascars, recruited in 1849 from the Honourable East India Company. By using Indian personnel, the Board of Ordnance was able to reduce the number of British gunners thereby making a considerable financial saving.

The outbreak of the Second Anglo-Chinese War in 1857 once again brought the matter of the defences of Hong Kong to the fore. The war was triggered by the boarding of a British-flagged ship, the *Arrow*, by the Chinese authorities. The Chinese refused to apologise and return the arrested crew members, so a joint naval and military expedition was dispatched to Canton and in 1858 the Treaty of Tianjin was signed by China with Britain, France, Russia and the United States. The treaty gave the right to foreign diplomatic missions to reside in Peking, but a joint British, French and American diplomatic mission attempting to implement the treaty was repulsed when the Taku forts at the mouth of the Peiho River opened fire on the allied ships.

This incident brought about the Third Anglo-Chinese War, a brief campaign that forced the Chinese to sign the Convention of Peking with each of the allied nations. Amongst other provisions, the Convention ceded Kowloon, opposite Hong Kong, to Britain, thus providing the extra protection for the harbour that the British commander of the garrison had deemed to be essential.

On annexation the only defensive structures on the Kowloon peninsula were a Chinese battery for eight guns at Tsim Sha Tsui and a fort at the tip of the peninsula. Initially the fort was occupied by the British and named Fort Victoria, but subsequently both the fort and the battery were demolished and by 1865 two batteries, East and West Batteries had been built in their place.

In 1860 the guns of the batteries were still the old 32-pdr SB guns that would have been familiar to Nelson at Trafalgar fifty-five years previously. However, in 1862 six of the new Armstrong 110-pdr RBL guns were ordered to be sent to Hong Kong to reinforce the defences. It would appear that a scheme for the general permanent defence of the colony was under consideration at that time, so the dispatch of the guns was accompanied by the instruction that no undue expense in installing these guns was to be incurred.[2]

Two of the new guns were to be installed on a spur of the hill above Belcher's Bay to command the channel between Green Island and Hong Kong Island, and to act in concert with two other guns which were to be placed on the 'commanding point' on Stonecutters Island to provide a cross fire to protect the western entrance to the harbour. The remaining two Armstrong guns were to be placed on the commanding feature on the Kowloon peninsula to watch Lyemun Pass, to defend the eastern entrance. However, by June 1862 the guns had not arrived although the ammunition had been delivered.[3]

The review of the Hong Kong defences in 1864 clearly indicated that the new guns had still not arrived and that the only existing defences at that date were Wellington and Murray Batteries in the town of Victoria itself. The defence review did, however, bring to a conclusion a dispute between the military and civil authorities over the allocation of land for defence purposes. In 1857 the Governor, Sir John Bowring, had been adamantly against the construction of gun batteries on what could be considered good commercial land. In a letter from a civil servant in Hong Kong to Herman Merivale, the Permanent Under-Secretary for the Colonies, it was stated that:

'Sir John Bowring is desirous that a definite understanding should be arrived at by the superior authorities whether Hong Kong is to be defended in case of attack by Men-of-War or by Land Fortifications; he considers the views advanced by the Commanding Royal Engineer with reference to the reservation of sites for batteries opposed to sound Colonial views and permanent interests, is of the opinion that such batteries are utterly valueless against a serious attack from civilized forces, and attributes the anxiety of the Commanding Royal Engineer on the subject to his unwillingness to remain idle while awaiting the more active service for which he was originally destined'.[4]

Despite, or perhaps because of, Sir John's disparaging remarks concerning the attitude of the Commanding Royal Engineer, the Secretary of State for War, Lord Panmure, disagreed with the Governor and a number of sites for batteries were allocated for the defence of the island. A total of twelve sites were selected, including the existing Wellington and Murray Batteries.

The sites selected were West Point, where there had been a temporary battery, and Belcher's Point to command the western approach to the harbour; Lyemun Pass and North Point to command the eastern approach; and Wellington and Murray Batteries and Kellett Island, where there had been an old battery, to prevent hostile ships from occupying the anchorage or cutting out ships. On the Kowloon side sites were selected opposite the island on the south-east point of the Kowloon peninsula, and opposite North Point to support the island batteries. Two sites were also selected on Stonecutters Island, one on the south-west corner of the island and the other on the north-east corner. A further site on the south-east corner was earmarked for military use should the GOC require it.

Hong Kong Harbour in 1875, with the old Royal Navy receiving ship HMS *Princess Charlotte* in the right of the picture, and her replacement HMS *Victor Emmanuel* to the left. (*Derek Bird*)

Despite the fact that Hong Kong continued to grow in commercial importance and had become the base for the Royal Navy's China Squadron little was done to fortify the island. The six Armstrong rifled guns eventually arrived only to be placed in store and the old smooth-bore guns and mortars of Wellington and Murray Batteries remained the sole defence of the colony.

The Russian Threat 1870-1905

As we have seen Anglo-Russian rivalry in Central Asia and Afghanistan resulted in a number of war scares in the 1870s and 1880s. The first such scare occurred in 1877 after the conclusion of the Balkan crisis and resulted in the signing of the Treaty of San Stefano in 1878. The treaty gave Russia unrestricted right of passage for its Black Sea Fleet through the Bosphorus into the Mediterranean. The British Government, however, did not recognize the treaty and the Mediterranean Fleet was used to threaten Russia.

The crisis threw into relief the matter of the defence of Britain's overseas possessions, and in April 1878 the newly formed Colonial Defence Committee, under the chairmanship of a retired First Sea Lord, Admiral of the Fleet Sir Alexander Milne, produced a report on the temporary defences of the coaling stations at the Cape of Good Hope, Mauritius, Ceylon, Singapore and Hong Kong.[5] The committee noted that the only guns immediately available for the defence of the coaling stations were sixty-one 7-inch 6½-ton RML guns.

Despite the Defence Committee in 1877 describing Hong Kong as second in importance in the list of coaling stations, the Hong Kong section of the report recommended the dispatch of only seven of these guns to the colony to be added to the six Armstrong 110-pdr RBL guns already there but not installed. These guns, together with some old 32-pdr SB guns were to be mounted in the following positions:

Green Island	2 × 7-inch 6½-ton RML guns
	1 × 32-pdr SB gun
Stonecutters Island West	2 × 7-inch 6½-ton RML guns
	2 × 32-pdr SB guns
Stonecutters Island East	2 × 32-pdr SB guns
North Point	3 × Armstrong 110-pdr RBL guns
Kowloon Dock	3 × 7-inch 6½-ton RML guns
Kowloon	3 × Armstrong 110-pdr RBL guns
Belcher's Bay	3 × 32-pdr SB guns

The committee recommended that 64-pdr RML guns should be substituted for the obsolete 32-pdr SB guns with the least possible delay.

There now occurred an unusual clash of views regarding the construction of new defences. The Colonial Office, in agreement with the Admiralty, instructed the Governor, Sir John Pope Hennessy, to implement the Milne Committee's recommendations. The acting commander of the garrison and the Commanding Royal Engineer disagreed with the Colonial Office's instruction to construct defences for the harbour; most unusually they maintained that all that was required was the updating of the existing batteries in Victoria.

The views of the two officers were firmly overruled by the Colonial Office mainly because events overtook them. On 3 April 1878 what was described as a 'Warlike' telegram was received by the Hong Kong authorities informing them that war between Great Britain and Russia was likely. Since there were no serviceable guns mounted in the batteries, immediate steps were taken to construct temporary battery positions by employing 2,000 Chinese labourers. The problem of arming the batteries seems to have been overcome by using naval guns stored in the dockyard, which included three heavy 9-inch 12-ton RML guns that were mounted in the new Bonham Road battery, and the Royal Navy also assisted by arming HMS *Victor Emmanuel*, the receiving ship anchored in the harbour, with six 64-pdr RML guns, two mounted on the upper deck and four on the deck below.

All the new temporary batteries were constructed with sandbag parapets with some in partially excavated positions with shell rooms beneath the parapets. All the guns, with the exception of six Armstrong 110-pdr RBL guns (probably the guns that were sent out fifteen years earlier) were mounted on Naval Service carriages and slides.

The temporary batteries were described as being of a 'very insubstantial and temporary character' and there can only be considerable doubt as to how effective these batteries would have been should they have been put to the test. The batteries were:

North Point	5 × Armstrong 110-pdr RBL guns
North Kowloon	5 × 7-inch 6½-ton RML guns
Kowloon	6 × Armstrong 110-pdr RBL guns
Stonecutters Island	5 × 64-pdr 70cwt RML guns
Bonham Road	3 × 9-inch 12-ton RML guns
Bonham Road West	2 × 7-inch 6½-ton RML guns
Wellington Battery	5 × Armstrong 40-pdr RBL guns
Naval Bay Battery	2 × 7-inch 6½-ton RML guns

All the guns were mounted on naval carriages and slides with the exception of the guns of Kowloon Battery which were on Land Service carriages and slides. All were mounted on wooden platforms with the racers for the naval carriages and slides only secured by 'fighting bolts'. The naval carriages and slides were described by Lieutenant Needham RN in a report to the Admiralty on the batteries constructed for the defence of Hong Kong as *'not being well suited for shore service, and secured as they are by fighting bolts only, are not in my opinion to be depended upon'*. The three 9-inch guns could not be used as no cog racers had been laid for the winch gear. The five 64-pdr 70cwt guns in the batteries on Stonecutters Island were Palliser conversion guns and were to be mounted on wooden common truck carriages, though in July 1878 none had been placed in position.[6]

In 1879 the Carnarvon Commission acknowledged the Milne Committee's view on the importance of Hong Kong but took three years hearing evidence before it produced its final report in 1881. As we have seen in the previous chapter the Commission sent Colonel William Crossman RE to Singapore and Hong Kong to report on the defences, while at the same time asking the Local Defence Committee and the War Office for their views. The Local Defence Committee recommended a total of ten permanent batteries, three on the Kowloon peninsula, four on Stonecutters Island and one each at North

Point, Belchers' Bay and Quarry Bay. Infantry positions were also proposed for Kowloon and Stonecutters Island.

Colonel Crossman recommended nine permanent batteries to be armed with RML guns. These batteries were:

Belcher Point	3 × 10-inch 18-ton RML guns
Kowloon Dockyard	4 × 10-inch 18-ton RML guns
Kowloon West	3 × 10-inch 18-ton RML guns
	1 × 64-pdr RML gun
Kowloon East	2 × 9-inch 12-ton RML guns
	1 × 64-pdr RML gun
North Point	3 × 9-inch 12-ton RML guns
	1 × 64-pdr RML
Quarry Bay	4 × 10-inch 18-ton RML guns
	2 × 64-pdr RML guns
Stonecutters Island Central	2 × 9-inch 12-ton RML guns
Stonecutters Island East	2 × 7-inch 6½-ton RML guns
Stonecutters Island West	3 × 10-inch 18-ton RML guns
	1 × 64-pdr Mk III RML gun

Because of Hong Kong's commercial and military importance, the Carnarvon Commission made it clear that Hong Kong should be adequately defended and garrisoned to make it strong enough to withstand an enemy attack for

A position for a 64-pdr RML gun at South Shore Battery on Stonecutters Island. (*Author*)

some time without reinforcement. The Commission, therefore, accepted Crossman's proposals for the defence of the colony.[7]

The total estimated cost for these batteries was £395,000, which included £25,000 for infantry positions. It was clear that this was considered by the War Office and the Colonial Office to be too great a sum to be spent on fixed defences in Hong Kong, and the Inspector General of Fortifications produced his own memorandum on the subject. The War Office Memorandum reduced the number of 10-inch RML guns from seventeen to twelve and increased the number of 9-inch RML guns from seven to nine, the number of 64-pdr guns to be reduced from six to three and removed the Kowloon East Battery from the list of batteries. This reduced the overall cost of the defences to £288,000, an overall saving of £107,000.

In Britain steps had now been taken both at the Royal Gun Factory at Woolwich and the Armstrong works at Elswick to develop heavy breech-loading guns and Lieutenant General Sir Alexander Clarke, the Inspector General of Fortifications, now proposed that the heavy gun to arm permanent batteries should be the new 9.2-inch BL gun that had been developed as a result of a request from the Admiralty. General Clarke recommended that these new guns should be mounted in the West Battery on Stonecutters Island and the Belcher's Bay and Quarry Bay batteries.

In 1885 the newly formed Royal Artillery and Royal Engineers Works Committee visited Hong Kong to advise on the defences. When they arrived, the committee found that the defences were in much the same state as when Colonel Crossman had inspected them four years earlier. The existing defences comprised just four batteries and a saluting battery, the latter armed with seven 32-pdr SB guns. The four defence batteries were:

North Point Battery	1 × 9-inch 12-ton RML gun
	2 × 7-inch 6½-ton RML guns
	1 × 8-inch RML howitzer
Kowloon Dock Battery	1 × 9-inch 12-ton RML gun
	2 × 7-inch 6½-ton RML guns
	2 × 8-inch RML howitzers
Stonecutters Island East Battery	2 × 9-inch 12-ton RML guns
	1 × 8-inch RML howitzer
Murray Battery	1 × 7-inch 6½-ton RML gun
	1 × 64-pdr RML gun
	2 × 8-inch SB guns
	2 × 10-inch SB howitzers

The role of the North Point and Kowloon Dock batteries was to prevent access to the harbour from the east, but it would seem that the old Possession Point and Kowloon East and West batteries were no longer armed, so only the Stonecutters Island battery and Murray Battery provided any form of defence from an attack from the west.

The RA and RE Works Committee were quite clear in their view that the existing defences were too close to the present, and no doubt future, harbour facilities and believed, as did the GOC, that it was essential that enemy ships should be prevented from passing Lyemun Point. The committee in its report recommended a number of changes to the War Office's approved armament including substituting a 6-inch BL gun for the proposed 9.2-inch BL gun at North Point, with two more 6-inch BL guns to be installed in a new battery to be constructed on Sai Wan Hill, overlooking the Lyemun Strait. The committee clearly felt that a number of reliable lighter breech-loading guns were a better form of defence than the single heavier 9.2-inch BL gun to defend the strait and to break up any attempt by an enemy force to land on the peninsula opposite.

Rather than install 9.2-inch BL guns as proposed by the Inspector General of Fortifications, the committee recommended that the new 10-inch BL guns should be mounted, two at Kowloon West with a third in a position south of the old Wellington Battery at a height of 400 feet (123m). Similar guns were to be mounted, two at Stonecutters West Battery together with two 6-inch BL guns; one at Stonecutters Central Battery with two 9-inch 12-ton RML guns; one at what was now termed Belcher's Upper Battery above Belcher's Bay, with a single 6-inch gun; and one at Fly Point, near Belcher's Point. All these guns were to be mounted *en barbette*.

A proposed 10-inch BL gun for Belcher's Lower Battery was cancelled but the battery was to retain two 6-inch BL guns on hydro-pneumatic 'disappearing' mountings. Finally, a 9.2-inch BL gun was proposed for a site,

Stonecutters West Battery 10-inch Mk I BL gun on Barbette Carriage Mk I c.1910. (*Author's Collection*)

also at a height of 400 feet (123m) to the south-east of Belcher's Point, which was to be Victoria Battery.

However, the Gunners and Sappers on the committee did not give up entirely the use of Heavy RML guns, although they did recommend the removal of all the 7-inch RML guns in the defences. The 9-inch RML guns currently mounted in Kowloon Dock and North Point Batteries were to be retained and, in addition to the two guns at Stonecutters Central Battery, five more were proposed for new batteries at Lyemun.

The committee recommended that the Lyemun batteries should be provided with defences against land attack but, bearing in mind the Treasury view of the overall expenditure on the defences of Hong Kong, these defences were to be such as not to incur any large expenditure in their construction. It would seem that this was the basis for the subsequent authority to construct, in 1894–95, the infantry redoubts at Lyemun and on the top of Sai Wan hill.

The 1878 Anglo-Russian diplomatic crisis had brought about the expansion of submarine mining in the British Army and the Milne Committee had recommended that a supply of submarine mines should be sent to Hong Kong to be laid between Green Island and Stonecutters Island. A detachment from 33 (Submarine Mining) Company RE had been sent to the colony in that year. A plan to recruit local Chinese personnel initially proved unsuccessful, so in 1882 the detachment was transferred to 23 Company RE, the Submarine Mining Depot Company. The detachment was subsequently formed into the Hong Kong Company of the Eastern Battalion RE in 1887 and the first Chinese personnel were enlisted in 1891.

As a result of, or perhaps even despite, the host of reports from commissions and committees, by 1886 the shape of the permanent fortifications of Hong Kong had been finalized. At a cost of £116,000, paid for by the Hong Kong Government, the permanent batteries were completed by the end of the century.

Although the importance of the commercial port and coaling station of Hong Kong was now fully appreciated, this was not the end of the financial quibbling between the two governments. In Hong Kong there continued to be considerable opposition in the Legislative Council to the size of the Imperial Contribution. In 1890 this sum was set at £40,000 per annum for three years, extended to five years on the understanding that the rate would be reconsidered. In 1896 the Colonial Office insisted that the colony's contribution to the defence costs should be set at 17½ per cent of the gross receipts from all sources of revenue less land sales.[8]

The Unofficial Members of the Legislative Council argued that the colony's municipal revenues should not be included when setting the Imperial Contribution, as was the case in the Straits Settlements where the municipal revenue of Singapore was excluded. The Colonial Office disagreed, arguing that in Hong Kong there was no municipal council, and the Hong Kong Government reluctantly accepted the Colonial Office's decision.

The New Territories and the Approach of War

In the 1890s Hong Kong was continuing to develop and, following acquisition of the Kowloon peninsula in 1861, the area quickly became urbanized. In 1898 China leased the New Territories to Britain and in the following year the War Office once again reviewed the defences of the colony.

By 1898, the year before the outbreak of the Second Anglo-Boer War, considerable work had been carried out on Hong Kong's permanent defences. In 1899 the defences of the colony comprised:

Eastern Entrance	Lyemun Redoubt	2 × 6-inch BL HP guns
	Lyemun Reverse	3 × 9-inch 12-ton RML guns
		2 × 6-pdr QF guns
	Lyemun Central	2 × 64-pdr Mk III RML guns
	Lyemun West	2 × 9-inch 12-ton RML guns
		2 × 6-pdr QF guns
Western Entrance	Stonecutters West	2 × 10-inch Mk I BL guns
		2 × 6-inch BL guns
		1 × 6-pdr QF gun
	Stonecutters Central	1 × 10-inch Mk I BL gun
		1 × 6-inch BL gun
	Stonecutter East	2 × 4.7-inch QF guns
	Stonecutters South Shore	2 × 6-pdr QF
	Belcher's Upper	1 × 10-inch Mk I BL gun
	Belcher's Lower	3 × 6-inch BL guns
		2 × 12-pdr QF
	Fly Point	1 × 10-inch Mk I BL gun
Inner Defences	North Point	2 × 9-inch 12-ton RML guns
	Victoria Battery	1 × 9.2-inch Mk IV BL gun
	Kowloon Dock	3 × 9-inch 12-ton RML guns
	Kowloon West	3 × 10-inch 18-ton RML guns
	Kowloon East	1 × 9.2-inch Mk IV BL gun[9]

A 6-inch Mk VI BL gun on a hydro-pneumatic mounting at Lyemun Redoubt. The redoubt is now the Hong Kong Museum of Coastal Artillery and the gun is a replica. (*Author*)

In the same year yet another committee was appointed to consider the defences and report to the Inspector General of Fortifications and the Inspector General of Ordnance. The committee, entitled 'Committee on Armaments of Certain Stations at Home and Abroad' considered the defences of four ports in Britain, together with Gibraltar and Hong Kong. The view of the committee was that in Hong Kong the defences of the western entrance were adequate, but those of the eastern entrance were deemed inadequate as the only modern guns in the defences were the two 6-inch Mk VI BL on HP mountings in Lyemun Redoubt. These guns were supported by two 9.2-inch Mk IV BL guns, also on HP mountings, both in the Inner Defences, one in Kowloon and the other in Victoria Battery on Hong Kong island.

The committee recommended that the 6-inch guns on 'slow' hydro-pneumatic mountings at Belcher's Upper and Lower Batteries, and on Stonecutters Island should be re-mounted on modern *barbette* mountings in order to increase their rate of fire. Similarly, it was recommended that the five 10-inch BL guns, currently mounted on Barbette Garrison carriages that also gave a slow rate of fire, should also be re-mounted on modern mountings providing what the committee referred to as a 'quick' rate of fire.[10]

Believing that the defences of the eastern entrance to the harbour were too weak to adequately defend the entrance, the committee also recommended that a new battery of two of the more modern 9.2-inch Mk X BL guns and two 6-inch Mk VII BL guns should be established on the Devil's Peak, part of the mainland north of Lyemun Passage which had recently been leased to Britain by the Chinese Government. While to further strengthen the eastern defences, it was proposed to construct the battery for two 6-inch BL guns on Sai Wan Hill, above the Lyemun redoubt, which had originally been recommended by the RA and RE Works Committee in 1885. These recommendations were accepted by the War Office and the Devil's Peak and Sai Wan batteries were completed by 1910.

Gough Battery 9.2-inch gun position on Devil's Peak seen from Devil's Peak Redoubt. The adjacent gun position was for a 6-inch gun. (*Author*)

Unusually the committee proposed a battery for two 6-inch guns on the Peak above Victoria. The battery, Pinewood Battery, was to be situated over 1,000 feet (307m) above sea level and, although constructed in 1902–03, it was short-lived in its coast defence

Gough Battery 9.2-inch Mk X gun practice firing c.1935. (*Author's Collection*)

Pinewood Battery, Hong Kong Island. Like Sai Wan Battery, Pinewood was originally a battery for two 6-inch QF guns and was then converted into a battery for two 3-inch AA guns. (*Author*)

role and, as we shall see, was declared surplus to requirements some three years later.

By 1896 the defences of the harbour had been further strengthened by additional minefields. The original plan for a single minefield between Green Island and Stonecutters Island had been modified so that the front of the main minefield ran from Belcher's Point to the western tip of Stonecutters, with mines at irregular intervals laid in the area of sea in front of the main belt between Green Island and Stonecutters Island. The eastern entrance at Lyemun Pass was also defended with mines. Originally it was the belief that the current running through the Passage was too strong, causing the mines to break loose, but this was found not to be the case and a front of main mine defence was laid between Devil's Peak and Lyemun Point with mines at irregular intervals in front of the main line.

The Submarine Mining Company RE took over the old Wellington Battery, which had been disarmed since 1877, as their barracks and established a launching station for the Brennan torpedo at Lyemun Fort. The Brennan torpedo, the world's first practical guided missile, was invented by an Irish-born Australian, Louis Brennan, in 1877. The torpedo was propelled by two contra-rotating propellers that were spun by rapidly pulling wires from drums inside the torpedo. The differential speed of the wires activated the rudder and steered the torpedo to its target to a maximum range of 2,000 yards (1,800m), at a speed of up to 27 knots (31 mph). The wires were connected to the shore station where there were steam-powered winding engines and an observation post. The Hong Kong station was one of only two Brennan torpedo stations outside the United Kingdom, the other being at Fort Ricasoli in Malta.

To defend the minefields a number of 6-pdr QF guns had been installed at Lyemun Reverse, Lyemun West, Stonecutters West, Stonecutters South Shore, and Belcher's Lower batteries. However, the committee believed that more powerful guns were required to defend the minefields and recommended that the two 6-pdr QF guns installed at the South Shore Battery and the single gun at West Battery, both on Stonecutters Island, should be removed and two more powerful 12-pdr QF guns mounted in the South Shore Battery in their place. For the eastern entrance four similar guns were proposed for a new battery to be constructed near the current Lyemun Reverse Battery.

It should, perhaps, be noted that at this time all the defences were sited to defend the harbour and the entrances to it. Any threat to the colony was believed to be from Russian or French forces based in the Far East and any idea of a threat from China was disregarded. Since the island was mountainous with virtually no communication between the southern shore and the populated north shore the Local Defence Committee considered that defences to protect the southern shore were unnecessary. Despite this view, however, in 1889 the Local Defence Committee felt it was necessary to recommend the construction of field redoubts above North Point Battery, on the hill above Belcher's Battery and other high points across the island, with one on the hill close to Kowloon East Battery, but there is no indication that these redoubts were ever completed.

Ten years later, in 1899, the Conference on Breech-Loading and Quick-Firing Guns proposed further changes to the armament of Hong Kong and the removal of all muzzle-loading guns together with three 6-pdr QF guns and two 6-inch BL howitzers, the latter part of the moveable armament of the colony. In the place of these guns three 9.2-inch BL, eight 6-inch Mk VII BL guns and six 12-pdr QF guns were to be mounted.[11]

The Owen Committee and the First World War

In 1905 the Owen Committee presented a second report on the armament of the defended ports abroad. The Committee's terms of reference required its members to consider long-range bombardment as the most likely method of attack on the colony, and, after considering the likelihood of such an attack, the committee's recommendations reduced the colony's armament to:

Eastern Entrance	3 × 9.2-inch Mk X BL guns on Mk V (15°) mountings
	3 × 6-inch Mk VII BL guns on CP (15°) mountings
Western Entrance	5 × 9.2-inch Mk X BL guns on Mk V (15°) mountings
	8 × 6-inch Mk VII BL guns on CP (15°) mountings

Since the current defences were sited to prevent an attack by enemy warships attempting to force their way into the harbour, the committee recommended the immediate reduction of the 6-inch battery at North Point; the two 6-inch Mk VI guns on HP mountings at Lyemun Redoubt; the 12-pdr QF guns at Centurion Battery on Stonecutters Island; and the quick-firing guns at Lyemun Reverse, Lyemun West, Stonecutters South Shore, and Upper Belcher's batteries. A battery for two 12-pdr QF guns built at the turn of the century in the Mid-Levels, Elliot Battery, together with the 6-inch QF guns of Sai Wan and Pinewood batteries were also declared redundant.

The Owen Committee's recommendations met with a howl of dismay from Vice Admiral Sir Hedworth Lambton, C-in-C China Station. In a strongly worded letter to the Governor dated 25 November 1908 he pointed out that, in view of the withdrawal of all the Royal Navy heavy units to Home waters as a result of the increasing threat from the new German navy, the defences of the important commercial port of Hong Kong were inadequate to counter a threat from either the Japanese or the United States navies.

In his letter Admiral Lambton used somewhat fanciful analogies to emphasise his point. If the defence of the colony was to depend on defeating an attack by bombardment from up to three modern battleships, then he believed the Owen Committee's recommendations were inadequate. With only three 9.2-inch BL guns to defend the eastern entrance, Admiral Lambton calculated that would mean that each gun must counter a broadside of fourteen guns (from an American *Louisiana*-class battleship, for example) from each of three enemy battleships.

'One gun against fourteen – what a preposterous proposal! Remember the position of these unhappy 9.2-inch guns is known in every foreign country to an inch, and the supposed smokelessness of their cordite charges is a purely comparative expression, and has just about as much relation to invisibility as a white elephant to Snow White.'[12]

Despite this 'broadside' from the C-in-C China Station, the Colonial Defence Committee continued to maintain that the defences were adequate, particularly in view of the Anglo-Japanese Alliance signed in 1902, which promised mutual support if either signatory became involved in a war with more than one foreign power. However, the five 10-inch BL guns, currently in place but no longer part of the approved armament, were allowed to remain in position.

The defeat of Russia by Japan in the war of 1904-05, and the signing of the Anglo–Russian Entente in 1907 meant that Britain's primary interest in the East was no longer the defence of India, but rather the defence of her possessions in the Far East. The rising power of Germany in Europe and the gradually decreasing economic power of Great Britain *vis-à-vis* Germany, France and Italy meant that it was no longer possible for Britain to maintain a battle fleet in eastern waters superior to either the newly emergent Japanese Navy or the United States Navy. To do so would give Germany naval supremacy in the North Sea, so the government accepted that it was essential to renew the Anglo-Japanese Alliance in 1911.

Although China had been defeated in a war with Japan in 1895 it was believed by British military planners to be a potential, if unlikely, threat to Hong Kong. This was particularly so after the fall of the Qing Dynasty in 1911, the coming to power of General Yuan Shikai as president of the new republic and the forming of the Canton New Army. So, in Hong Kong, attention turned to landward defence against possible Chinese, or even Japanese, aggression, and in 1910 the GOC Hong Kong, Major General Charles Anderson, proposed the construction of a line of blockhouses to run along the Kowloon ridgeline from Devil's Peak to Lai Chi Kok Pass. These blockhouses were to act as an initial line of defence and to enable artillery observation parties to bring fire to bear on the valleys north and east of the line. By 1912 authority had been given for the construction of thirty blockhouses along the line proposed by General Anderson. These blockhouses appear to have been built to a similar design as that used for the blockhouses in South Africa during the Second Boer War.[13] To protect the batteries on Devil's Peak an infantry redoubt armed with machine guns was built on the top of the hill.

At the start of the First World War the only threat to Hong Kong was the German East Asia Squadron commanded by Admiral Graf von Spee, but with the entry into the war of Japan on the Allied side and the destruction of the German East Asia Squadron at the Battle of the Falkland Islands in December 1914 any threat was removed.

As the war progressed a number of improvements were made to the fixed defences, while at the same time, regular troops of the garrison were gradually withdrawn to Britain and reliance for the manning of the guns became the responsibility of units of the Hong Kong and Singapore RGA. On

Stonecutters West Battery showing two 6-inch Mk VII guns c.1925. (*Author's Collection*)

Stonecutters Island an additional 6-inch BL gun was added to the West Battery and the 10-inch BL guns withdrawn. The 10-inch gun at Belcher's Point was also withdrawn, and two 4.7-inch QF guns added to both the Lyemun Pass Battery and Centurion Battery on Stonecutters Island. In the latter case this required the reconstruction of the old 12-pdr QF gun emplacements.

By 1917 the armament of Hong Kong was:

Western Entrance	Mount Davis	5 × 9.2-inch Mk X BL guns
	Lower Belcher's Point	2 × 6-inch Mk VII BL guns
	Upper Belcher's Point	1 × 6-inch Mk VII BL gun
	Ferry Battery (Kowloon)	4 × 12-pdr QF guns
	Stonecutters West Battery	3 × 6-inch Mk VII BL guns
Eastern Entrance	Devil's Peak	3 × 9.2-inch Mk X BL guns
	Pak Sha Wan Battery	3 × 6-inch Mk VII BL guns
	Lyemun Pass West	2 × 4.7-inch QF guns
	Lyemun Pass Reverse	2 × 12-pdr QF guns

However, the 12-pdr QF guns at Ferry Battery and Lyemun Pass reverse had actually been removed and were on loan to the Royal Navy.[14] In 1918 the Ferry Battery was condemned as useless as it was inside the limits of the harbour and, if attacked, would be masked by the shipping and junks anchored there.[15]

Mount Davis Battery c.1935. The photograph shows two of the five 9.2-inch Mk X BL guns on Mk V (15°) mountings. (*Author's Collection*)

The Inter-War Years

In early 1920 the Chief of the Imperial General Staff, Field Marshal Sir Henry Wilson, forwarded to Winston Churchill, the Secretary of State for War, and the Cabinet his views on the defence of British bases in the Far East, particularly Hong Kong. The Field Marshal believed that with Japan neutral it was possible that the garrison of Hong Kong might have to face a stronger attack from the Chinese mainland, while if Japan was hostile it would be impossible to hold the colony against a determined attack for the period of three months, which the Royal Navy believed would be the length of time before a relief force could arrive. Therefore, the strength of the garrison should be based on defending the colony from a Chinese *coup de main*, possibly engineered by Japan. In the briefing papers supporting the memorandum, however, no change was proposed in the fixed defences since there was no revision of the scale of naval attack.

However, the desperate financial situation faced by post-war Britain was such that in 1919 the government ordered the three services to draft their annual financial estimates on the assumption that the country would not be involved in a major war for the next ten years. By the end of the decade and at the insistence of the Treasury the 'Ten Year Rule' was placed on a daily-moving basis, so continuing to constrain defence expenditure.

Even so this was not enough for the government which proceeded to sign a number of international treaties aimed at arms limitation. The most important, and the one that would have a lasting effect on Britain's position as a world power, was the Washington Naval Treaty of 1922. The Washington Treaty resulted in a major reduction in the size of the Royal Navy, but also had an effect on the fixed defences of Hong Kong. One clause in the treaty limited the construction of coastal defences in Asian colonies, thus limiting any attempt to improve or change Hong Kong's coastal defence batteries.

The Washington Treaty ended for good the threat of an unwinnable naval arms race with the United States, but it also had the effect of ending the Anglo-Japanese Alliance, thus presenting the British military planners with the apparently insuperable problem of facing a potential enemy, Japan, without being able to improve the defences of the British bases in the Far East.

This problem came to a head initially as a result of a review of the defences carried out in 1927. As part of the review of the defences of ports at home and abroad by the Joint Oversea and Home Defence Committee, Hong Kong was ranked second to Singapore in a list of ports where the defences needed improvement. The Chiefs of Staff Committee considered the recommendation that the 9.2-inch and 6-inch guns currently *in situ* should be brought up to date by installing modern mountings that would increase the elevations of these guns to 35° for the 9.2-inch guns and 45° for the 6-inch guns respectively, so increasing the maximum ranges of these guns.

The question was: did the modernizing of the guns and the necessary modification of the emplacements offend against the clause relating to the ban on the construction of new fortifications? The Chiefs of Staff believed that it did not and argued that since the battleships of some of the navies of the signatory nations had been modernized changing the coast defence guns was no different. Indeed, not to do so would place the defences in an inferior position *vis-à-vis* the battleships. While this was generally accepted within the Cabinet, initially the Foreign Office demurred, only eventually accepting the argument that under the treaty gun emplacements were not regarded as fortifications *per se*, though disused emplacements had to be destroyed.

Needless to say, because of the ever-deteriorating national financial situation, no steps were taken to modernize the garrison's guns, though the threat of air attack was beginning to be appreciated, and a token number of anti-aircraft guns, four 3-inch (76mm) AA guns, was sent to Hong Kong to be manned by a reinforced section attached to 12 Heavy Battery RA. The old 6-inch battery positions at Sai Wan Hill and the Peak were converted into AA battery positions, each mounting two of the newly arrived guns.

In 1927 the Joint Planning Sub-committee (JPC) of the Chiefs of Staff Committee considered the defence of the colony. The sub-committee accepted as a basis for their study of the defences that Great Britain would

Sai Wan Battery, Hong Kong Island. Originally designed as a battery for two 6-inch QF guns, it was then converted into a position for two 3-inch AA guns. After the Second World War it was changed again into a battery position for four 3.7-inch HAA guns. The 1970 photograph shows the positions for two of the latter guns. (*Author's Collection*)

fight Japan alone after a long period of tension before the outbreak of war. In addition, it was assumed that the Washington Treaty did not prohibit the garrison including aircraft and that China could not, or would not, intervene.

In these circumstances the JPC believed that Hong Kong should be held at all costs against a Japanese invasion, most probably from the Chinese mainland, until the arrival of the main fleet from Britain. To do this would require a minimum garrison of eight infantry battalions and five squadrons of aircraft.

A further report three years later accepted the same controlling factors and confirmed that the main objective of the garrison should be to hold the harbour facilities, which meant holding Hong Kong Island and part of Kowloon. This, the committee suggested, could be done with a smaller garrison of six battalions and five squadrons of aircraft and by updating the coast guns. Since the primary threat was considered to be an attack on Hong Kong Island from the New Territories, one aspect of the overall defence plan included a proposal to build three defence lines in the New Territories. The forward defence line was to run from Starling Inlet to Shenzhen; the second, or intermediate line, would cover some 16,000 yards (14,770m) in the area of Tai Mo Shan, the highest peak in Hong Kong; and the third, and final, line to run along the ridge of hills from Tide Cove in the east to Gin Drinker's Bay in the west. However, the after effects of the Great Depression put paid to this plan.

By 1932 the political scene in Europe was becoming more threatening. After Hitler's rise to power in Germany and the Japanese occupation of Manchuria, the British Government reviewed the defences needed for the nation and the Empire. The 'Ten Years Rule' was abandoned and a Defence Requirement Sub-committee of the Committee of Imperial Defence was established. In a Review of the Defence of Ports it was proposed to regroup the existing fixed defences in Hong Kong, placing the main priority on the defence of Hong Kong Island. In 1934 it was decided that, for financial reasons, these changes should be carried out over a period of the next five years, that is between 1934 and 1939, and also because the demand for new guns and mountings throughout the Empire was greater than Britain's current manufacturing capability.

The proposed change meant that the defences were to comprise eight 9.2-inch CB guns on 35° mountings; six 6-inch CD guns on 45° mountings; and eight 3.7-inch HAA guns. Three of the 9.2-inch guns were to be mounted in a new battery on the Stanley peninsula in the south of the island, with a completion date set for 1937.

Needless to say, with Britain's limited capacity to manufacture guns and mountings and the increased demand for guns, this ambitious plan was never realized. However, with increased emphasis being placed on the defence of Hong Kong Island work commenced on the new battery at Stanley, the armament for which was to come from re-deploying two of the five guns from Mount Davis Battery and the gun from Gough Battery on Devil's Peak. All three guns were to be mounted on new Mk VII 35° mountings, but Stanley Battery was the only 9.2-inch gun battery to receive modern mountings before war broke out in 1939. A second new counter-bombardment battery was built on D'Aguilar peninsula armed with two 9.2-inch BL guns moved from Pottinger Battery on Devil's Peak with the old Mk V 15° mountings. This battery was not completed until late in 1941.

Three new 6-inch BL gun close defence batteries were also constructed on Hong Kong Island with some of the guns being transferred from existing batteries. Collinson Battery, on the island's east coast, was armed with two 6-inch Mk VII BL guns moved from West Battery on Stonecutters Island, while the new Jubilee Battery, built at the foot of Mount Davis, was armed

Chung Hum Kok Battery No.2 gun position. The overhead cover was to protect the gun crew from the blast of No.1 gun, positioned immediately above No.2. Even when camouflaged this gun position must have been clearly visible to an attacking warship. (*Author*)

with three similar guns, two from Belcher's Battery and one from Pak Sha Wan Battery.

The third close defence battery, sited west of Stanley and overlooking Chung Hom Kok beach, was also armed with two 6-inch Mk VII BL guns. Interestingly, because of being built on a steep cliff face the two gun emplacements were built one above the other. This necessitated the construction of a semi-circular concrete shield over the lower, No 2, gun to protect the gun crew from the blast of the upper, No 1 gun.

Major General Frederick Barron, Director of Fixed Defences at the War Office, visited Hong Kong in 1934, and in 1935 he produced a report on the colony's defences which he declared to be deplorable, though he noted that the new battery at Stanley was under construction. The report noted that the GOC China had recently prepared and forwarded to the War Office a plan for the defence of the New Territories that involved the construction of a line of pillboxes, wire obstacles, signal communications and the necessary roads along the line of the Kowloon ridge. This would become the infamous Gin Drinker's Line.[16]

General Barron believed the real threat to the colony came from a Japanese invasion of the New Territories and he proposed the construction of close defence batteries to defend possible landing places at Starling Inlet, Port

The Gin Drinker's Line. The photograph shows the entrances to two tunnels, Regent Street (left) and Shaftesbury Avenue (right) which connected with a command post and firing positions. (*Author*)

Shelter and Castle Peak Bay. A 6-inch BL gun battery on 45° mountings was proposed for Mount Hallowes, on the northern tip of the Sai Kung peninsula, in a counter-bombardment role.

In considering the anti-aircraft defence General Barron was of the view that sixteen 3-inch AA guns, which were to be replaced in due course by the more modern 3.7-inch HAA guns when they became available, would be sufficient for the defence of the colony. These were to be supported by thirty-six AA searchlights and, intriguingly, by six acoustic mirrors. These were concave-shaped half spheres made of concrete designed to locate acoustically approaching aircraft and were the forerunners of radar. The mirrors were to be sited on Bluff Head, Cape D'Aguilar and Mount Davis on Hong Kong Island, and at Tai Wan Tau on the Clearwater Bay peninsula, Tai Po, and Fanling in the New Territories, but these were never built.

For defence against MTB attack General Barron recommended seven of the new Twin 6-pdr QF AMTB equipments for defence of the western entrance and three for the eastern entrance, but none of these equipments were to be allocated to Hong Kong.[17]

In 1931 Japan had invaded and occupied Manchuria and three years later renounced the naval treaties of 1922 and 1930, following this in 1936 by signing an Anti-Comintern Pact with Germany. This raised the spectre of a Japanese alliance with Germany in any future war between Britain and Germany. The question now arose as to whether Hong Kong was still an important naval base and, if so, should it be reinforced, or indeed, abandoned if it could not be defended. This was important as Hong Kong was now within range of Japanese bombers based on Formosa.

In 1936 the JPC and the Admiralty had completed a joint study on a proposed British strategy in a war with Japan with the Royal Navy representatives firmly advocating that the colony should be defended. This was a view accepted by the Chiefs of Staff Committee, despite a dissenting view of one of the authors of the study, Wing Commander Arthur Harris (later Marshal of the Royal Air Force Sir Arthur Harris), that Hong Kong could not, under any circumstances, be held against a determined Japanese attack.

However, in late 1937 the Sino-Japanese conflict escalated into a full-scale war and the Japanese occupied Nanjing and the area around Shanghai. The Foreign Office view was that should the Japanese move south and occupy Canton (Guangzhou) then Hong Kong would be indefensible. As a result, the Chiefs of Staff Committee decided that the defences of Hong Kong should be concentrated on holding Hong Kong Island and the Kowloon peninsula south of the Kowloon ridge of hills. Major General Arthur Bartholomew had already received permission to commence construction of a line of fixed defences, pillboxes and OPs, along the line of the Kowloon ridge. This was roughly the third and final line of defence proposed by the JPC in 1930, and also proposed by General Barron in 1935. Later known as the Gin Drinkers Line, the line of defences was to stretch from Gin Drinkers Bay in the west to Tide Cove in the east and was to consist of some ninety pillboxes with eleven headquarters bunkers and three OPs. In the event only thirty-eight pillboxes, one headquarters bunker and one OP were completed before the construction of the line was abandoned in 1938.

In May 1937 the guns of the coast defences and anti-aircraft defences were described in a Cabinet minute as being in existence and were:

Coast Defences:	3 × 9.2-inch (35°) BL guns
	5 × 9.2-inch (15°) BL guns
	11 × 6-inch (15°) BL guns
	4 × 4.7-inch QF guns
	14 DELs out of 23 approved
Anti-Aircraft Defences	10 × 3-inch AA guns
	18 AA searchlights[18]

The use of the phrase 'in existence' was perhaps somewhat optimistic as a year later the list of the approved coast defences of Hong Kong showed that Stanley Battery, Jubilee Battery and Collinson Battery were still under construction.

The new batteries at Chung Hum Kok, Jubilee, and Cape Collinson were to have been armed with the new 6-inch Mk XXIV BL guns on 45° mountings but, as there were none of the new guns currently available, these batteries were armed with the older Mk VII guns redeployed, as we have seen, from other batteries in the garrison.

In 1938 further consideration of the value of defending Hong Kong continued with the Royal Navy insisting on the value of the colony as a base, and War Office and the Royal Air Force maintaining its vulnerability to attack, especially should the Japanese occupy Canton. Indeed, it was clear that the Royal Air Force could not provide aircraft for the colony's defence, not least because the only possible sites for airfields, other than Kai Tak, lay north of the Kowloon ridgeline, making it impossible to hold them against Japanese air and land attack.

The Foreign Office, however, supported the Navy since, while appreciating the vulnerability of Hong Kong, believed that to abandon the colony would involve an enormous loss of prestige in the Far East and indicate to the Japanese Government Britain's lack of will to defend its Asian colonies.

The final plan adopted was that Hong Kong Island should be defended, with the Gin Drinker's Line occupied only as a delaying position. The regrouped gun batteries were to provide the main fixed defences supported by additional beach defences, including seventy-two coastal pillboxes most of which had adjoining Lyon light (beach searchlight) positions. The garrison was to be maintained at four infantry battalions supported by the personnel of the Hong Kong Volunteer Defence Force (HKVDC). This force had been formed in 1878 as the Hong Kong Artillery and Rifle Volunteers and by 1938 the HKVDC had a strength of 2,200 officers and men, in five artillery batteries, an engineer company, seven infantry companies, an armoured car platoon and Signals and Army Service Corps detachments. The personnel of four of the artillery batteries manned four of the coast defence batteries and one anti-aircraft machine gun battery.

The naval defences were to comprise a flotilla of four light destroyers with motor torpedo boats, and naval fixed defences. These defences consisted of anti-submarine booms, underwater indicator loops stretching from Port Shelter to Lantau Island to detect approaching enemy submarines, and a number of minefields with floating contact mines and remote-controlled

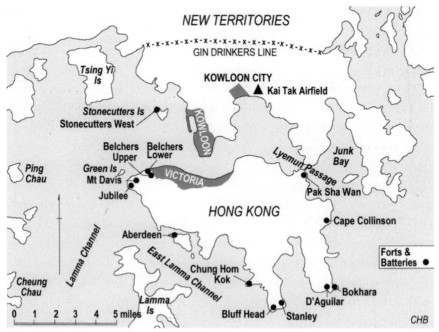

Map of the defences of Hong Kong in 1941. (*Charles Blackwood*)

mines fired from observation posts ashore. Shipping access was to be limited to the East Lamma and Tathong Channels.

War with Japan

At the outbreak of war with Germany on 3 September 1939 the garrison consisted of four infantry battalions, four artillery regiments, with a number of minor units and the HKVDC. The infantry battalions were:

2nd Battalion The Royal Scots (2 R Scots)
1st Battalion The Middlesex Regiment (1 Middlesex)
5th Battalion The 7th Rajput Regiment (5/7 Rajputs)
2nd Battalion The 14th Punjab Regiment (2/14 Punjabis)

The Middlesex Regiment was a machine-gun battalion armed with 0.303-inch (7.6mm) Vickers machine guns.

The artillery regiments were:

8th Coast Regiment RA (12, 30 & 36 Coast Batteries)
12th Coast Regiment RA (20 & 24 Coast Batteries)
5th Anti-Aircraft Regiment RA (7, 17 & 18 AA Batteries)
1st Hong Kong Regiment Hong Kong & Singapore RA (1 & 2 Mountain Batteries and 3 & 4 Medium Batteries)

The mobile artillery of the garrison was manned by 1 Regt HK&SRA and the regiment was armed with 3.7-inch pack howitzers and 6-inch howitzers. There was also an independent battery, 965 Defence Battery RA (formerly 35 Mobile Coast Defence Battery RA), which was armed with 2-pdr anti-tank guns and 18-pdr QF field guns to defend the island's beaches.

A number of improvised batteries, which were constructed and armed in 1941 as the onset of war with Japan approached, were manned by personnel of the HKVDC. These batteries were:

Cape D'Aguilar	No 1 Battery HKVDC	2 × 4-inch BL Naval guns
Bluff Head	No 2 Battery HKVDC	2 × 6-inch BL Naval guns
Belcher's Point	965 Defence Battery RA	1 × 6-inch BL Naval gun
		2 × 4.7-inch QF guns
Aberdeen	No 3 Battery HKVDC	2 × 4-inch BL Naval guns

In addition, the 6-inch CD gun battery at Pak Sha Wan was manned by men of 4 Battery HKVDC.

The anti-aircraft guns of 5th AA Regiment RA were distributed in a number of positions each of two guns, with 3-inch AA guns at Chung Hom Kok, Pinewood Battery, Brick Hill and Shouson Hill. The 3.7-inch HAA guns were deployed at Wong Nai Chung Gap and at a position in the Mid-Levels in Central, and two 4.5-inch HAA guns at Waterfall Bay. Two 3-inch AA guns were manned by 5 Battery HKVDC at Sai Wan Hill under command of 5 AA Regiment.

Under the 1938 Defence Plan three of the infantry battalions were designated the Mainland Brigade with the role of carrying out a delaying action in the New Territories before withdrawing to Hong Kong Island, which was to be held by 1 Middlesex and the HKVDC.

The fall of France in 1940 and the declaration of war by Italy meant that no fleet could be sent to the relief of either Singapore or Hong Kong in the event of war with Japan. Governor Northcote was of the opinion that Hong

Kong could not be held against Japanese mass bombing and he recommended the demilitarisation of the colony. However, the Chiefs of Staff argued that to demilitarize the colony would discourage Chinese resistance and that the possible loss of prestige due to its fall would be less serious than the loss of prestige due to its demilitarization.[19]

The new C-in-C Far East, Air Chief Marshal Sir Robert Brooke-Popham, was a strong supporter of the view that the Japanese could be deterred from attacking Hong Kong if the garrison was suitably reinforced, but Winston Churchill disagreed, believing there was no way of holding or relieving the colony.

The international situation changed dramatically in 1941 with the German invasion of the Soviet Union. The British Government now saw supporting China as vital in order to prevent Japan becoming allied with Germany against the Soviet Union, and this changed the Cabinet's and the Prime Minister's views on reinforcing Hong Kong.

In the autumn of 1941 the departing GOC British Troops in China, Major General Arthur Grasett, a Canadian by birth, was convinced that the current garrison of four battalions was insufficient to successfully defend Hong Kong. The question was, therefore, where could reinforcements be found, since the garrisons of Tianjin and Shanghai had already been withdrawn and sent to Singapore. General Grasett proposed that the Canadian Government should be asked to provide two or more battalions to reinforce the colony.

After some debate his suggestion was accepted and the Dominion Office formally requested Canada to provide two battalions for Hong Kong. The Canadian Government agreed to provide the battalions, the Royal Rifles of Canada and the 1st Battalion The Winnipeg Grenadiers, collectively known as C Force. Prior to their move to Hong Kong both battalions had been on garrison duty, the Royal Rifles in Newfoundland and the Winnipeg Grenadiers in Jamaica, and both had received only the minimum of training before arriving in Hong Kong only three weeks before the Japanese attacked.

The arrival of the Canadian units meant an immediate review of the Defence Plan and this resulted in the Canadian battalions taking up positions on Hong Kong Island while carrying out intensive training. The island garrison now consisted of the Canadians, 1 Middlesex and the bulk of the HKVDC.

At 0800 hours on 8 December 1941 Japanese aircraft attacked Kai Tak airfield destroying the few out-dated RAF aircraft stationed there and a number of civil aircraft. Radio intercepts had warned the authorities in Hong Kong of a build-up of Japanese troops on the border, so the Mainland Brigade had been deployed to its war positions and demolitions activated. The 38th

Japanese Infantry Division commanded by General Sakai, comprising 228th, 229th, and 230th Infantry Regiments and supporting troops, crossed the border, moving quickly to attack the Gin Drinkers Line held by the three battalions of the Mainland Brigade rather than with a garrison of six battalions as had originally been envisaged.

On the night of 9 December 228th Infantry Regiment attacked and captured the Shing Mun Redoubt, a key position in the Gin Drinkers Line and held by only a single platoon of 2 Royal Scots. This early penetration of the line forced the defenders into a fighting withdrawal and the New Territories were evacuated on 12 December. During the withdrawal the Japanese in the area of the Shing Mun Redoubt were engaged by the mobile artillery of the HK & SRA and the guns of the Stonecutters West and Mount Davis batteries. The Royal Navy supported the troops of the Mainland Brigade with the gunboat HMS *Cicala* using its 6-inch guns to prevent Japanese troops moving along Castle Peak Road, the coastal road leading to Kowloon from the west.

With the return of the Mainland Brigade to Hong Kong Island General Maltby took the opportunity to re-form the garrison into two brigades, East and West, with the inter-brigade boundary dividing the island along a line running from North Point through Jardine's Lookout, Wong Nai Chung Reservoir to Stanley Mound and Chung Hum Kok on the south shore. The West Brigade, with its headquarters at Wong Nai Chung Gap, comprised 2 Royal Scots, 2/14 Punjabis, 1 Winnipeg Grenadiers with elements of 1 Middlesex and the HKVDC. East brigade, with its headquarters at Tai Tam, consisted of 5/7 Rajputs, the Royal Rifles of Canada and the remaining elements of 1 Middlesex and the HKVDC.

Since the Japanese Navy had complete command of the sea, General Maltby felt forced to plan on a linear defence of the island with a large proportion of both 5/7 Rajputs and the Winnipeg Grenadiers deployed in defence of the southern beaches. This substantially reduced the number of troops available to oppose the Japanese assault on the north shore when it came.

However, the Japanese paused for four days and relied upon their heavy artillery to soften up the British defences while preparing for what they knew would be an opposed crossing to the island. With the capture of Devil's Peak on the mainland, the Japanese had obtained a magnificent observation position overlooking Lyemun and North Point. The Japanese gunners manning 240mm (9.4-inch) howitzers and 150mm (5.9-inch) guns targeted the British artillery positions and pillboxes on the north shore. In return the British batteries on Mount Davis and Stanley Battery shelled Devil's Peak and targets in Kowloon. On 13 December the Fire Command Post on Mount

Davis was destroyed by three 240mm shells and No 3 gun, the top gun, was put out of action by a direct hit from a 240mm shell that failed to explode.

On 14 December the two 4.7-inch QF guns of Belcher's Battery were put out of action and the Mount Davis and Pak Sha Wan batteries were heavily shelled. The following day Pinewood anti-aircraft battery was bombed and the guns destroyed. That evening Pak Sha Wan engaged Japanese reconnaissance parties attempting to cross to the island.

Mount Davis Battery was again heavily shelled on 16 December and the Battery Plotting Room was hit. The next day, with the plotting room back in action, counter-battery fire was carried out on Devil's Peak, Gun Club Hill in central Kowloon and the Kowloon waterfront in conjunction with Pak Sha Wan Battery. In return the Japanese maintained a bombardment using their heavy guns, while smaller calibre guns engaged the pillboxes on the north shore.

The artillery duel continued throughout the daylight hours of 18 December with the Japanese guns concentrating on the pillboxes, the guns of the fixed defences and the garrison's moveable artillery. General Maltby was of the view that the Japanese attack would come in the Victoria area, though many of his senior staff officers believed the Japanese would cross from Devil's Peak to North Point, the shortest crossing. However General Maltby continued to maintain a linear defence with 5/7 Rajputs occupying the North Point/Lyemun defences, 2 Royal Scots the Victoria area and 1/14 Punjabis the shoreline west of Victoria.

On the night of the 18/19 December leading elements of the 38th Japanese Division crossed to the island taking the British defenders by surprise. Crossing to Shau Kai Wan, 229th Regiment quickly captured the anti-aircraft battery at Sai Wan Fort, while other crossings were made by 228th Regiment at Tai Koo and by 230th Regiment at North Point. The latter regiment moved rapidly along Sir Cecil's Ride towards the high ground and the Wong Nai Chung Gap.

After fierce fighting in which the commander of West Brigade, the Canadian Brigadier Lawson, was killed outside his headquarters bunker revolver in hand, the Wong Nai Chung anti-aircraft position was captured. Isolated pockets of British and Canadian troops continued to hold out in the North Point, Shau Kai Wan and Wong Nai Chung Gap areas, and the Pak Sha Wan battery held out for a further three days.

The Japanese continued their drive towards the south coast and by late afternoon on 21 December had reached Deepwater Bay and Repulse Bay, driving a wedge between East Brigade, now holding the Stanley Peninsula, and West Brigade continuing to occupy Victoria and the west of the island. By late evening of that day the Japanese occupied the centre of the island, including Stone Hill that overlooked Stanley and, most importantly, they now controlled the main reservoirs that supplied the island's fresh water.

Fighting continued throughout 23 December with East Brigade units being slowly pressed back into the Stanley peninsula despite desperate counter-attacks by the Royal Rifles of Canada supported by guns of the moveable artillery and the 6-inch guns of the emergency battery at Bluff Head. In West Brigade's area the Japanese continued to push westwards occupying Leighton Hill and Mount Cameron and bringing Central under artillery fire.

By 25 December the British-held territory was reduced to the western third of the island, together with Little Hong Kong, the Stanley peninsula and Chung Hum Kok. House to house fighting continued around Wan Chai, but at 15.30 hours on that day General Maltby advised the Governor that further resistance was useless and the colony was surrendered to the Japanese.

The defence of Hong Kong had always been a 'forlorn hope'. It could be said that General Maltby's defensive plan was defective. He viewed the Japanese command of the sea as a threat which could not be ignored and that landings were possible anywhere on the south shore as well as the north. This meant that troops were deployed to meet what turned out to be an illusory threat and, as a result, counter attacks against the main Japanese threat were rarely carried out in more than reinforced platoon strength. It can also be said that running the inter-brigade boundary along the approach to Wong Nai Chung Gap meant that a co-ordinated defence of this vital ground was not possible. Nevertheless, for seventeen days the garrison fought bravely, inflicting heavy casualties on the Japanese invasion force. The medium and mountain guns of the moveable artillery fully supported the garrison, as did a number of guns of the fixed defences which, unlike the guns of Singapore fixed defences, were adequately supplied with high-explosive and shrapnel ammunition.

As the British gunners withdrew from the fixed defences, they destroyed the majority of the serviceable guns with the exception of two 9.2-inch guns of Stanley Battery that were in action until the surrender and a single 6-inch gun of Pak Sha Wan Battery which was found intact after the capture of the battery. The two 9.2-inch guns were subsequently kept in operational condition by the Japanese and, indeed, were provided with concrete overhead cover 4 feet (1.23m) thick resembling a beehive in shape.

The Post-War Defences

In 1946 Colonel F.W. Rice was sent to the Far East to inspect the remains of the fixed defences at Singapore and Hong Kong and to recommend what form any future defence should take for each colony. The three options were to re-fortify the colony; to only establish an examination service battery; or to de-activate the coast defences entirely. Colonel Rice reported that only the three coast guns used by the Japanese were capable of reuse and that the Japanese had removed the other unserviceable guns for scrap. After brief consideration the War Office selected the third option and the decision was taken that the colony would no longer be defended by guns in fixed defences.

The strategic situation changed dramatically in 1949 when the Chinese Communist Party defeated the Nationalists and came to power in China. The British Government, aware of the vulnerability of Hong Kong, authorized a major reinforcement of the Hong Kong garrison. The garrison was increased to the strength of a division with the arrival of the Headquarters 40th Infantry Division and supporting troops. The division consisted of three infantry brigades, 26 Gurkha Infantry Brigade, and 27 and 28 Infantry Brigades each supported by a field artillery regiment armed with 25-pdr gun-howitzers,

Stanley Battery 9.2-inch Mk X BL gun. The photograph was taken in 1946 and shows the very thick concrete carapace built over the gun by the Japanese, and which must have restricted the gun's traverse considerably. (*Author's Collection*)

with a medium artillery regiment armed with 5.5-inch medium guns as divisional troops.

The anti-aircraft defence of the colony was the responsibility of 27th HAA Regiment RA comprising three batteries, two static and one mobile, each armed with 3.7-inch HAA guns. The mobile guns, based at Stanley Barracks, were to be deployed to positions at Tate's Cairn and Isthmus Camp, with the static guns on sites on Stonecutters Island, Brick Hill, Sai Wan Hill (Sai Wan Fort) and Mount Davis. At Sai Wan Fort the 3-inch AA and old 6-inch BL gun positions were adapted to mount the modern 3.7-inch guns. At the other positions simple concrete platforms were laid, each with a number of concrete lockers for ammunition.

During the Korean War between 1950 and 1953 units of the garrison served in Korea as part of the United Nations force but, with the end of the war and a gradual improvement in relations with China, the decision was taken to disband 40th Infantry Division in 1957 and the Hong Kong garrison was reduced to one infantry brigade supported by three Royal Artillery regiments, two field and one medium regiment. However, by late 1963 the artillery element of the garrison had been reduced to one light (field) regiment, and this unit was finally withdrawn in 1976 when the role of the garrison changed from defence of the colony to assisting the Royal Hong Kong Police in internal security duties.

Appendix

Artillery Guns and Mortars

Smooth-Bore Guns & Mortars

Guns

Type	Weight* cwt	Length feet	Calibre inches	Range yards	Comments
12-pdr	29	7.6	4.62	1,700	At 5° elev
18-pdr	41	9	5.29	1,770	At 5° elev
24-pdr (1)	50	9.5	5.82	2,000	At 5° elev
32-pdr (1)	58	9.5	6.41	2,260	At 5° elev
56-pdr	98	11	7.56	2,260	At 5° elev
68 pdr	95	10.8	8.12	2,500	At 5° elev
8-inch Shell Gun	65	9	8.05	1,920	At 5° elev
10-inch Shell Gun	86	9.33	10	2,000	At 5° elev

Mortars Land Service

Type	Weight* cwt	Length feet	Calibre inches	Range yards	Comments
8-inch	9	2.10	8	690–3,000	Range at 45° with varying charges. Weight of shell 40lbs
10-inch	15.5	2.33	10	690–3,000	Range at 45° with varying charges. Weight of shell 84lbs
13-inch Land Service	37.25	3.67	13	690–3,000	Range at 45° with varying charges. Weight of shell 200lbs

Rifled Muzzle-loading Guns

Type	Weight* cwt	Length feet	Calibre inches	Range yards	Comments
64-pdr (2)	58	10.58	6.30	3,000 (3)	
64-pdr (2)	71	10.22	6.30	3,000 (3)	
64-pdr	64	9.8	6.39	3,000 (3)	Mark III
	tons				
7-inch	6.5	11	7	3,000 (3)	Weight of shell 112lb
7-inch	7	12.5	7	3,000 (3)	Weight of shell 112lb
9-inch	12	13	9	3,000 (3)	Weight of shell 250lb
10-inch	18	15	10	3,000 (3)	Weight of shell 400lb
11-inch	25	15	11	3,000 (3)	Weight of shell 530lb
12.5-inch	38	18.68	12.5	3,000 (3)	Weight of shell 800lb

Quick-firing Guns

Type	Weight* cwt	Length feet	Calibre inches	Range yards	Comments
6-pdr	7	8.13	2.24	7,500	
Twin 6-pdr	10	9	2.24	11,300	Hotchkiss
12-pdr	12	10.3	3	8,000	Weight of shell 12.5lbs
	tons				
4.7-inch	2.05	16.17	4.70	10,800	Weight of shell 45lbs
6-inch	6.50	20.77	6	10,900	Weight of shell 100lbs

Breech-loading Guns

Type	Weight* tons	Length feet	Calibre inches	Range yards	Comments
6-inch Mk IV & VI	5	14.45	6	10,000	Weight of shell 100lbs
6-inch Mk VII CP Mtg (15°)	7.50	23.26	6	12,000–19,700	Weight of shell 100lbs
6-inch Mk XXIV on Mtg Mk V	7.50	23.26	6	24,500	Weight of shell 100lbs
8-inch Mk VIIIa Barbette Mtg	11.50	19.25	8	9,000	Armstrong Weight of shell 210lbs
9.2-inch Mk IV on Mtg Mk I (15°)	23	25.85	9.20	16,000	Weight of shell 380lbs
9.2-inch Mk X on Mtg Mk V (15°)	28	36.86	9.20	21,000	Weight of shell 380lbs
9.2-inch Mk X on Mtg Mk V II (35°)	28	36.86	9.20	29,000	Weight of shell 380lbs
10-inch Mk III on Mtg Mk IV (15°)	29	28.5	10	11,500	Weight of shell 500lbs
15-inch Mk I on Mtg Mk II (45°)	100	54.16	15	42,000	Weight of shell 1,938lbs

Field Guns

Type	Weight cwt	Length feet	Calibre inches	Range yards	Comments
15-pdr BLC	8	7.66	3	5,750	Weight of shell 14lbs
18-pdr QF	8	8.08	3.30	9,300	Weight of shell 18.5lbs (4)

Anti-Aircraft Guns

Type	Weight cwt	Length feet	Calibre inches	Range feet	Comments
LAA					
40mm L60	3.81	9.80	1.57	5,000 (6)	Weight of shell 2lbs
HAA					
3-inch QF (5) Mk III	20	11.66	3	26,000 (6)	Weight of shell 28lbs
	tons				
3.7-inch QF on Mk III Carriage	9.1+	16.25	3.7	32,000 (6)	Weight of shell 28lbs
4.5-inch QF MkII on Mk1a mtg	16.5+	17.58	4.45	44,000	Weight of shell 54lbs

* Barrel Weight

+ Overall Weight

Notes:

1. Blomfield gun
2. Palliser conversion
3. Effective range
4. Shrapnel shell
5. Mobile mounting
6. Effective ceiling

Notes

Archival Sources

BL   British Library
OIOC   British Library Oriental & India Office Collection
OUP   Oxford University Press
REL   Royal Engineers Library, Chatham
RGS   Royal Geographical Society, London
RHL   Rhodes House Library, Oxford
RSAA   Royal Society for Asian Affairs
TNA   The National Archives, Kew
USNA   United States National Archives

Introduction
  1. TNA CAB 11/118
  2. Ibid
  3. TNA CAB 7/6
  4. TNA WO 32/6358
  5. TNA CAB 7/2
  6. TNA PRO 30/6/122

Chapter 1: Bermuda
  1. TNA WO 55/928
  2. TNA WO 55/1551/1
  3. TNA WO 55/1551/2
  4. TNA WO 55/928
  5. TNA WO 55/1551/2
  6. Ibid
  7. Ibid
  8. TNA WO 55/929
  9. NAM Acc. No. 6807-169
 10. Ibid
 11. TNA WO/538
 12. USNA, DNA, Record Group 59, Records of Department of State, Communications from Special Agents 1784-1908, Microfilm 37, Reel T-12, 25 July 1838–21 July 1842.
 13. Ibid
 14. Ibid
 15. Quoted in Hogg, Ian V., *Coast Defences of England & Wales*, David & Charles, Newton Abbott, 1974, p.46

16. Jervois, *Report on the Defences of Canada and British Naval Stations in the Atlantic* Pt II, para.52, Quoted in Crick, Timothy, *Ramparts of Empire*, The Exeter Press, Exeter, 2012, p.148.
17. TNA WO 28/348
18. TNA CAB 11/11
19. Ibid
20. TNA WO 32/6358
21. Ibid
22. TNA CAB 11/11 Pt.9
23. TNA CAB 11/11 Pt.12
24. TNA CAB 80/25

Chapter 2: Jamaica
1. Buisseret, David, *The Fortifications of Kingston 1655–1914*, Bolivar Press, Kingston, 1971, p.29
2. TNA CO 137/82
3. Judah, G.F., *Rock Fort, Fort Castille, Fort Nugent*, Kingston, Jamaica, No Date. BL 010480.de.47
4. TNA CO 137/116
5. Ibid
6. TNA WO 55/1554
7. Ibid
8. TNA WO 44/121
9. TNA WO 55/934
10. Ibid
11. TNA CAB 7/1
12. TNA CAB 7/4
13. TNA CAB 11/8
14. Ibid
15. TNA WO 32/6358
16. TNA WO 95/5446
17. Ibid
18. Ibid
19. TNA WO 176/28

Chapter 3: St Helena
1. Jackson, E.L., *St Helena*, Ward Lock, London, 1903, p.190
2. Janisch, H.R., *Extracts from St Helena Records*, St Helena, 1885, 31 March 1787
3. Ibid, 12 November 1737
4. Ibid, 28 November 1695
5. Ibid, 12 January 1717
6. Brooke, *History of the Island of St Helena*, Kingsbury, Parbery & Allen, London, 1824, p.317
7. Ibid, 24 July, 1734
8. TNA CO 700 St Helena 8a

9. Brooke, p.282
10. Jackson, p.185
11. Ibid, pp.185–186
12. TNA WO 55/2827
13. Jackson, p.189
14. Mellis, G.W., *Views of St Helena Illustrative of its Scenery and History*, Vincent Brooks, London, 1857, p.44
15. TNA WO 396/1
16. Ibid
17. TNA WO 78/5401

Chapter 4: Antigua and St Lucia
1. Desmond V. Nicholson, *Forts of Antigua and Barbuda*, DVN Fund, Antigua, 1994, p.2
2. TNA CO 152/20
3. Ibid
4. Ibid
5. Ibid
6. TNA WO 55/923
7. TNA MPH 1/618
8. TNA CAB 7/4
9. TNA ADM 52/1544
10. TNA WO 55/938 & WO 55/238
11. TNA WO 55/938
12. TNA PRO 30/6/122
13. TNA CAB 7/11
14. TNA PRO 30/6/122
15. TNA CAB 7/4
16. TNA WO 106/6332
17. TNA CAB 38/6/99
18. Ibid
19. CAB 38/6/114
20. TNA WO 33/1006
21. Canadian Forces in Bermuda & St Lucia 1914-1919, Report No 87, Historical Section (GS) Army HQ, Ottawa.

Chapter 5: Ceylon
1. TNA WO 55/1552/1
2. BL OIOC IOR/H/338
3. P.M.Brigham & H.R.Cottle, *History of the Public Works Department Ceylon 1796–1913*, Vol 2, Colombo, 1921, p.35
4. TNA WO 55/1552/1 & MPH 1/619
5. Ibid
6. BL OIOC IOR/F/4/1331/52587
7. Brigham & Cottle, Vol 2, p.20

8. Pridham, Charles, *An Historical, Political, and Statistical Account of Ceylon and its Dependencies*, T.& W. Boone, London, 1849, p.602
9. TNA WO 55/1552/2
10. TNA WO 80/12
11. TNA WO 33/19
12. Ibid
13. Ibid
14. TNA PRO 30/6/122
15. TNA CAB 7/2
16. TNA WO 106/6332
17. TNA ADM 127/140
18. Ibid
19. TNA CAB 9/1 Pt 1
20. TNA CAB 9/1 Pt 2
21. TNA CAB 16/1
22. TNA CAB 5/5
23. Ibid
24. TNA WO 196/5
25. TNA WO 192/166
26. TNA CAB 80/32
27. TNA Ibid

Chapter 6: Mauritius
1. TNA WO 55/892
2. D'Unionville, Raymond M., *Letters of Sir John Abercromby Sep 1810 – Apr 1811*, Journal of the Mauritius History Society, 1969, p.60
3. TNA WO55/893
4. TNA CO 167/166
5. TNA WO 55/893
6. TNA CO 700 Mauritius 7
7. TNA WO 44/66
8. TNA WO 55/892
9. Abercromby Letters, p.59
10. TNA WO 44/66
11. Ibid
12. TNA WO 44/532
13. TNA WO 44/508
14. TNA WO 78/90
15. TNA CAB 7/1
16. TNA WO 78/4917
17. TNA WO 33/415
18. TNA WO 78/5403
19. TNA WO 78/4380
20. TNA CAB 80/32
21. TNA WO 192/40
22. TNA CAB 80/25

Chapter 7: Ascension Island
1. TNA WO 44/499
2. REL *Notes on the Island of Ascension*, Professional Papers of the Royal Engineers, Vol IV, 1840, pp.116–130
3. Ibid
4. RHL *Captain Bate's Log 1835*, Mss.Atlan.R.I.
5. RGS *Communication on the Island of Ascension*, Captain H. Brandreth RE, RGS Journal, London, 1835, pp.243–262
6. TNA ADM 123/84
7. Ibid
8. TNA CAB 7/4
9. Ibid
10. TNA ADM 116/314
11. Ibid
12. Ibid
13. TNA ADM 116/680
14. Ibid
15. TNA CO 968/25/2

Chapter 8: Singapore
1. Wurtzburg, Charles Edward, *Raffles of the Eastern Isles*, OUP, Singapore, 1954
2. BL OIOC IOR/E/4/807
3. Cameron, John, *Our Tropical Possessions in Malayan India*, Smith Elder & Co, London,1865
4. TNA CO 273/8/502-509
5. Ibid
6. TNA CO 273/35
7. TNA CO 273/53
8. TNA CO273/73
9. TNA CAB 7/1
10. Ibid
11. Ibid
12. TNA CO 129/205
13. TNA CO 273/137
14. TNA CAB 11/128
15. Turnbull, C.M., *A History of Modern Singapore, 1819–2005*, NUS Press, Singapore, 2009, p.170
16. TNA WO 106/132
17. TNA WO 78/5366
18. Simpson, Brigadier Ivan, *Singapore – Too Little Too Late*, UMCB Publications, Kuala Lumpur, 1981, p.26
19. Ibid p.208
20. TNA WO 203/6034
21. TNA WO 32/11031

Chapter 9: Hong Kong

 1. RSAA RE Letter Books, RSAA/M/184
 2. Ibid
 3. Ibid
 4. Ibid
 5. TNA CAB 7/1
 6. TNA ADM 125/27
 7. TNA CAB 7/4
 8. TNA WO 33/61
 9. TNA CAB 7/6
10. Ibid
11. TNA WO 32/6358
12. TNA CAB 11/57
13. TNA CO 537/739 & Weir, Rob, *British Blockhouses in Hong Kong*, Surveying & Built Environment, Vol. 22, Nov 2012, pp.8–18
14. TNA WO 78/5354
15. TNA CO 537/736
16. TNA WO 106/111
17. Ibid
18. TNA CAB 53/29
19. TNA COS 40/834

Glossary

À fleur d'eau	at sea level
AMTB	anti-motor torpedo boat
Batter	(of a wall) its inclination from the base
Barbette	position in which guns are mounted to fire over a parapet wall rather than through embrasures in the wall.
Bastion	a defence work projecting outwards from the main walls of a defended place.
BL	breech-loading
BLC	breech-loading converted
Caponier	covered passage constructed across, or projecting into, a ditch.
Carronade	a short-barrelled smooth-bore gun designed for use in confined spaces such as gun decks of ships and small casemates.
Casemate	a bomb-proof vaulted chamber built in the ramparts of a fort to contain guns, or to provide barrack accommodation.
CASL	coast artillery search light (term used post-1941).
Cavalier	high platform, mounting guns, built on a bastion or curtain wall.
CB	counter-bombardment
CD	close defence
CD/AA	close defence/anti-aircraft.
Chase	the part of a gun barrel forward of the trunnions
CID	Committee of Imperial Defence
CMB	coastal motor boat
CO	Commanding Officer
Counterguard	extensive outworks, usually triangular and open at the rear, which cover the faces of bastions, ravelins and redans.

Counterscarp	outer wall or slope of a ditch
Cwt	hundredweight
DEL	defence electric light (term used pre-1941 for search lights)
DPF	depression position finder
DRF	depression range finder
Embrasure	opening in a parapet or wall through which a gun can be fired
Epaulement	a covering mass raised to give protection from flanking fire
Escarpe	see Scarp
Gabion	a cylindrical wicker or metal basket filled with earth and used for field fortification.
GHQ	General Headquarters
Glacis	open slope extending from the ditch or moat giving a clear field of fire to the defenders
GOC	General Officer Commanding.
Gorge	rear, whether open or closed, of any defensive work
Grillage	heavy framework of cross-timbering as a foundation for a building in treacherous soil
HAA	heavy anti-aircraft
HKSRA	Hong Kong & Singapore Royal Artillery
Holdfast	a steel plate secured into the ground by long vertical bolts sunk into a concrete base on which heavy guns in fixed positions were secured.
JPC	Joint Planning Committee
LAA	light anti-aircraft
Machicoulis/ Machicolation	gallery projecting from a wall with openings between the corbels through which musketry fire can be brought upon an enemy at the base of the wall.
Mantlet	a protective screen covering an embrasure
Martello Tower	a small, circular tower, mounting a gun, and usually sited on the coast to prevent a hostile landing
Merlon	solid part of a parapet between two embrasures
Monitor	a shallow-draught warship armed with heavy guns
MTB	motor torpedo boat.
OC	Officer Commanding

OP	observation post
Orillion	projection from the face of a bastion
Parapet	stone or earth breastwork designed to give defenders on a wall or tower protection from enemy fire and observation.
Pdr	abbreviation of 'pounder', referring to the weight of a shell fired by a gun
PF	position finder
Pulau (Malay)	island
QF	quick-firer
RA	Royal Artillery
Racer	circular or semi-circular horizontal metal rail along which the wheels of a traversing platform for a heavy gun move.
Ravelin	triangular outwork, usually placed in a ditch in front of a curtain wall.
RBL	rifled breech-loading
RE	Royal Engineers
Redan	a triangular work in advance of a main fortification
Redoubt	a small fortified work, standing alone without bastions, usually designed as an infantry stronghold
RGA	Royal Garrison Artillery
RML	rifled muzzle-loading
SB	smooth-bore
SBML	smooth-bore muzzle-loading
Scarp	inner wall or slope of a ditch
SL	search light
Tampion	wooden stopper for the muzzle of a gun
Tenaille Trace	succession of redans joined at right angles to form a front of defence which resembles the teeth of a saw
Terreplein	area on top of a rampart or tower and surrounded by a parapet where guns are mounted
Traverse	a defensive barrier, usually a wall or earth bank, placed at right-angles to the main line of defence in order to protect the defenders from flanking fire.
Trunnion	horizontal cylindrical projections from a gun barrel which provide the rotational axis for elevating the barrel in its cradle.

Bibliography

General

Baker Brown, Lt Col W., *History of Submarine Mining in the British Army*, (Chatham, Royal Engineers Institute, 1910).

Coad, Jonathan, *Support for the Fleet – Architecture and Engineering of the Royal Navy's Bases*, (Swindon, English Heritage, 2013).

Crick, Timothy, *Ramparts of Empire: the Fortifications of Sir William Jervois Royal Engineer 1821–1897*, (Exeter, The Exeter Press, 2012).

Gardiner, Robert (Ed), *All the World's Fighting Ships 1860-1905*, (London, Conway Maritime Press, 1979).

Hogg, Ian V., *Coast Defences of England & Wales*, (Newton Abbott, David & Charles, 1974).

Hogg, I.V. & Thurston,L.F., *British Artillery Weapons & Ammunition 1914–1918*, (London, Ian Allen, 1972).

Hughes, Maj Gen B.P., *British Smooth-Bore Artillery*, (London, Arms and Armour Press, 1969).

Hughes, Maj Gen B.P. (Ed), *History of the Royal Regiment of Artillery, Between the Wars 1919–1939*, (London, Brassey's (UK), 1992).

Hughes, Quentin, *Military Architecture*, (London, Hugh Evelyn Ltd, 1974).

Kirby, Maj Gen S. Woodburn, *The War Against Japan Vol I*, (London, HMSO, 1959).

McConnell, David, *British Smooth-Bore Artillery, A Technological Study*, (Ottawa, Parks Canada, 1988).

Maurice-Jones, Col K.W., *History of Coast Artillery in the British Army*, (London, Royal Artillery Institution, 1959).

Schofield, Victoria, *Wavell, Soldier and Statesman*, (Barnsley, Pen & Sword Military, 2010).

Treatise on Service Ordnance 7th Edition, (London, HMSO, 1908).

Bermuda

Harris, Edward Cecil, *Bermuda Forts 1612–1957*, (Bermuda, Bermuda Maritime Museum Press, 1997).

The Great Guns of Bermuda, (Bermuda, Bermuda Maritime Museum Press, 1992).

Bermuda Forts, Fortress Issue 1, (Liphook, Beaufort Publishing Ltd, May 1989).

Willock, Col Roger USMC, *Bulwark of Empire*, (Bermuda, Bermuda Maritime Museum Press, 1988).

Jamaica

Buisseret, David, *The Fortifications of Kingston 1655–1914*, (Kingston, Bolivar Press, 1971).

Judah, G.F., *Rock Fort, Fort Castille, Fort Nugent*, (Privately published, Kingston, Jamaica, no date).

St Helena

Brooke, Thomas H., *History of the Island of St Helena*, (London, Kingsbury, Parbery & Allen, 1824).

Jackson, E.L., *St Helena*, (London, Ward Lock, 1903).

Janisch, H.R., *Extracts from St Helena Records*, (St Helena, 1885).

Mellis, G.W., *Views of St Helena Illustrative of its Scenery and History*, (London, Vincent Brooks, 1857).

Antigua & St Lucia

Dingwall, R.G., *The Military Complexes of Antigua, Volume 1, 1632–1900*, (Calgary, Dingwall Resources Ltd, 2016).

Nicholson, Desmond V., *Forts of Antigua and Barbuda*, (Antigua, DVN Fund, 1994).

Ceylon

Brigham, P.M. & Cottle, H.R., *History of the Public Works Department Ceylon 1796–1913, Volume II*, (Colombo, Public Works Department, 1921).

Nelson, W.A., *The Dutch Forts of Sri Lanka*, (Edinburgh, Canongate, 1984).

Pridham, Charles, *An Historical, Political and Statistical Account of Ceylon and its Dependencies*, (London, T. & W. Boone, 1849).

Mauritius

D'Unionville, Raymond M., *Letters of Sir John Abercromby Sep 1810 – Apr 1811*, (Port Louis, Journal of the Mauritius History Society, 1969).

Grant, Charles Viscount de Vaux, *History of Mauritius, or Isle of France, and the neighbouring islands*, (London, G. & W. Nicol, 1801).

Jackson, Ashley, *War and Empire in Mauritius and the Indian Ocean*, (London, Palgrave Macmillan, 2001).

Ascension Island

Brandreth, Capt Thomas RE, *Communication on the Island of Ascension*, (London, Journal of the Royal Geographical Society, 1835).

Hart-Davis, Duff, *Ascension: the Story of a South Atlantic Island*, (London, Constable, 1972).

Notes on the Island of Ascension, Professional Papers of the Royal Engineers, Volume IV, (Chatham, Royal Engineers Institute, 1840).

Singapore

Cameron, John, *Our Tropical Possessions in Malayan India*, (London, Smith Elder & Co, 1865).

Farrell, Brian, *The Defence and Fall of Singapore*, (Singapore, Monsoon Books Pte Ltd, 2015).

Glendinning, Victoria, *Raffles and the Golden Opportunity 1781–1826*, (London, Profile Books, 2012).

Grenfell, Russell, *Main Fleet to Singapore*, (Singapore, OUP, 1987).

Hack, Ken & Blackburn, Kevin, *Did Singapore Have to Fall? Churchill and the impregnable fortress*, (Abingdon, Routledge, 2003).

Harfield, Alan, *British & Indian Armies in the East Indies (1685–1935)*, (Chippenham, Picton Publishing (Chippenham) Ltd, 1984).

McIntyre, David, *The Rise and Fall of the Singapore Naval Base* (London, The Macmillan Press, 1979).

Murfett, Malcolm H., Miksic, John N., Farrell, Brian P., Chiang, Ming Shun, *Between Two Oceans, A Military History of Singapore from 1275 to 1971*, (Singapore, Marshall Cavendish Editions, 1999).

Simpson, Brig Ivan, *Singapore Too Little Too Late*, (Kuala Lumpur, UMCB Publication, 1970).

Smith, Colin, *Singapore Burning, Heroism and Surrender in World War II*, (London, Penguin Books, 2006).

Stubbs, Peter, *Fort Siloso*, www.fortsiloso.com

Wurtzburg, Charles Edward, *Raffles of the Eastern Isles*, (Singapore, OUP, 1954).

Hong Kong

Banham, Tony, *Not The Slightest Chance, The Defence of Hong Kong 1941*, (Hong Kong, Hong Kong University Press, 2005).

Bard, Solomon Matthew, *Notes on the History of Hong Kong's Coastal Defences during the British Administration, with special reference to Lei Yue Mun*, (Hong Kong, Hong Kong Museum of Coastal Defence, 2015).

Ko, Tim Keung and Wordie, Jason, *Ruins of War, A guide to Hong Kong's Battlefields and Wartime Sites*, (Hong Kong, Joint Publishing (HK) Ltd, 1996).

Kwong Chi Man and Tsoi Yiu Lun, *Eastern Fortress, A Military History of Hong Kong 1840-1970*, (Hong Kong, Hong Kong University Press, 2014).

Lovell, Julia, *The Opium War*, (London, Picador, 2011).

Ochterlony, John, *The Chinese War; an account of the operations from the commencement to the Treaty of Nanking*, (London, Saunders & Otley, 1844).

Rollo, Maj Denis, *The Guns and Gunners of Hong Kong*, (Hong Kong, Gunners Role of Hong Kong, 1991).

Siu Kwok Kin, *Forts and Batteries. Coastal Defence in Guangdong during the Ming and Qing Dynasties*, (Hong Kong, Hong Kong Museum of History, 1997).

Stewart, Evan, *Hong Kong Volunteers in Battle*, (Hong Kong, Blacksmith Books, 2005).

Index

Abercromby Hill, 91, 95
Abercromby, Gen Sir John, 135, 144
Abercromby, Gen Sir Ralph, 135
Acoustic Mirrors, 239
Admiral Hood's Tower, 106
Admiralty, Board of, xxi, xxvi, 9, 10, 23, 46, 77, 84, 95–5, 98, 109–10, 123–24, 126, 129, 160–61, 169–70, 174–78, 188, 190, 199, 200–201, 220, 223, 240
Admiralty Works Department, 171
Agincourt, HMS, 22
Air Ministry, 201–202
Albert Battery, 149–53
Alexandra Battery, 16, 24–5, 27
American War of Independence, 85, 90
Amiens, Treaty of, 39, 90, 92
Amsterdam Bastion (Colombo), 102
Amsterdam Bastion (Trincomalee), 106
Anderson, Maj Gen Charles, 232
Anglo–Japanese Alliance, 152, 198, 231, 235
Anglo–Russian Entente, 232
Anglo–Spanish War, 34
Antigua, 85–6, 94
Apostles Battery (Jamaica), 36, 40, 43–50
Apostles Battery (St Lucia), 96–7
Armstrong, Sir William, xiv, xvi, 120, 193, 223
Arthur Battery, 122
Ascension Island, 159–60, 164, 166–67, 169, 170–72, 175–76, 179
Ascension, HMS, 160, 164
Aurora Bastion, 111
Australian Army:
    22 Inf Bde, 209–10
    27 Inf Bde, 209–10

Back Bay, 103, 105
Banks' Lines, 59, 61, 71
Banks' Platform, 57, 59
Bank's Valley, 57, 59–61
Barney, Capt George RE, 43–4
Barker, Lt Col RE, 48–9, 117
Bartholomew, Maj Gen Arthur, 240
Bastion Fanfaron, 144
Bate, Capt William RM, 160, 162, 164
Barron, Maj Gen F.W., 128, 203, 238, 240
Baticaloa, 101, 108, 130

Batterie Condé, 140, 149
Bastion Battenburg (Battery), 102, 111, 114–15, 120–21, 125
Batterie de L'Anjou, 140
Batterie du Roy, 136
Batterie Fanfaron, 136
Battery Abercromby, 142–43, 148
Batu Berlayer AMTB Battery, 206, 211
Beane USAF Base, 100
Bedford Battery, 171–72, 174–77, 179
Belcher's Battery, 230, 232, 238, 246
Belcher's Bay, 217, 220, 222–24
Belcher's Lower Battery, 224, 226–27, 230, 233
Belcher's Point, 218, 222, 224, 229
Belcher's Upper Battery, 224, 226–27, 233
Belfry Hill, 110, 118
Bencoolen, 181
Bentinck, Lord William, 108, 182
Berhala Reping AMTB Battery, 206
Berlayer Point, 191, 213
Bermuda, 1–4, 7, 9, 12–13, 17, 25, 30, 45, 51
Bermuda Militia Artillery, 28–30
Bermuda Volunteer Engineers, 30
Berkley's Platform, 57, 64
Best, Capt Samuel BE, 182
Beting Kusah AMTB Battery, 203, 205–206
Bird Battery, 155, 158
Black Prince, HMS, xi, 22
Black River Bay, 138, 140, 142, 148
Blakang Mati, 180, 182, 184, 189–93, 196, 203, 209, 211, 213
Blakang Mati East Battery, 191, 195
Blakely, Alexander, xv
Blake's Island, 81, 83
Blockhouse, The, 168
Blockhouse Battery, 86
Bluff Head, 239, 247
Bluff Head Battery, 243
Blundell, Governor, 184
Boer War, 77, 226, 232
Bonham Road Battery, 220–21
Boucher Redoubt, 90–2
Boxer, HMS, 73
Brandreth, Capt Henry RE, 161–64
Brennan Torpedo, 229–30
British Army:

Royal Artillery:
  1st Battalion, 4
  2nd Battalion, 4
  Invalid Battalion, 4
  5th AA Regiment, 243
  6th Coast Regiment, 128
  7th Coast Regiment, 206
  8th Coast Regiment, 243
  9th Coast Regiment, 206
  12th Coast Regiment, 243
  16th Defence Regiment, 206
  27th HAA Regiment, 249
  43rd LAA Regiment, 130
  55th LAA Regiment, 130
  65th HAA Regiment, 130
  2 Heavy Battery, 54
  10 Heavy Battery, 53
  12 Heavy Battery, 235
  14 LAA Battery, 128
  25 Coast Battery, 157
  25 Heavy Battery, 157
  965 Defence Battery, 243
  Hong Kong & Singapore RA, 153, 206,
    232, 243
  St Helena Coast Battery RA, 78–9
Royal Garrison Artillery:
  3 Garrison Company, 28
  56 Company, 153
  66 Company, 52–3
  Ceylon–Mauritius Battalion, 125
  West Indian Battalion, 51
Royal Engineers:
  4 Company, xxv
  23 Company, 49, 225
  27 Fortress Company, 27
  33 Company, xxv, 225, 229
  43 Company, 157
  44 Fortress Company, 52
  Eastern Battalion, xxvi, 225
  St Helena Fortress Company, 70
Infantry:
  27th (Inniskilling) Regiment, 91
  1/53rd Regiment, 70
  2/66th Regiment, 70
  91st Regiment, 70
  Middlesex Regiment, 1st Battalion,
    242–43, 245
  Royal Scots, 2nd Battalion, 242, 245
  Shropshire Light Infantry (TF), 4th
    Battalion, 198
  West India Regiment, 45, 53, 72, 98
Brigades:
  26 (Gurkha) Infantry, 248
  27 Infantry, 248
  28 Infantry, 248
  East, 245, 247
  Mainland, 243–45
  West, 245–47

Divisions:
  40th Infantry, 248
Breakneck Valley, 57, 63, 69
Breda, Treaty of, 80
Bridges, Lt Col RE, 106
Brooke, Governor, 67, 69
Brough, Lt Col RA, 137
Brough & Buchanan Report, 140, 143–44
Brownrigg, Gen, 106
Bryce, Maj Gen Sir Alexander, 139–40
Buchanan, Lt Col RE, 137
Buildings Bay Battery, 15–16
Bukit Timah, 209, 211
Buona Vista, 203, 212
Buona Vista Battery, 203–204, 206–207, 209
Burt, Governor William Mathew, 85

Cable & Wireless Ltd, 176, 179
Calcutta, 181, 184
Calder Harbour AMTB Battery, 207
Calder Passage, 203
Campbell, Maj Gen Archibald, 36–7
Canadian Army:
  6 Company RGA, 99
  Royal Canadian Army Medical Corps, 99
  C Force, 244
  Royal Rifles of Canada, 244–45, 247
  Winnipeg Grenadiers, 1st Battalion,
    244–45
Cannonier's Point, 133, 138, 144–45, 148
Canton, 214, 217, 240–41
Cape D'Aguilar Battery, 243
Cape of Good Hope, ix, 5, 69, 164–65, 175,
  180, 219
Captain, HMS, xiii
Castle Harbour, 2, 17–18
Castle Island, 2–4, 17
Castlereagh, Lord, 40
Castillo, Sir James, 37
Castries, 90–3
Castries Harbour, 88, 93–4, 99–100
Caudan Battery, 144–45
Causeway, The, 199, 207–10
Cavalier Battery, 118, 120
Cavendish, Thomas, 57
Centurion Battery, 321–32
Ceylon, ix, xxv, 101, 104–105, 111–12, 114,
  117, 120–21, 128–29, 132, 219
Ceylon Artillery, 132
Ceylon Artillery Volunteers, 125
Ceylon Defence Force, 125
Ceylon Garrison Artillery, 125, 128, 132
Ceylon Infantry Regiment, 188
Changi, 202–203, 208
Changi Battery, 205–206
Changi Fire Command, 205–206, 210
Channel Battery, 136, 146–47
Chapel Hill, 110, 116, 126–28, 131

Chapel Hill Battery, 129
Charles Fort, 2
Chief of the Imperial General Staff, 234
Chiefs of Staff Committee, xxx, 129, 153, 235, 240
China Squadron RN, 214, 219
Chubb's Rock, 61, 71
Chuenpi, Convention of, ix
Chung Hom Kok, 238, 243, 247
Churchill, Winston, 234, 244
Cicala, HMS, 245
Ciceron Redoubt, 90, 93, 95
Citadel Battery, 118, 120
Civilian Shore Wireless Service RN, 176
Clappenburg Island, 106–107
Clappenburg Point, 116, 131–32
Clarence Bay, 160, 162–63, 174
Clarke, Lt Gen Sir Alexander, 223
Clarke, Maj Gen Sir Andrew, 117
Cleghorn, Hugh, 105
Cleland's Line, 37
Cochrane, R Adm Thomas, 109
Cockburn, Adm Sir George, 70, 160
Codrington's Battery, 81, 83
Cole, Sir Lowry, 137
Collinson Battery, 237, 241
Collyer, Capt George RE, 184
Colombo, 101, 106–108, 110–17, 120–22, 124, 126–28, 130–31, 199, 213
Colombo Fort, 103, 105, 111, 113
Colombo Harbour, 122–23, 127, 129, 132
Colombo Town Guard, 125
Colpetty Battery, 132
Colonial Defence Committee, ix, xxix, xxx, 76, 94, 98, 115, 120–21, 148, 190, 219
Colonial Office, x, 111, 187, 191–92, 194, 220, 223, 226
Comfort Cove, 162, 172
Comfortless Cove, *see* Comfort Cove
Committee of Imperial Defence, xxx, 98, 126, 199, 202–203, 237
Convention of London, 180
Coolidge USAF Base, 89
Coote, Lt Gen Sir Eyre, 40
Cottage Battery, 169–71
Cow Bay, 26
Cox's Battery, 66
Crabb's Peninsula, 88
Crimean War, xi, xxviii, 194
Cross Hill, 160, 163, 165–66, 168–72, 174, 178
Crown Point (James Town), 59
Crown Point (Sandy Bay), 61–2
Crownhill Fort, xxiii
Cul–de–Sac Bay, 90, 92–3, 97
Cunningham, Lt Col RE, 4–5, 8, 142
Cunningham Tower, 138, 140, 142, 147, 150
Cuyler, Brig Gen, 87

Dalling, Maj Gen John, 36–7
Daniel's Head, 17–18, 22
Darkdale, RFA, 78
Dawson, Capt William RE, 104, 107–108
Debutts, Capt RE, 4–5
Defence Committee, xxviii–xxx, 16–18, 25–7, 46, 48–9, 74–5, 94, 112–14, 220
Delft Bastion, 102
Destroyers for Bases Agreement, 30, 55, 100
Devastation, HMS, xiii
Devonshire Redoubt, 2–3
Devil's Peak, 228–29, 232–33, 237, 245
Diamond Hill Battery, 131–32
Diego Garcia Anti–Raider Battery, 158
Dockyard, Bermuda, 6, 8, 15, 21–2
Dominica, 85
Dow's Hill, 86
Drunkenman's Cay, 47
Du Casse, Adm Jean–Baptiste, 33
Durnford, Lt Andrew RE, 3
Dutch Battery, *see* Portuguese Battery
Dutch Bay, 103
Dutch East India Company, *see* VOC

East, Capt J.W. RM, 162, 167
East Battery (Hong Kong), 217
East Battery (St Helena), 65–6
East Indies Squadron RN, 126
East Lamma Channel, 242
Eastern Battery, 118–19
Eastern Entrance (Hong Kong), 226, 231, 233
Eastern Redoubt, *see* Fort Albert
Eastern Telegraph Company, 171, 176
Edgar's Bungalow Battery, 216
Egg Island, 70
Elephant Island, 131–32
Elephant Point, 110, 116, 128, 131–32
Elephant Ridge, 110, 117, 126, 128
Elliot Battery, 231
Elswick Ordnance Company, xix, 120, 193, 223
Emden, SMS, 198
English Bay, 178
English Bay Company, 178
English Harbour, 80, 82–8, 94
Enkhuysen Bastion (Colombo), 114–15, 121
Enkhuysen Bastion (Trincomalee), 104, 111
Entrenchment, 83
Eolus Bastion, 111, 115, 117
Esher Committee, xxx

Faber Fire Command, 204, 206, 210–11
Fairfax–Ellis, Lt Col RA, 48–9
Falklands, Battle of, 125, 153, 176, 232
Falmouth, Antigua, 80–1, 83, 87
Fanfaron Bastion, 146, 148
Fanshawe, Lt Col Edward RE, 8–9

Farquar, Maj William, 181
Fay Battery, 156
Ferry Battery, 233
Ferry Point, 6, 17
Fisher, Adm 'Jackie', 28, 51
Fitz, Albert, 11–12
Flagstaff Battery (Bermuda) 22
Flagstaff Battery (Colombo), 111, 114, 122, 124
Flagstaff Battery (Trincomalee), 118–20
Floating Dock No 1, 22–3
Fly Point, 224, 226
Forts:
    Adelaide, 145, 152, 184
    Albert, 9, 12, 15, 19, 24–5, 27, 30
    Augusta, 35, 37, 41, 43–5
    Barrington, 85
    Berkeley, 83–4, 86, 88
    Blanc, 135–38, 143
    Brownrigg, 106
    Byam, 83
    Canning, 184–85, 188–89, 191–92
    Carlisle, 33
    Castile, 39
    Castillo, 37
    Charles (Antigua), 81
    Charles (Jamaica), 33–6, 43, 46
    Charlotte (Antigua), 86–8
    Charlotte (St Lucia), 92–5
    Clarence (Ascension), 165–66
    Clarence (Jamaica), 38, 40, 43–4, 48, 50–1, 53–5
    Cockburn, 160–63, 165
    Connaught, 193, 195–97, 202, 204, 206, 209
    Cumberland, 143, 148, 153
    Cunningham, 5–6, 8, 12–13, 15–16, 18, 24–7
    Frederick, 103, 108, 111, 114–16, 119–22, 126, 132
    Fullerton, 182–85, 187–88
    George (Antigua), 81, 87–8
    George (Bermuda), 9, 12, 19, 24, 27
    George (Jamaica), 34
    George (Mauritius), 138, 142–46, 149–58
    Hamilton, 20–1, 24
    Harman, 83
    Hayes, 175–76, 178
    James (Antigua), 81–3, 85
    James (Jamaica), 33
    Johnston, 37–8
    Langton, 16, 19–21, 24–6
    McDonald, 106
    McDowell, 106, 108
    Marlborough, 181
    Monk, see Fort George (Antigua)
    Murdoch, see Murdoch's Battery
    Nugent, 39, 43, 51–2

Ostenburg, 103, 106, 108, 111, 114–17, 120
Paget, Upper, 5
Palmer, 192, 195–96
Pasir Panjang, 193, 195–96
Popple, 3, 5
Prospect, 15, 19–21, 24
Rocky, 46
Rodney, 90, 93
Rupert, 33
Serapong, 193, 197
Shirley, 86
Siloso, 193, 195–97, 204, 211, 213
St Catherine, 5–6, 8–9, 12, 15, 17, 19, 24–5, 27
Tanjong Katong, 192–93
Thornton, 168–71, 176
Victoria (Bermuda), 12, 15, 19, 24–5, 27, 29–30
Victoria (Hong Kong), 217
Victoria (Mauritius), 149–53
Walker, 33
Warren, 164, 166–69
William (Antigua), 83
William (Bermuda), 7, 9
William (Jamaica), 34
William (Mauritius), 138, 144, 147–52
Fort de France, 89
Fraser, Capt RA, 4
Freemans Bay, 85
French Battery, see Ostenburg Point Battery
Fyers, Lt Col RE, 139

Galle, 101, 105–106, 108, 110–14, 117
Galle Face, 124
Galle Face Battery, 120–22, 125, 127, 132
Galle Fort, 103, 108, 111
Gallwey, Lt Gen T.L., 95, 116
Ganteaume, Adm, 39
Garrison, The, 161
General Brownrigg's Tower, 107
Georgetown (Ascension), 161, 165–66, 168, 172, 177
Georgetown (Penang), 198
Gibraltar Shield, 14
Gillman, Lt Gen Sir Webb, 202–203
Gin Drinkers Bay, 237, 240
Gin Drinkers Line, 228, 240–41, 245
Gladstone, William Ewart, xxiv, 118
Gloire, La, xi, 111
Goat Hill (Antigua), 82, 85
Goat Hill (Ascension), 162, 165, 167
Goat Island, 55
Goat Pound Ridge, 63–4
Gomm, Maj Gen Sir William, 145–46
Goodenough, Maj Gen W.H., 21, 25, 50
Gough Battery, 237
Government Hill, 184

Governor's Island, 4
Graf Spee, 55
Grand Port, 133–34, 157
Grand River North West, 135, 137–38, 140, 142, 148–49
Grand River South East, 156
Grasett, Maj Gen Arthur, 244
Great Fort George, *see* Fort George (Antigua)
Great Sober Island, 110, 116–17, 119–20, 122, 131–32
Great Sound, 4–5, 21
Green Mountain, 159, 161, 164–65, 168
Gregory's Battery, 66
Grinfield, Lt Gen, 92
Gros–Islet Bay, 90, 93
Guangzhou, *see* Canton
Guard Battery, 115, 121

Half Moon Battery (St Helena), 59–60, 64, 72, 74
Half Moon Battery (Trincomalee), 118–19
Hambantota, 106
Hamilton, 2, 5–6, 19, 26
Hammenheil, 109
Hanover Lines, 43, 46–8, 50
Harris, V Adm Sir Robert, 175
Hayes Hill, 165, 167–70
Hayes Hill Battery, 165, 167–68, 172
Hector, HMS, 130
Hemphill, Col A.J., 12
Hennessy, Sir John Pope, 220
Hercules, HMS, 216
Hermes, HMS, 130
High Knoll Fort (Battery), 69, 71, 74–5
Hog Fish Cut, 3, 17–18, 22–3
Holland Bastion, 104
Hollyhock, HMS, 130
Hong Kong, ix, xxvi, 123, 199, 212, 214, 216–17, 219, 221–23, 225–27, 230–32, 234–37, 240–41, 243–45, 248
Hong Kong Artillery, 241
Hong Kong Rifle Volunteers, 241
Hong Kong Volunteer Defence Corps (HKVDC), 241, 243, 245
Hood, Commodore Samuel, 92, 106
Hood, HMS, 177
Hood's Tower, 128
Hood's Tower Battery, 128, 132
Hoorn Bastion, 102
Horse's Head, 61–2
Hurd, Lt RN, 4

Île aux Aigrettes, 155, 158
Île de France, 133–34
Île de la Passe, 133–34, 137–38, 141, 144–45, 156

Île aux Tonneliers, 135–38, 142, 153
Indian Army:
    5th Light Infantry, 198
    14th Punjab Regiment, 2nd Battalion, 242, 245–46
    7th Rajput Regiment, 4th Battalion, 242, 245–46
    44 Infantry Brigade, 210
    III Indian Corps, 208–209
    Madras Artillery, 215
    Madras Engineers, 215
Inner Defences, Hong Kong, 226–27
Inspector General of Fortifications, xviii, xxvii–xxviii, 41, 46, 48, 95, 114, 116–17, 120, 137–39, 168, 192, 223–24, 227
Ireland Island, 2–3, 8, 22, 24, 26–7, 29, 30

Jaffna, 101, 105–106, 108
Jamaica, xxv, 32, 36, 38, 42, 48, 50–1, 55, 94, 244
Jamaica Militia Artillery, 50–5
James Fort, 58
James Town, 57, 59, 62–3, 67, 72–3, 77–9
James Town Lines, 71
Japan, 126, 153–54, 198, 200–201, 232, 236, 239
Japanese Army:
    5th Division, 209
    18th Division, 209
    38th Division, 245–46
    Imperial Guards Division, 210
    228 Infantry Regiment, 245–46
    229 Infantry Regiment, 245–46
    230 Infantry Regiment, 245–46
Jervois, Sir W.D., 13–14, 16–17, 19–21, 113–14, 188–89, 193
Johnston, David, 37
Johore, Sultan of, 203
Johore Battery, 203, 205–207, 209, 211
Jubilee Battery, 237, 241
Jurong River, 208, 210

Kandy, 104–107
Keane's Battery, 87
Kellett's Island, 215–16, 218
Keppel Harbour, 199, 203
King William's Fort, 57, 59
King's Castle, 2–3
Kingston, 32, 34–7, 40–4, 48–9, 51, 53–4, 99
Klippenburg Bastion (Colombo), 102, 111, 115, 121
Klippenburg Bastion (Galle), 111, 115, 117
Knowles, Capt Charles RN, 83–4
Korean War, 249
Kowloon, 217–18, 220–21, 226, 236, 238, 240–41, 245
Kowloon Battery, 221

Kowloon Dock, 220, 222–26
Kowloon East, 222–24, 226, 230
Kowloon North, 221
Kowloon West, 222, 226
Krupp, Friedrich, xix, 188

Labrador Battery, 204, 206, 211–12
Ladang AMTB Battery, 207, 211
Ladder Hill, 63, 65, 67, 69, 71–3, 75
Ladder Hill Battery, 78
Ladder Hill Fort, 67, 70–1, 74–6
Laffan, Col RE, 112
Lake, Capt ME, 182–84
Lake's Battery, 183–84
Lambton, V Adm Sir Hedworth, 231
La Preneuse Tower, 142
La Toc Battery, 96–7
La Toc Peninsula, 94–7
Lawson, Brig, 246
League of Nations, 127, 200
Leeward Islands, 80, 82, 85
Lemon Valley, 57, 63–4
Lemon Valley Fort, 64, 69, 74
Lemon Valley Lines, 63, 71
Lewin, Maj Gen Earnest, 203
Lewis, Lt Col J.F. RE, 172, 175
Lilly, Christian, 33
Little Plum Point Battery, 47
Little Sober Island, 110, 116, 121, 123, 130
London Naval Disarmament Conference, 200
Longfield, Maj R.J. RA, 78
Lookout Battery, 86
Lowe, Sir Hudson, 70
Lyemun Central Battery, 226
Lyemun Pass, 218, 228–29, 232, 245
Lyemun Redoubt, 226–28, 231
Lyemun Reverse Battery, 226, 230–31, 233
Lyemun West Battery, 226, 230–31, 233

Macdonald, Ramsey, 200
Mahébourg 133, 137–38, 144, 148, 154–57
Main Channel, see Narrows, The
Maitland, Gen, 106
Malacca, 180, 183
Malay Regiment, 1st Battalion, 211
Maltby, Maj Gen C.M., 245–47
Manaar, 101, 105, 108–109
Mann, Gen Gother, 137
Maria Hill Fort, 3
Martel, Peter, 35
Martello Towers, xxii, 5–8, 42–3, 65, 106, 138, 147, 150, 162, 182
M'Arthur, Lt RMA, 164
Martinique, 89, 94, 98–9
Masked Battery, 85–6
Matale, 106, 108

Matara, 101, 105, 108–109
Mathew, Governor William, 82–3, 85
Mauritius, ix, xxvi, 105, 133–35, 137, 145–46, 148, 152–55, 157, 184, 219
Mauritius Anti–Raider Battery, 155
Mauritius Coast Regiment, 157
Mauritius Territorial Force, 155, 157
Mauritius Volunteer Artillery, 153, 157
McCallum, Capt RE, 191
Meadows Battery, 96–7, 100
Middle Ground, 86–7
Middle Point, 59, 72, 77–8
Middleburg Bastion, 111
Milne, Adm of the Fleet Sir Alexander, 219
Minto, Lord, 181
Missiessy, Adm, 39–40
Monk's Hill, 81, 83, 87
Moon Bastion, 103
Morne Fortune, 91, 95–7
Morne Freeland Battery, 93
Morne Chabot, 95–6
Morse, Gen, 41
Mosquito Point, 35
Mount Batten Battery, 122, 124
Mount Davis, 214, 233, 237, 239, 245–46, 249
Mount Davis Battery, 237, 245
Mount Faber, 183, 189, 192
Mount Faber Battery, 183, 185, 188–89
Mount Faber Mortar Battery, 185, 188–89, 191
Mount Imbeah Battery, 185, 188
Mount Palmer, 183–84, 189–91, 193
Mount Palmer Battery, 185, 188
Mount Serapong, 184, 189–93, 203
Mount Siloso, 189–92
Mulcaster, Lt Col RE, 137
Munden's Battery, 58, 71
Munden's Hill, 58, 74–5
Munden's Hill Battery, 72, 74, 76
Munden's Point, 57, 61, 73–4
Munroe Battery, 122, 124
Murdoch's Battery, 164–65, 167–68
Murray, Adm, 4
Murray Battery, 215–16, 218–19, 223–24
Murray, Gen Sir Thomas, 110
Murray's Anchorage, 4–5, 8, 12, 15, 17
Mutwall Battery, 122, 124
Mutwall Point, 114, 120–21

Nanking, Treaty of, ix, 214
Napier, Capt RM, 169–70
Napoleon Bonaparte, ix, 70, 87, 160, 164, 180
Narrows, The, 4–6, 17–18, 22, 24, 26
Naval Bay Battery, 221
Naval & Military Defence Committee, see Defence Committee

Nelson Battery, 50–1
New Harbour, 180, 182–84, 189, 193, 196, 199
New Territories, 226, 236, 238–39, 243, 245
Nicholls, Lt Col Edward, 160
Nicholson's Cove, 109–110
Nick Battery, 156
North Caribbean Force, 55
North East Advanced Battery, 47
North Point Battery, 223–25, 230–31
Nugent, Lt Gen George, 39

Old Harbour, 41–2
Old Woman's Valley, 70
O'Meara's Battery, 93
Opium Wars, 214, 217
Ord, Sir Harry, 188
Ordnance, Board of, x, xvi, xxvi–xxviii, 10, 38, 40, 44, 86, 110, 138, 146, 217
Orsini Affair, 111
Oso (Siloso Point) AMTB Battery, 206, 212–13
Ostenburg Face Bastion (Battery), 118, 120, 122
Ostenburg Point, 110, 116–17, 120, 122, 130
Ostenburg Point Battery, 123, 131–32
Ostenburg Ridge, 110, 116, 119, 122, 127
Oversea Defence Committee, xxx, 199, 201, 235
Owen, R Adm, 108
Owen Committee, xxi, 28, 51, 124–25, 152, 196, 230–31

Paget's Fort, 2–3
Paget's Island, 5, 22
Paixhans, Col Henri–Joseph, xiv–xv
Pak Sha Wan Battery, 233, 238, 243, 246
Palisadoes, The, 33, 48
Palisadoes Battery, 48–9
Palliser, Maj, xvi–xvii
Palmerston, Lord, 214
Panama Mounts, 30, 55, 88
Panjdeh Incident, 118, 193
Panmure, Lord, 218
Parham Harbour, 88
Paris, Treaty of, ix, 90
Pasir Laba Battery, 204, 206, 209
Pasir Panjang, 191, 209, 211
Pasley, Gen Sir Charles, 13
Patton, Governor, 69
Patton's Battery, 71
Pearl Harbor, 129
Pearl's Hill, 184
Peking, Convention of, 214, 217
Pellew, R Adm Sir Edward, 109
Pembroke Fort, 2
Penang, 181, 183, 198, 207

Pengerang Battery, 205–206
Peniston's Redoubt, 2
Penn Battery, 50
Percival, Lt Gen A.E., 207, 209–11
Petite Montagne, 138–39
Phillips, Lt Col RE, 168–69
Pigeon Island, 90–1, 93–4
Pilot Station Tower, 124
Pinewood Battery, 228, 231, 243, 246
Pointe de Galle, see Galle
Pointe du Diable, 138, 156
Pointe aux Feuilles, 156, 158
Pointe L'Harmonie, 140
Port Henderson Hill, 33, 35
Port Louis, 133–40, 143, 145–49, 152–155, 184
Port Mathurin, 155, 158
Port Royal, 32–4, 37, 40, 45–7, 94, 99
Port Royal Point Battery, 46
Port Shelter, 229, 241
Portuguese Battery (St Helena), 67
Portuguese Battery (Trincomalee), 118, 120
Possession Point, 224
Pottinger Battery, 237
Powell's Valley, 65, 69
Prevost Redoubt, 90, 92
Priest's Peak, 152, 157
Prince of Wales, HMS, 207
Prince of Wales's Line, 43, 46–9
Prince William Henry's Polygon, 37, 41–2, 46
Prospect Hill, 16, 18–19
Prosperous Bay, 57, 66–8
Pujet, Capt Peter RN, 109
Pulau Brani, 184, 190, 196
Pulau Hantu AMTB Battery, 206, 211
Pulau Tekong Besar, 202–203, 208
Pulau Tekong Kechil, 203
Pulau Sehajat AMTB Battery, 206
Pulau Ubin, 203, 208
Pyramid Point, 162, 174

RA & RE Works Committee, xxix, 24–5, 223–24, 228
Raffles, Sir Stamford, 181, 184
Ralfe, Capt BA, 182
Rat Island, 81–2, 85
Regent's Battery, 116, 118–21
Regiment du Meuron, 105
Reid, Col RE, 10–11
Rennell, Maj James, 64
Repulse, HMS, 207
Repulse Point Battery, 60
Resolution, HMS, 4
Retreat Hill, 6–7, 9
Réunion, 137, 145, 155
Riau, Sultan of, 181

Riau–Linnga Islands, 181
Rice, Col F.W., 213–14, 248
Richards, Commodore F.R. RN, 167
Ricochet Battery, 164
Ridge Battery (Antigua), 86, 118–19
Ridge Battery (Trincomalee), 122
Road Fort, 83
Roberts, Governor, 58
Robinson, Sir Hercules, 187
Rock Fort, 36–7, 39, 41–4
Rockhouse 9.2in Battery, 124–25, 127
Rockhouse 6in Battery, 127, 132
Rocky Point Battery, 46–55, 99
Rodney, Adm, 90–1
Rodney Battery, 96
Rodrigues, 154, 158
Rotterdam Bastion, 102
Royal Battery (Hong Kong), 215–16
Royal Battery (Mauritius), 136, 138, 140,
    142–43, 146–48, 150, 152–57
Royal Carriage Department, 145, 170
Royal Gun Factory, xv, 120, 145, 193
Royal Marines:
    HQ 1 AA Brigade, 129–30
    1st HAA Regiment, 129–30
    1st RMMNBDO, 129
    22 LAA Battery, 130
    Royal Marines, 77–8
    Royal Marine Artillery, 162
    Royal Marine Mobile Force, 175
Runaway Bay, 82
Rupert's Bay, 60–1
Rupert's Hill Battery, see Munden's Hill
    Battery
Rupert's Valley Line, 61
Russo–Japanese War, 153

Saddle Battery, 93
Sai Wan Battery (Fort), 228, 231, 245, 249
Sakai, Gen Takashi, 245
Salt Pond Battery, 48–9
Salt Pond Hill, 37, 48
San Stefano, Treaty of, 189, 219
Sandy Bay, 61–2, 69
Sandy Point, see Tanjong Katong
Santa Domingo, 32, 39
Scandal Point, 182
Scaur Hill, 24, 30
Sea Face Battery, 74
Seche Battery, 93
Sentosa Island, 180
Serapong Spur Battery, 197, 204, 206
Seven Years War, 89, 133
Seville, Treaty of, 34
Seychelles, 129
Sherwin, Lt RA, 4
Shing Mun Redoubt, 245

Shipley, Brig Gen Charles RE, 40–1, 43–4,
    86, 93
Shipley's Battery, 92
Shirley Heights, 88
Shirley, Maj Gen Sir Thomas, 85
Sierra Leone, 51, 176
Signal Hill, 154, 157
Silingsing Battery, 197, 204, 206
Silingsing Point, 196
Simmons, Lt Gen Sir Lintorn, 46, 114, 121
Simpson, Brig Ivan, 208
Singapore, xx, xxv, xxx, 113, 126, 130,
    154, 180, 182–86, 188–90, 193–95, 197,
    199–202, 204, 206, 208, 213, 219, 235,
    243, 247–48
Singapore Artillery Volunteers, 196
Small's Battery, 38
Smith's Fort, 2, 5
Somerville, Adm, 130
Soufriere Bay, 93
South Battery, Fort Canning, 184
South Caribbean Force, 55, 100
South East Point Battery, 85–6
Southampton Fort, 2
Spanish Fort, 42
Spanish Point, 6, 19, 21, 26
Spanish Succession, War of, 83
Spanish Town, 33, 37
Sphinx Battery, 205–206, 209, 211
Sprague's Platform, 57, 64
St David's Battery, 27–9, 31
St David's Island, 3, 22, 25, 30
St George's, 2–3, 10, 15, 22, 30
St George's Island, see Blakang Mati
St Helena, iv, 57, 70–2, 74–5, 77, 160,
    168–69, 176
St Helena Artillery, 70
St Helena Regiment, 69–72
St John's, 80–3, 85, 88
St Lucia, 50–1, 89, 91–2, 94–5, 97–9, 135
Stanley, 237–38, 247
Stanley Battery, 237, 241, 245, 247
Star Bastion, 103, 117
Stewart Battery, 122
Stonecutter's Island, 217–18, 224–25, 227,
    229, 231–32, 249
Stonecutter's Island Central Battery, 222,
    224–26
Stonecutter's Island East Battery, 220,
    222–23, 226
Stonecutter's Island South Shore Battery,
    228, 231
Stonecutter's Island West Battery, 220–24,
    226, 230, 232–33, 237, 245
Straits Settlements, 182, 187, 189, 194
Straits Settlements Volunteers, 209
Stuart, Col James, 105

Submarine Mining, xxv, 22, 49, 51, 116, 148, 192–93, 225
Suez Canal, 113, 165–66
Sugar Loaf Point, 57, 59
Sun Bastion, 103
Sungei Sembawang, 199
Swarts Bastion, 103
Swinton, Col, 62
Sydney, Lord, 86

Tanjong Johore AMTB Battery, 207
Tanjong Katong, 182, 184, 187, 189–90, 192, 196
Tanjong Katong Battery, *see* Fort Tanjong Katong
Tanjong Pagar, 191–92
Tapion Rock, 93
Tartar Steps, 160
Tathong Channel, 242
Tekong Besar Battery, 205–206, 209, 211, 213
Tenedos, HMS, 130
Tengah Airfield, 211
Tenku Hussain, 181
Teregeh Point, 190
Teregeh Point Battery, 193
Thompson's Valley, 65
Thunderer, HMS, xiii
Tianjin, Treaty of, 217
Tide Cove, 237, 240
Tombeau Bay, 137–38, 140, 148–49
Tombeau Point Battery, 149–50, 153
Town Cut Battery, 3, 5
Town Face Battery, 74
Town Guard Artillery, 125
Trafalgar, HMS, xiii
Traveller's Hill, 169–70
Tricolor Battery, 93
Trincomalee, 101, 103, 105–106, 108–16, 118, 120–23, 125, 126–31
Triton Bastion, 111, 115, 117
Trou Fanfaron, 144
Tsim Sha Tsui, 217
Turk's Cap, 66

U–66, 88
U–124, 177
U–161, 100
Up Park Camp, 43
US Army:
    28th Coast Artillery Battalion, 178
    327th Coast Artillery Battalion, 55
    425th Coast Artillery Battalion, 55
    426th Coast Artillery Battalion, 178–79
    38th Combat Engineer Regiment, 178
    91st Infantry, 3rd Battalion, 178
    Composite Force 8012, 178
    Task Force 4612, 177
Utrecht Bastion, 114–15

Vampire, HMAS, 130
Vanguard, HMS, xiii
Venables, Gen Robert, 32
Vernam USAF Base, 55
Victoria, 218, 220, 228, 246
Victoria Battery (Hong Kong), 225–27
Victoria Battery (Jamaica), 48–51
Vieux Fort, 100
Vieux Grand Port, *see* Grand Port
Vigie, 90, 93–7, 100
Vigie Battery, 96–7
Villa de la Vega, *see* Spanish Town
Villeneuve, Adm, 39–40
Virginia Company, 1–2
VOC, 101, 104, 180–81

War Office, xvi, xix, xxi, xxviii–xxix, 14, 17, 28, 48, 50–51, 71–2, 77–9, 114, 124–29, 148, 153, 157, 169–71, 176, 188–95, 203, 212, 221, 223–24, 228, 238, 241, 248
Warrior, HMS, xi, xiii, 22
Warwick Camp Battery, 31
Washington Treaty, 126, 199–200, 235–36
Watering Point, 112, 114
Waterpas Bastion, 102
Watts, Lt Col RE, 107
Wavell, Gen Sir Archibald, 207, 209, 211
Wellington Battery, 215–16, 218–19, 221, 224, 229
Wellington, Duke of, xxviii, 8, 10
West Africa Squadron RN, 160, 164
West Battery (Hong Kong), 217
West Battery (St Helena), 65
West Point, 216, 218
Western Battery, 119–20
Western Entrance (Hong Kong), 226, 231, 233
Western Redoubt, 7, 12–13
Wetherill's Point, 88
Whale Bay, 18, 22
Whale Bay Battery, 22, 24–5, 27
Wheeler, Sir Charles, 81
White's Redoubt, 92
Whitfield, Maj Gen, 189
Whitworth, Joseph, xv–xvi
William & Mary Battery, 65
Wilson, Field Marshal Sir Henry, 234
Windward Islands, 89

Yamashita, Gen, 211
Young's Valley, 63, 69
Yuan Shi Kai, Gen, 232
Yule, Capt Henry BE, 183

Zeeburg Bastion (Battery), 103, 118